An Ordinary Catholic

A View From The Pew

D0974067

Thomas A. Nelson

ISBN: 1475016743

ISBN 13: 9781475016741

Library of Congress Control Number: 2012904548
CreateSpace Independent Publishing Platform
North Charleston, South Carolina

Contents

Preface

Sometimes sheep will bleat. Sometimes the ordinary will sound off. Sometimes the unlikely will occur. This memoir is just such an improbable effort, an outcry, a voice from the pew. It is the story of turmoil, a labor of faith endured over many decades by an ordinary Roman Catholic who has struggled to reconcile the conflicts between his Church and his lived experiences. It speaks amid an ongoing crisis in that Church. The urge to tell this story has been simmering for several years. It is about my life as a committed Catholic and my journey of faith; a story of a continuing struggle to reconcile a Church that proclaims its infallibility, yet preaches a doctrine that seems opposed to reality—and sometimes even Jesus himself. It is necessarily about my family, while also about my Church and me.

Writing about me is not something I particularly relish, as I recognize that very common ailment of unbridled ego and its annoying consequences, aware that it is always lurking to ensnare me. I try constantly to curtail it, however being ordinary, I have not always been successful at it. Restraining my personal vanity is an affliction for which corrective therapy is ongoing; I firmly believe that our egos tend to be irrepressible and too often get in the way of being loving Christian persons. Thus, I fear this memoir business. Talking or writing about myself runs the risk of violating my resolve, yet any memoir or autobiography is the essence of such self-focus, and I am determined to tell my story.

Therefore, despite that self-perceived conundrum, I have undertaken this unlikely task. I am doing it to resolve that nagging urge to sound off. I am also driven by a desire to pass on to others the many hard-won lessons I have learned in eighty-two years of living, and the resulting faith evolution—that of an ordinary Catholic, one who has decided to do some trumpeting of his journey, in order that the views of the ordinary might get some visibility.

Writing about the Church is also a personal discomfort. It is definitely from the perspective of a progressive Catholic, and I make no claims to be unbiased. Nor do I pretend to be any touted academic, or some kind of expert. I only claim to be someone who sees things from the vantage point of the pew; of one who is concerned about the crisis in the Church; one who loves the Church. I claim to be nothing more than typical of what the Church can expect from a well-educated laity: a Catholic-educated Catholic with a BSME and an MBA as academic credentials. That is where I come from. I am the product of sixteen years of the best Catholic schools. I am still a committed Catholic, the father of six children, grandfather to twelve, and great grandfather to three. I was married for nearly fifty years, widowed for two years, and remarried now for more than five years. Both my late wife and my current spouse came from traditional Catholic backgrounds that have mirrored my own. It has been a fulfilling combination—enhancing to my lifelong Catholicism. I am definitely enjoying the reflection, and I think the accumulated experience of more than eighty years as an every Sunday, Holy Day, and more Catholic is sufficient qualification for some commentary and observations.

I do not write to the hierarchy. It is very unlikely that the hierarchy would have any concern for this peasant's view, and it is a mutual affection. Traditionalists will disagree with me, some even aghast with my claim to be Catholic; progressives may lament that I am not more avant-garde. Nevertheless, the story I tell is prevalent in the pew. It is a common story of a common Catholic —an "Ordinary Catholic" who talks about some things about which the Church would prefer silence. Some may see it as a ranting—more fuel feeding the flames of the conflagration between traditionalists and progressives in our mutual dispute to define an authentic Christianity. However, I submit that the traditionalist view is well represented by the current magisterium from its bully pulpits. The issues I confront, these leaders dismiss with silence or an indefensible doctrine. I cannot be silent. I hope that at some point in the future, progressives and traditionalists can come together in a common understanding, but failing that, it is my prayerful hope that we can at least coexist in a loving manner that recognizes our mutual sincerity.

The lessons I have learned have stimulated the views expressed in this book. I have learned how to think for myself and to evolve into a version of an adult faith. I no longer accord my thinking to those who claim divine direction for their pseudo-infallible truth. I have studied uncensored Church history and had my former delusions further destroyed by current Church leaders and their various abuses of authority. The mythical unchanging, infallible, ultimate truth image of the Church of my youth is gone. What I have found in its place is an unlikely reality, a reality that has resulted in a precious gift—a new level of faith and commitment that has given me much joy while challenging me continuously.

My position as an ordinary Catholic gives me a degree of freedom that most folks in the clerical realm and some others in positions of assigned authority do not have. I know more than a few clergy, including bishops, who hold in their hearts many of the same convictions regarding the current state of the Roman Catholic Church that I do. Among others, there are also people in the academic world whose position restrains them from speaking out. They are all mostly silent. They must remain silent or suffer dire consequences. They are bound by a commitment, but it is a commitment that often demands a surrender of independent thought; it is a commitment enforced by fear. If they allow their wheel to do any squeaking at all, it is a muffled sound that will most likely be unheard. Their fate confines them to be quiet dwellers in closets of concealment. Society politely calls it discretion.

I am unabashedly cavalier about discretion. I write in this memoir of the things I see, just as I see them. I have long ago cast off fear. Even in my period of introversion, I was driven to speak the observed data as my first priority. While I try always to be kind, the sensitivities of the listener are secondary to disclosing the facts. If I may not always draw correct or popular conclusions from the data, I am always passionate about reporting the data exactly as I witness it. While I may at times be strident, I hesitate to apologize for that. I am comfortable with this stance because I find exemplary models of stridency in the prophets of old. Therefore, though I may be no prophet, I will tell it as I see it.

To understand my criticisms of the Church, it might be helpful to consider my perspective:

The institutional Roman Catholic Church over the centuries has evolved into a rigid aristocracy in the most classical sense. With the ongoing death of collegiality, this aristocracy is today, a virtual dictatorship. The current structure consists of a caste-like division into three levels. The pope, the emperor-king, leads the aristocratic elect, the hierarchy. The cardinals are the princes, and the bishops are the dukes. Next, there is the low-level clergy, the priests and deacons. The priests are the knights who have to do the menial work of their parishes, assisted by the deacon-squires. Finally, at the lowest level is the ignorant laity, the ordinary folks who are assigned the stature of peasants and serfs. Male laity are the peasants. Female laity are the serfs, the very lowest on the ladder. Any deviation or rebellious conduct from below is dealt with severely by the next higher level in the structure. Aristocracy is a form of governance that long ago became obsolete. In the civil realm, the remnants of that ancient condition, the dictators of today, face a rising tide of rebellion—witness the Arab Spring; the Church is not immune to this trend.

History shows that past papal utterances consistently deplored democracy and some of the most fundamental civil rights. The Church has been on the wrong side of history many times in the past and continues that pattern today. It clings to its aristocratic rule for a variety of reasons, but it is obviously the antithesis of the servant-of-all dictum envisioned by Jesus. Popes do not serve peasants and serfs, but the peasants do sometimes rebel.

This ordinary peasant has something to say about this condition. Due to my vocational choice, I have long suffered my assigned, demeaning status. I could have gone for the aristocracy, but I felt unworthy. It was an unworthiness bred by a strict Catholic upbringing that instilled a very negative self-image and taught me not to think, but to submit, acknowledge my sinfulness, and to simply believe and obey. Ridding oneself of that submissiveness after many years has yielded some unique benefits. Despite the lowly state of being just an ordinary Catholic layman and being shrouded in obscurity, I have encountered an unforeseen, irrepressible, and delightful result. A new freedom to think has emerged, which has been a refreshing and delightful experience. Coupled with the blessing of a gay son, who was a major catalyst in this process, I have definitely awakened from a long intellectual coma. This is a new state, unique mostly to contemporary peasantry; generally, people of higher rank do not enjoy this life-giving freedom, and members of the aristocratic hierarchy are now powerless to threaten ordinary peasants—those no longer comatose. Excommunication imparts little fear these days to the awakened ranks. Most peasantry probably would not be deemed significant enough to warrant such notoriety anyway.

Therefore, this is about an ordinary view, a voice that is quite prevalent. When ordinary people tire of injustice, they can be quite capable of precipitating the demise of an aristocracy or dictatorship. When it happens in the civil realm, it is termed revolution. It happened before in the Church, and it was labeled the Reformation. Past attempts to reform or end the aristocracy have generally failed, but today is different. The technology-bred revolution in communication has precipitated an amazing transfer of power to the ordinary among us, and perhaps an end to the privileged Roman royalty is in sight. Like the aristocracies of old, an unseen revolution seems imminent. The abuses of the ruling elite have been plentiful and plain to see; their arrogance and self-perceived immunity have blinded them to the reality of the portent, but many of us ordinary Catholics see the glaring dysfunction. It is what I am writing about—that and the alternative.

The alternative to our aristocratic Catholicism is a Jesus-inspired Christianity with an emphasis on love. It is a religion that we have drifted away from somewhere along the way—to "love one another" as He loved us. If I have learned anything, it is the primacy of love. Someday soon, I pray and expect that my cherished Catholic Church will return to such a Pauline principle, with or without the hierarchy. Perhaps it can only be accomplished through schism. However, it is the essence of the Jesus story, "the greatest love story ever told." This conviction, this hope is lurking in many hearts in the Church, suppressed by authority, but sprouting persistently— everywhere. It is expressed very well by the words of even some of the aristocracy. The late Cardinal George Basil Hume in his 1995 "Note on Church Teaching Concerning Homosexual People" said of it:

> To love another is in fact to reach out to God who shares His lovableness with the one we love. To be loved is to receive a sign or share of God's unconditional love. To love another, whether of the same sex or of a different sex, is to have entered the area of the richest human experience. [1]

That does not sound like the views that commonly come out of Rome these days. It sounds more like many laity I know.

---

1   Cardinal Basil Hume, "A Note on the Teaching of the Catholic Church Concerning Homosexual People, *Catholic News* (February 4, 2007). http://jameslau88.com/a_note_on_the_teaching_of_the_catholic_church_concerning_homosexual_people.html.

Introduction

The Catholic Church is in a state of profound turmoil today. Nearly fifty years after the Vatican II Council, it is in the midst of an historical crisis, which surely conflicts with the goals established by those prescient fathers. Few would dispute that the sexual abuse scandal and cover-up, the declining number of priests, the departure of many devoted laity, and the ongoing repugnance of the younger generation reflect a state of serious decline. More than thirty-five million people in the U.S. identify as former Catholics. It is a worldwide phenomenon, exacerbated by the "see no evil, hear no evil" stance of Church leaders, who seem focused on the past and bent on distracting critics with irrelevant issues and silly reforms such as the "new missal." It is partly my intent in this book to address in a frank and open manner what they apparently do not want to address. It is time to expose the root factors behind this phenomenon. The views expressed here are not those of some high-ranking authority or academic scholar, but an ordinary one—a perspective from the pew. It is one born of lived experiences. It is about reforms that resonate with many of the laity. It is also about why such reforms are unlikely to come from the top. It is simply a voice from the pew, from an Ordinary Catholic. Change is happening; that change, whether from the top, the bottom, or somewhere in between, will produce a Church very different from historical norms. It is an extraordinary period.

Another reason for this book is to pass on the story of my life experiences, which have so profoundly influenced my faith—the how and why of that impact. These experiences, some of which could be termed bizarre, explain the evolution of my understanding of God and how to live. It is why I am now a Church rebel and the reasons for the reform I believe to be so necessary. I relate them in the hope that others might in some way benefit from what

I have learned and that my expression might further the cause of reform. I also hope to impart to my children and their children some of the benefits of these hard-won lessons.

I have not attempted to relate every incident or experience that has affected my faith evolution, only the most meaningful ones. I include things that may seem quite remote from faith-related things. Some are definitely mundane. Some are more obvious as a faith-influencing factor. I tell a bit of my early years, my Catholic schooling, to establish a starting point that is very *traditionally* Catholic. I tell of the ordinary things that every family experiences because these ordinary incidents are relevant. They are all part of the stresses of daily life—the things that make one think—the experiences that form the eventual understanding of life's meaning.

I dwell at length on my son being gay and on the injustices perpetrated by an uncaring Church that seems militantly opposed to his dignity as a human being. My son's story in many ways is a common one. That he survived his trauma is testimony to my many blessings, and an uncommon one among his gay brethren only because of such a good outcome—through common grace in an uncommon way. He and his story have been a major factor in my faith evolution. I have learned more from my son being gay than any other circumstance of my life.

The death of my first wife was another life-changing encounter. Fifty years of marriage makes an indelible impact on who you are, what you think, and your faith. You cannot survive its ending without being changed. I am still pondering that phase of my life.

The views I express in the end chapters of this book reflect some of my conclusions. The Catholic Church has had a profound impact on every aspect of my life and thinking, and in the process, I have come to see that my Church, too, suffers from the inadequacies of being human. Despite my pejorative views, it is still very dear to me, and I owe her much. It is where I started and it has established the foundations of who I am. I anticipate my Catholicity will endure to the grave, but certainly not in the manner I had expected.

Chapter 1

An Activist

"Moderation is a fatal thing. Nothing succeeds like excess"
—OSCAR WILDE

It started out as an ordinary Sunday, but I still can't believe how that day turned out. It marked a huge change from who I once was, because I have always thought of myself as a quiet kind of guy. In fact, when I was younger, I definitely tended to be rather introverted, and you probably could have predicted my characteristic social restraint. Being raised a strict traditional Catholic, I absorbed completely that well-known Catholic guilt complex. I was unprepared for any life outside of my protective Catholic mental cave. It was a cave whose walls of well-instilled doctrine were rock solid and the confinement allowed no perception beyond the cave. That was just fine, as It was a satisfying and undemanding place and I seldom cared to venture outside of it. Oh, I could speak up when the occasion demanded, but I was more comfortable sitting back and letting other folks do the ranting, if ranting was called for. I abhorred making a scene; anonymity was my natural preference, besides, I had enough to do raising my six kids, trying to get ahead at work, and fulfilling all the life fantasies I'd authored in my very Catholic youth. Perhaps some of my reticence to come out of my cave came from a lack of passion about contemporary affairs, but my excuse was that I preferred a nice "live and let live" policy. So, when others were marching in support of their passionate causes, I was more apt to be sitting in the comfort of my living room watching them on TV and shaking my head—just a good churchgoing, ordinary Catholic and anything but radical.

For many years, my life followed that path. It was the path of a typical ordinary suburban guy who knew the rules of his faith and tried to follow them—Mass every Sunday and Holy Day, regular confession, and all the nuances of family life that implied. Any trips outside the cave were rare and when they did occur, they generally involved something beyond my control. However, unexpectedly and deceptively over time, that shtick disappeared. What happened that particular Sunday though was something beyond.

My wife would certainly attest to my growing verbosity as I have gotten older, yet more than that, much more than that, I have been afflicted with this passion—for the cause. It's been a creeping thing that came up surreptitiously, and it's definitely the fault of my gay son. Because of him and who he is, it seems, I've undergone a major life transformation. I have gone from that quiet suburban caveman to being really steamed. He has been the catalyst of a rapid evolution in my faith, and indeed in my very persona. It's really quite amazing, this transformation. Before I discovered he was gay, I was that normal, quiet, submissive citizen—one who might mumble a little discontent now and then, but never speak out blatantly in public and seldom peek out of that Catholic cave. True, I could discuss political postures enthusiastically when the situation demanded it, but it was never outside of small group gatherings or one-on-one situations. I would certainly never even think about speaking out on issues involving homosexuality or anything critical of the Church. (Actually, any conversation that touched on human sexuality was cloaked with an inherited Victorian restraint.) Indeed, all of my family were quiet, comfortable Americans, and under my incessant direction, focused primarily on the many things for which we had to be thankful. It was by stealthy and persistent avoidance that little passion was generated, and quiet control was constantly the unspoken goal. Activism? Not a chance. Nevertheless, gradually, after discovering we had a gay child, my wife and I both evolved toward a more activist stance as we tiptoed out of our self-defined closet. We had become involved in ministry to the gay community with a growing passion for advocacy, but it had been a fairly sedate existence at the outset. In addition, despite a growing dissatisfaction with Catholic dogma in a number of areas, we both remained mostly just ordinary, compliant Catholics.

Then that Sunday in October 2004 arrived. It marked a major exclamation point in my personal journey of faith. I was shot out of the lurking shadows of my cave with cannon-like suddenness. It still startles me when I recall it. A growing activism suddenly exploded, and I returned to that cave only to roll a blocking boulder to seal the door from reentry. There is no going back. I have not been the same since.

I had gone to the nine thirty Mass, the most popular and well-attended one at our parish. Nearly every seat was taken. I was alone, my wife was at home in the final stages of a terminal brain cancer, a condition that had cast a depressing pall over my whole being. Despite this, I had trudged to Church, hoping to find some relief from the tragedy that I knew was so imminent. I had not yet comprehended the terrible reality of the nightmare, which was marching so inexorably toward me, and my soul was whimpering in the agony of witnessing her steady decline. My prior days had been filled with private weeping, and the thought of her death was incessantly with me as I moved slowly down the aisle, searching for an open seat in the sea of unseen faces. Finally I found a place close to our usual area near the front of the church. We had always tried to sit close to the altar because of my wife's preference. My own natural inclination was to find an obscure place in the rear, but I had grown accustomed to sitting up front where we could see and hear well. I had decided it's one of the few public accommodations where you don't have to pay a premium for front-row-center seating. As I sat down, I remember trying to relax. I was in an escape mode enshrouded by my cloud of sadness, struggling for some measure of comfort, a little sleepy, and hoping for an inspirational and peaceful experience.

Inspirational it certainly turned out to be. Peaceful it was not.

It was just a short time into the service when it happened. After the scripture readings, our visiting assistant priest told us that in lieu of the usual homily, we were to be treated to a recorded message from the cardinal. The purpose was to cajole us into voting for Michigan's Proposition II, the state constitutional amendment banning gay marriage, which was on the ballot in the coming election. Understand that by this point in my experience of being the father of a gay son, I had been well tuned into the cacophony of the Church's demeaning theology and society's self-righteous moralistic railing, all opposed to fundamental human rights for gay people like my son. Now it appeared that I was about to receive a forced dose of this rationalized bigotry, a terrible affront to a long-developed personal sensitivity—and in my own church! The taped message began with the cardinal droning: "And God created them male and female…"

Suddenly I went from a comfortable, relaxed, and harmless pew occupant, an ordinary Catholic, into a never before encountered feeling of a terrible rage. I was overwhelmed with emotion. This was not going to pass. There was a tremendous rush of adrenalin, a tingling sensation unlike anything I had ever experienced before, and it seemed as if someone had lifted me up bodily. A surge of emotion was crying out inside of me with a fury I had never experienced: *"Enough! Enough! No more silence!"* I found myself driven—marching directly to the altar with an unstoppable resolve. There was no reticence, no hesitation or thought other than to cry out against this terrible assault on my family, which was happening in this unlikely place. I quickly reached the center of the altar, mounted several steps to the top, turned, and faced the congregation. I literally shouted out, my voice shaking with much emotion, overriding the cardinal's recording: "This is a message of hate. It hurts me. It hurts my family. It hurts my friends. I come to this place to hear Christ's message of love. Today I hear only hate. I cannot stay and listen to it."

With that, I descended the steps and marched out—down the main aisle in a defiant military manner, almost daring any usher or person to accost me for my interrupting outburst. I looked to the left and the right, as many people directly in the eye as I could, hoping to emphasize my message, and expecting some kind of reaction. There was none. To a person, they all looked astonished. They were dumbfounded, frozen in place, even the ushers. Nothing like this had ever happened before at our quiet, comfortable, suburban church.

It had certainly never happened to me before either. By the time I traversed the parking lot and got into my car, I took a deep breath and began to calm down. My immediate reaction was, "Holy cats! Who did that? What did I do? How did that happen? Was that me? I can't believe what I just did!" I had blatantly and publically violated every tenant of my philosophy of polite passivity. I felt like I had just jumped off a fifty story building and awakened abruptly, still alive, in the front seat of my car. The memory stuns me still.

The sequel started thirty minutes later, after I got home. The phone rang. It was my pastor. I heard him through my lingering daze apologizing: "Tom. I'm so sorry. I will never again do anything that will hurt a single parishioner. I apologize to you..." His unwavering support for me was unexpected, and it continues to this day. It has cemented our mutual respect and friendship—a memorable experience. Much later, I heard from some of my fellow parishioners, my neighbors. Their comments were consistently positive and usually began with, "Wow! That took guts..."

It was a surreal affair that astounded me that I could ever do such a thing, and I'm still impressed by the response it generated. I'd like to think that it was "guts," but I know better now. That wasn't me. After reflecting on it, I concluded it was the Spirit that day who used me to send a message. I'm absolutely sure of it. I may have come out of my cave, but I'm not a gutsy guy, yet maybe, just maybe, I'm a little bit more of an activist now, a sometimes tool of the Holy Spirit. Could that be? Maybe I do stand guilty of that self-defined mocking label of an activist, a label I often scorned in my prior years of comfortable complacence. Certainly, a dramatic new direction in my life had begun. How did that happen?

I can now look back at more recent times, and recall the many trips to the state capitol to lobby my state senators and representatives. I remember all the marches and demonstrations my wife and I have participated in, the letters to the editor and articles I've written, all on behalf of the gay community and my son. I look back and I say to myself, "Good Grief! That has all the earmarks of an activist. You've even been seen on TV!" Maybe I should start feeling good about my dedicated efforts and myself. Then I realize: It's the Spirit working through me, telling me what to say and what to do. I am only a receptive, grateful tool. It's the way the Spirit works, apparently. Still, how did I become that tool? What has happened? Now, when I consider it, I see a consistent pattern emerge. The Spirit has been leading me, often when I didn't realize it, and maybe toward a place where I did not want to go. Yes, I've gone from being an ordinary Catholic to some kind of budding activist—not a full-blown activist, for sure. (I've never been to jail. Real activists are arrested for their protesting.) I'm more ordinary. Still, how my activism happened and where my evolution has led me is quite an amazing story. It is the story I want to tell you.

Chapter 2

A Gift

"The most astonishing thing about miracles is that they happen"
—G. K. CHESTERTON

"**B**less me father, for I have sinned. It has been one day since my last confession…" I was about eleven or twelve years old when I whispered those fear-filled words in the anonymous darkness of the confessional box after a thirty-minute wait in the long line of fellow classmates. It was the early forties and I was well along in my Catholic elementary school education. It was Sacred Heart School in Dearborn, Michigan. The big, red-brick building with the wide-eyed triple-tall windows, which required a ten-foot pole to open in the warmer months, housed the parish elementary and high schools for us west end Catholics. It was one of the largest structures in the city, located on the west side, (the colloquial "best side" of the city) and was divided from the east by the Ford estate and the Henry Ford Museum. Blue-collar residents were "east-siders," while we west-enders came from mostly white-collar families. The east side Catholics had their Saint Aloysius, but the west end had Sacred Heart with the vaunted Immaculate

Heart of Mary nuns. Sacred Heart invariably won the academic contests but not always the football games.

I was born the middle of three boys in Detroit, Michigan. It was October 1929, virtually the day the stock market crashed, marking the onset of the great depression. I don't think that economic disaster made any conscious impact on me in the ensuing early years, at least none that I was aware of, but it has always impressed me when reflecting back on my life. I was born in a time of turmoil and I have lived through many epic events since. Shortly after my birth, the family moved to the Long Island area for a brief period, and thence to Bethesda Maryland. We returned to Michigan in 1935 and took up residence in Dearborn. It was destined to be our home for more than twenty years. I immediately entered Sacred Heart School in the first grade and those early years of parochial school proved to have the most profound effect on my life. It marked the true beginning of my faith journey, a journey that continues to this day.

Rt to Lt, Bruce, Tom, and Bill, Circa 1935

Like most of my fellow student adolescents, I was thoroughly indoctrinated by the nuns in the ritualized list of mortal sins. Daily

Mass was a standard routine for all, along with weekly confession. Religion classes were a primary focus, where we learned all the rules, if not the reasons. Throughout this disciplined cadence, most of us experienced inevitable failures as we tried our best to live up to the demanding dogmatic standards. That we were sinners was a given; that was thoroughly ingrained. The slightest faults could quickly mushroom into prescient panics that we were hellbound. Visions of the horrors of hell were aptly dramatized by the nuns, and our examinations of conscience were guided classroom affairs, following which we would all march off to the confessional cubicles in the nearby church. This scenario was an effective tool, which tended to create a constant state of intense fear, an accepted approach for reducing our egos to levels considered necessary for good discipline. It was a real and vivid fear of going straight to hell for all eternity, should sudden death find us unprepared with the stain of mortal sin on our souls. Thus, it was natural and logical to rush to an always available confession whether scheduled or not, no matter what the interval. Fear was a popular motivator, and it is still promoted by some today, but nothing like the rigid routine of those days. In retrospect, parochial school was an experience that branded my understanding of authority and spirituality, and it established a diminished level of self-confidence that has taken me a lifetime to moderate.

The fear was mixed with many more positive elements, which I still cherish today. If you survived the fear factor and managed to emerge mentally intact, the disciplined atmosphere was truly an effective educational tool. I spent several of those early years as an altar boy. The five o'clock rising to make the one-mile walk in the dark to church and serve the six thirty a.m. Mass meant that on those days, you'd be attending mass twice, since everyone started the school day by attending the eight o'clock Mass as well. The discipline I accepted without question; it was standard procedure. My older brother had preceded me down the same path, and I was thrilled to be included in that fraternity of privileged boys who were allowed to be so close to the Lord on the altar.

As an altar boy, one had to arrive at church at least fifteen minutes before Mass to assist the priest in vesting. No tardiness was tolerated. The younger servers were assigned the earlier six thirty Mass; the more senior boys got the privilege of serving the later eight o'clock service It was three days on this schedule, then a week off. It made for a long day, and if you were noted to be slouching in your pew during the ensuing eight o'clock school Mass, there was always a sentry nun standing by to correct your posture. Stern discipline was never considered a severe thing. It was simply the routine.

Our parish pastor during those grade school years was a large, elderly man with snow-white hair who exuded the essence of authority as his consistent characteristic. I remember him as having some other indelible traits. One in particular that I have not forgotten was his penchant to start off every Sunday Mass in a booming voice, announcing an introduction which always ended with the statement, "and there is no pew rental in this church." He made the phrase seem like one word, it was so automatic. Of course, I had no idea what the heck "pew rental" was. I did not even realize that "pew rental" was two words. Apparently, pew rental had died an evolutionary death in Catholic practice prior to my time, and our pastor was emphasizing the charitable implications of the demise of this tax. His vibrant voice and dominating demeanor consistently evoked an aura that left little doubt exactly who was in charge.

At least every quarter, the pastor-father would visit each classroom at our school to dispense the period's student report cards individually. It was an epic event for most of us. We would all stand when he entered the room and would greet him in perfect unison with "Good morning Father!". The ensuing ritual entailed a formal reading of your report card in full detail to the whole class. Father would seat himself behind the teacher's desk, which seemed under-sized for his over-sized bulk. Then he would begin to select from the deck of student report cards by first calling out the student's name. Each student when called would stand and remain at rigid attention, while his results in every subject were broadcast for all to hear. While any subpar academic performance was usually overlooked by the father, if the final notation included the proclamation: "Tuition paid in full," it always resulted in the comment, "a very good report card!" However, the full public disclosure of any low grades was a class-entertaining humiliation. It served as an effective motivation to improve. That humiliation paled in comparison, however, to what the father would have to say to you if your parents had been untimely in your tuition payments. Fortunately, I never suffered on either count, but just observing the whole process had a definite, repressive effect on everyone. You never questioned authority and if you were not afraid of failure, you simply did not understand. I can smile about it now and cherish those memories, yet by the time I moved on to high school, my self-confidence was in complete collapse and I had withdrawn into my self-constructed retreat, my mental cave, a committed introvert. It proved to be a lengthy stay. Fear of failure is a powerful genie of repression.

My parents were quite atypical of the standard Catholic model because theirs was a mixed marriage. Dad was non-Catholic and Mom was the product of a strict Dutch Catholic upbringing. A mixed marriage in those days was anathema. It meant no church wedding was allowed; they were married privately in the parish rectory, minus any Mass of celebration; devoid the usual wedding festivities and more like a private religious justice-of-the-peace affair. Dad was the youngest in a family of five boys and three girls. They were firmly Christian but not regularly affiliated with any denomination. When the occasion demanded it, they preferred a Presbyterian perspective. Despite the dire predictions and warnings my Mom received from her parish priest about marrying a non-Catholic, she enjoyed both parental acceptance of her choice and Dad's promise to raise the children Catholic. They were married June 25, 1925. No two people were more in love and recalling their relationship, I still marvel at the loving union that unfolded over their lifetime. None could have been more successful. It was storybook love that never seemed marred by conflict. Their marriage was another standard of perfection, which I absorbed as my own, and I found it hard to emulate.

Both my parents were, in a way, the direct opposite of my early Catholic school environment. Complementing their own loving relationship, they provided a thoroughly nurturing home uniquely filled with exclusively positive feedback and love. It was definitely offsetting to the negative aspects of my parochial school experience. Criticism was just not part of Mom and Dad's inventory of interpersonal skills. Their discipline was never harsh and rarely apparent; it just seemed to be a by-product of a very orderly household. The high standards they set were mainly through their example and goals articulated, always in a loving way. They had an innate way of making goodness the sole attractive behavior and making you feel you were the best. Even now, it astonishes me when I realize, over all the years, I never witnessed any displays of anger or discord between them. I recall with much nostalgia how my dad would sing to my mother as he routinely went about some menial household task, and my mom would respond with some worshiping gesture of affection. They seemed to be in a perpetual state of love for one another and their mutual generosity made unconditional loving behavior a universal norm for my two brothers and me. I still marvel when I recall their patience, a patience that seemed never ending. I recall that only once in my life did my father raise his voice to me in frustration at some repeated misbehavior. My childhood home was one of the greatest blessings of my life and set personal standards for me that surpassed all other dictums. In retrospect, it was a tough act to follow.

Dad was a gentle man with a rare sense of humor. It was impossible to be glum for long when in his presence. His non-Catholic status was accepted without question. He wasn't a churchgoer, but his unrelenting Christian living was always evident. I remember when, for some work-related reason, he would retire early along with us boys, we would see him kneel at his bedside for his night prayers. We considered it normal practice. Sometimes his Sunday absence in Church from the rest of us, however, was a source of minor guilt feelings for me because I would envy his privilege of sitting in the family car reading his newspaper while we were all attending Sunday Mass. I considered my envy to be a venial sin at least. Dad finally succumbed to our constant cajoling and prayers for his conversion. He finally joined the Catholic Church following his retirement at age sixty-five. Bishop Fulton Sheen had significant influence on his decision at the time.

While I might denigrate the atmosphere of fear I experienced in my early Catholic schooling, and the long-lasting scars I feel I incurred, there is much for which I am grateful. The nuns who taught us, at a dedicated sacrifice of themselves, as I now well understand, imparted much more than fear. I learned well in a rare, disciplined academic atmosphere. It's easy to criticize a fear-based philosophy from today's perspective, but in those days, it was more of a cultural standard. On the whole, I would not trade it for any alternative, and I am unequivocally grateful for that early blessing.

During that second decade of my life, the world became embroiled in World War II. This epical event greatly altered our family life and that of all Americans at the time. Rationing, seven-day workweeks, constant prayers for our armed forces—these were the mundane. However, there were more life-changing experiences that have remained vivid for me over a lifetime. The material disciplines seemed insignificant. My brothers and I were spared having to fight overseas by reason of our young age. Yet, as the war progressed, we gradually became aware of the unique horror of that war. Gold stars appeared in some neighborhood windows. Then, paralyzing portraits formed in my mind from news media reports and from family dinnertime discussions that left indelible impressions, which still evoke intense emotional response in me. The images of human beings emerging from the death camps as virtual living skeletons…the mournful mounds of naked dead bodies…the realization of the complicity of so many in the horrors of the Holocaust…these were stupefying events and remain faith-shaping encounters that I wish to always remember. It is still mystifying. It is right and useful that *we remember.* It forever condemns the culture of silence, a silence that can still terrify my soul.

My blessings continued when Mom and Dad decided my educational progress needed a different element and they enrolled me in the all-male Jesuit-run University of Detroit High School. It was not an anachronistic event. The Jesuits provided me with a new perspective and I began a long process of overcoming my introversion—recovering a bit of self-confidence. I developed a modicum of intellectual certitude and I credit the Jesuits with introducing me to the beginnings of independent thinking—a phenomenon which matured over the years that has both delighted and plagued me ever since. Critical thinking was still in the future, and I remained mostly in my cave, my safe place, but soon I was learning apologetics for the first time. This was a distinctly new and intellectually stirring event and began a process of putting some flesh on the skeleton of my young faith.

One day, one of my Jesuit teachers, attempting to dramatize the reality of the existence of God through the argument of design, brought a tabletop radio to class. He placed the radio on his desk, and then proceeded to take a screwdriver and remove the chassis from the enclosure, exposing the impressive circuitry and radio tubes within. Then he posed the question: "Who designed this circuitry? Who assembled it? How long do you think we'd have to sit and wait for the atoms in the atmosphere to coalesce into this functioning radio without the designer and manufacturer?" We all agreed. It would be a fool's wait. He then proceeded to the concluding question: "Is not the universe far more complex than this puny radio? Is it not rational that the universe also required a designer? Who is that designer? Think." Think, I did, and I have often recalled that incident as fodder for meditation. It was an introduction to critical thought, but I had a long way to go.

I remember also the Jesuits introducing me to the importance of intent when considering moral choices. The story they told us:

A Dominican priest went in to his confessor and asked, "Father, is it all right if I smoke while I pray?" The confessor quickly replied, "Oh no my son. That would be irreverent; a venial sin at least."

A Jesuit priest went in to his confessor and asked, "Father, is it all right if I pray while I smoke?" His confessor confidently replied, "Of course, my son. That is commendable. There are no restrictions on prayer."

That little anecdote had more than a minor impact on my understanding of Church doctrine in the following years.

My education continued through the university years, first at the nearby Jesuit-run University of Detroit. Lacking any certain career goal, my father convinced me that an engineering path was right. He had concluded that my mechanical interests and hands-on tendencies were appropriate to a mechanical engineering destiny. I agreed. I'm not sure that was an accurate assessment, but it sufficed to make a necessary decision, and I had no other bent. Actually, because of an early interest in chemistry, I started out in chemical engineering, but after my first encounter with the challenges of quantitative chemical analysis and a better understanding of the career portents of chemical engineering, I quickly determined that my future would best lie elsewhere. I decided that mechanical engineering was definitely the correct choice. In later years, I would lament that I had never considered medicine. By the time I discovered this yearning, however, I was already well into the beginnings of my large family, and the idea of returning to school full-time was an impossibility. While I never achieved my dream of becoming a doctor, it definitely resulted in an intense and active interest in medicine over the years, one that found its outlet in personal study and observation.

Mechanical engineering became the default choice and after two years with the Jesuits, I matriculated to the University of Notre Dame in 1950. Mom and Dad again felt my educational progress demanded a change, and that it should entail an away-from-home environment and perhaps a return to an all-male setting. (Notre Dame was not yet coed in those days) Actually, my intense relationship with a young woman at the time probably provided a major motivation for my parents to send me off. It was another blessing, as for the first time in my life, I was on my own and the experience was not inconsequential. It also accomplished what may or may not have been the secondary objective. The young woman I was seeing soon turned her attentions elsewhere, and I was too involved with my new circumstances to be much concerned. It was a natural progression of maturation for us both.

Notre Dame was a new and unique experience. At that time, in addition to its all-male status, it maintained a military-equivalent discipline. We often bragged that the only school with more strict discipline than Notre Dame was the U.S. Naval Academy. While we might outwardly grumble and complain, internally we generally accepted it and were unabashedly proud of it. One dorm requirement for undergraduates living on campus was to sign in on a roster at least three times a week, every week, any time prior to eight o'clock in the morning. The sign-in sheet was just outside the dormitory chapel, where there was always an eight o'clock Mass. Now you didn't *have* to attend Mass, but the impetus was there, and we got the message, if not always the grace. Notre Dame was good. By the time my graduation neared, I had developed a fairly rigid Church-doctrine-instilled stance on most things, reinforced with the naive belief that my certitude had university-level credibility. Critical thinking remained in infancy, however. While not yet anywhere near being an extrovert, I had at least developed a determination to achieve and a modicum of self-confidence. Nevertheless, I still had a long way to go.

Military service loomed. It was now the Korean War and I knew I was probably going to be drafted for the "police action" raging on that far away peninsula. As another implausible blessing though, several years previously, I had enlisted in the Naval Air Reserve, simply because I loved to fly. The Naval Air Reserve gave me the chance to be in the air nearly every weekend as an enlisted man at the Naval Air Station, Grosse Isle, Michigan. I was flying free of charge. It was the answer to a dream at the time, and it turned out to be an unanticipated blessing.

It later developed that, because of my status as an enlisted person in the Naval Air Reserve who was also attending college, I was eligible to apply to Officer Candidate School and subsequent active duty as a naval officer. It certainly seemed preferable to the draft, so I applied. As luck would have it—or as I prefer to believe, as the Spirit blessed me—the interviewing officer board for applicants was headed by a Notre Dame graduate. I was one of two persons chosen out of 250 applicants! This did fine things for my ego. Despite my complete wonderment, I was on my way to become the first naval officer in our family.

Life as an officer in the U.S. Navy was another important part of my education. I found myself in an unwarranted position of leadership—in many cases over men much older than me, with far more naval experience than myself. It was a leadership condition that demanded an exhibition of self-confidence that I had long struggled to achieve. I soon enough became comfortable with the unavoidable reality and at least managed an effective facade of self-confidence. However, more important to my education, I also eventually discovered that the adulation and respect that go with being clad in a naval officer's uniform could be quite distorting. The constant "Yes sir, no sir" "Mr. Nelson, etc." irresistibly stimulated my vanity, and I realized, it could easily blind one to reality through such incessant nurturing. It was a fantasy land experience that I have often pondered over the years, and I believe that most people in positions of power and respect will encounter a very difficult challenge to maintain any semblance of reality and personal humility because of adulation. A realistic perspective of one's humanity requires exceptional intellectual awareness in such situations. It is not easily done and it requires extraordinary effort. No one is immune. It can be a delusional fog—the higher the office, the thicker the fog. I have witnessed many victims in public life. The examples in today's world are legion. I consider such folks less celebrity and more victims. I have learned to be wary of all adulation.

An incident occurred early in my tour that I now recall as the seeds of an activism to come. It involved a confrontation with racism. It is fair and accurate to state that my parents, despite their innate goodness, held some culturally induced prejudices toward African Americans. Today, one would say that they were simply unwitting participants in the prevailing aphotic phenomenon in American culture that we now recognize as "white privilege." Mostly unspoken and mild, they were nevertheless conventionally prejudiced. It stemmed from not only the segregated culture in which they were raised, but also the common white view of the time that the American Negro was created less capable. Still, they always came down on the side of tolerance when challenged, and never were guilty of passing on their prejudices in any conscious manner. I formed my own views, and in significant ways, they differed from my parents. Dad, being a staunch Republican and in the upper ranks of management, was antiunion.

I was the opposite, but I kept that opposition to myself. When it came to race, I was distinctly sympathetic toward any minority that I thought was getting the short end of it. I had made some close friendships during my period as an enlisted man in the Naval Air Reserve, some of whom were African American, and I had decided that not only were my black friends great guys, some of them just might be more capable than me. It was not a common perspective among many of my peers and I did not advertise my differing view. It was not challenged in the mostly "polite" circles I inhabited, but that day in Norfolk, it was challenged.

I had been assigned to attend a special U.S. Navy school in Norfolk, Virginia, for a one-week period at the outset of my tour of duty in Rhode Island. The routine was intense and left little time for outside diversion. However, on the one weekend, which was part of the schedule, I had sufficient time off to seek a little recreation. I decided to do some sightseeing in downtown Norfolk and, being dependent on public transportation, I boarded a bus for the trip into town. The bus was nearly empty, there being only two or three other occupants, and I chose a seat in the back where I could stretch out more easily. We had traveled little more than a couple of blocks when the driver stopped the bus in the middle of the block, did not open the doors, got up, and came back to me. He said, "Sailor. You don't want to sit here. This is where the niggers sit." My reaction was abrupt and clear as my anger popped like a cork. I told him with in a loud, dismissive voice with no attempt to hide my disgust. "You just go back to driving, buster. I'll sit where I damn well please!" He was obviously taken back, but shrugged and went back as admonished, shaking his head at the ways of the younger generation. I remember that because it was the first time I had ever really stepped out of my Catholic cave to defy publically a culture I saw as wrong. I remember being surprised at the extent of my anger. I was incensed and I was just not going to be silent. It was a hint of things to come. Years later, as I watched on TV, I was cheering the freedom marchers and Rosa Parks for their heroic efforts to right such wrongs. However, I was cheering from the comfort of my living room. I was not capable of public exposure yet. It would take many years and a gay son to unleash my passion.

Another incident occurred during my active-duty tour that had a subtle influence on my faith in later years. It involved a friend who was a Catholic, and with whom I had many long and lively conversations about our Catholic faith in the officers' wardroom during our regular coffee breaks. He was a subordinate, a warrant officer who came from an intense Italian Catholic background, and had many close relatives living in Italy. I sensed that his deference to me as a higher-ranking officer restrained any really frank expressions of his apparent discontent with our Church. Yet, I soon understood that he did not accept Church dogma as unquestioningly as I did. When I would make some righteous revelation of my rigid doctrinal certitudes, he would often shake his head slowly and quietly say, "Tom, you just don't understand Rome, and how it really is. It's not what you think." When I pressed him on that, he would simply add, "You're not Italian. You wouldn't understand." I was puzzled, and did not know how to reply or what to think about what he was implying. I knew my Church. Nothing could divert my thinking from an unflinching doctrinaire stance. Little did I realize how I would recall his bemusement later in my life. I now realize that the Italian-bred clerical mindset and other self-protective instincts of Church leaders in Rome are the product of a complex interaction of a variety of factors, mostly historical.

To be fair to my Italian brethren, I am not sure any of it has a great deal to do with being Italian. Probably of greater consequence is the "old boys' club" mentality—clericalism. Whatever its roots, my fellow officer's Italian background was instrumental in stimulating an arousal of some critical thought. I pondered what he had said and wondered about why he thought I "wouldn't understand." His refusal to elaborate only deepened my puzzlement. While I mostly dismissed the incident at the time, the memory of his attitude persisted. I sensed that he was trying to spare me some kind of exposure to reality or delusion about my faith. Now, many years later, I'm doing the smiling as I recognize how drastically I've changed from my early perspective of a flawless Church hierarchy. It is certainly not Italian roots that have spawned the recognition of a Roman hierarchy that seems to live in a world apart, espousing a deluded doctrine far from any relevance to the reality of life for ordinary folks. If I don't understand them, I would add that they don't understand me—and folks like me. However, like the smoking Jesuit, I know there are differing approaches to most issues of faith.

During my short naval career, I continued a courtship with my future wife, Trish, via the U.S. mail. Trish was a neighborhood friend whom I'd begun to pursue prior to my tour of active duty and things had quickly moved to serious. She was an elementary school teacher with a background not unlike my own. Our families were close and we had grown up as neighbors and childhood play-mates. Also Catholic to the bone, with sixteen years of Catholic schooling from Sacred Heart elementary and high school and four years at Marygrove College,[2] we saw most things through the same lens. After my call to active duty, despite the distance that separated us, we fell completely in love. Before my two-year tour of duty was up, we were engaged to be married, but some six months before our scheduled marriage I received some devastating news from her.

Trish had been suffering from a severe cough for some weeks and she was quite frightened, as she had been coughing up blood. A visit to her doctor resulted in some very bad news. The diagnosis had come back. Trish was suffering from tuberculosis. Trish's dad was a physician and she was under the care of the best the Detroit medical community had to offer. The diagnosis was certain. Both X-ray and skin tests were positive. Being prior to the era of antibiotics, the best that could be expected was a long quarantined confinement at the Herman Kieffer TB Sanitarium in Detroit. Death was a distinct possibility, if not a probable outcome. It was a terrible tragedy for us both. We talked for a long time via telephone and with an unflinching resolve born of our mutual firm faith, we concluded that our only solution was a miracle. OK, let's get at it, we agreed. I would make a novena to the Blessed Mother and Trish would too, to the limits of her confinement. I prayed over the ensuing days with greater intensity than I had ever imagined I could. I was driven by an unyielding urgency that I had never before experienced in my entire life. I made promises to Our

2 Marygrove College website: http://www.marygrove.edu/

Lady that I probably never quite accomplished. Trish did her best, too, in praying to Our Lady. Two weeks passed and the doctors repeated the X-rays and skin test as a final step in the long commitment to the TB sanitarium.

They were amazed. Both the X-ray and the skin test were now negative. Trish's cough was gone. She told me how, as she lay in bed in the hospital room, fearful of the terrible verdict, her dad and several other physicians gathered round and examined the before-and-after X-rays, which were displayed side-by-side on an illuminated viewing screen. "Look!" the doctor exclaimed. "On this film—here is your lesion, clearly evident—but over here, the latest one—perfectly clear! Your latest skin test is negative also! We can't explain it! We just don't understand it!"

We did. We understood what had happened. Our Blessed Lady had intervened. We had gotten our miracle. Anyone who says that miracles don't happen in this modern age just hasn't had one happen to them. Trish and I knew. It happened to us.

This incident was one that would affect my spirituality throughout a lifelong recollection. The supernatural is real and it is always lurking behind our self-constructed veils of personal versions of reality. It was the first of five extraordinary spiritual gifts in my life, and I don't think I'm in any way special. I think perhaps I simply talk about it more, or maybe somehow I'm a bit more perceptive—better attuned to it. I suspect there are more unnatural interventions than we realize. They seldom get any press, probably because most folks are too reticent to talk about it. Like a UFO phenomenon, if you happen to experience one and talk about it, you are mostly regarded as mentally challenged, or worse. I've concluded that a child-like faith can have its advantages. Reality cannot always be defined simply by rational argumentation. Sometimes we need to admit to the existence of mystery and accept those things that defy explanation—things that are simply not in the realm of the natural. Some would call this faith.

In another light, miracles surely abound. We are accustomed to defining miracles as occasions of the supernatural, but much more common miracles surround us all, every day. We just do not see them as such. Who would deny that life is a miracle? Virtually all of creation is a miracle. When one considers the billions of people currently living on earth, and then realizes that none of us is identical in either appearance or personality, it seems logical to conclude that such diversity is miraculous. The diversity of our universe is infinite—a miracle that fails to penetrate our veil of blindness. It is a blindness common to us all. We see, but we do not see.

Chapter 3

Again

"Grace is given to heal the spiritually sick, not to decorate spiritual heroes"
—MARTIN LUTHER

"Are you pregnant again? Why aren't you on the pill?" Trish and I heard those very shocking words from our assistant pastor after Sunday Mass one weekend in late May. We had stopped to talk with him as he stood just outside the church to greet departing parishioners. He was a close friend whom we both admired and respected, and Trish was several months along on the road to our sixth child in eight years of marriage. It was a startling question he posed, one that, even from someone we regarded as a persuasive progressive, we wouldn't have expected. It was still very unlikely in our minds that any Catholic priest would ever suggest that we should be using artificial contraception. Even in those times, when Vatican II was opening the doors a bit to new perspectives, we were still very much confined by the rigid demands of dogma. Our Catholic upbringing held us unwaveringly captive. We had struggled for some time about such a decision. We had reason to. Trish's health was at serious risk with this new pregnancy. Father Mike was aware of our dilemma, as we had discussed the Church's teaching on it, but he probably did not know fully the physical risk Trish was facing. She had recently undergone extensive surgery on her legs to remove varicosities that were deemed potentially life threatening. She had endured more than 250 separate incisions and was advised to avoid any further pregnancies for at least five years. This latest pregnancy was simply another discordant failure of the Church-touted rhythm method. Trish's monthly cycle wasn't monthly and it certainly was not rhythmic. Her engineering husband who, with his atypical medical interest and study, had certainly provided technical support in terms of temperature etiology, charts, and thorough supervision of the process. Her doctor had advised her that the rhythm method simply was not feasible for her, and that we should be using artificial contraception. She had replied, "Doctor, if the Lord sends them to me, I'll accept them." The doctor was quick to answer, "Honey, He'll send them."

Send them He did. Six children in eight years; it was a pace we both knew couldn't continue. That eight-year period also included two midterm miscarriages for a total of eight pregnancies in eight years. For Trish, despite her vulnerable physiological risk, pregnancy was an annual affair. The two of us had frank and open discussion about all aspects of the issue, and we admitted, of course, the big problem was Church teaching. Our committed Catholic convictions effectively blocked any choice of conventional contraceptive measures. We both held similar views on Church teaching and while we were united in our rejection of the Church's argument that "natural family planning" was God's plan, we were reluctant to employ forbidden alternatives. Natural family planning surely didn't seem like a plan to us, and it was anything but natural. We had come to know its futility and frustrations. Personally, I had grudgingly concluded that even if I couldn't accept the Church's argument from nature as rational, I simply had to accept it as a matter of obedience to the superior authority to whom I had accorded my decision making. Trish held similar views, albeit not as firm as my own, since she was the one in the line of fire. Yet we were both convinced the magisterium was one step down from God, and they were definitely in our driver's seat; artificial contraception was a serious sin. We had only one solution left and thus began a period of total abstention from physical intimacy. It promoted a gradual, imperceptible distancing between us and helped sow the seeds of a coming discord. It was a hard and challenging time that would lead to an unnecessary and severe stress to our relationship, one that nearly destroyed our marriage.

While Trish endured her unremitting health challenges of our rapidly growing family, I was beginning to encounter some of my own. One evening after work, I told Trish I was going to bed early. I wasn't feeling too great. A short time later, she came into the bedroom to check up on me and she immediately knew something was amiss. I was breathing very rapidly, sweating, and beginning to feel some weird paralysis creeping into my hands and feet. She said, "I'm calling the doctor," and I didn't object. I was frightened at this totally new and unaccustomed feeling of helplessness.

The doctor arrived a few moments later. It was in those times long ago when house calls were still routine, and even better for us, the doctor was a close neighbor who lived just a block away. He was a younger man like me, who also happened to know my physician father-in-law. I remember being impressed at the suddenness of the crisis and a strange feeling of calm that came over me as a result. After a few minutes of examination, the doctor turned to Trish, who was standing by with the little ones huddled close around her, and said: "Please call for an ambulance, and then I think you should call your parish priest." That really got my attention and I began to think seriously that it was my time. Amazing! It was so abrupt and unexpected. I recall thinking: "You know not the hour." My prior feeling of calmness began to drift into a sense of urgency and excitement. I began to experience strong emotion, along with a feeling of joy, creep into whole body. Was this really it? Was my tour over? I remember my reaction being: "Well, if it is, there's not a damn thing you can do about it. So just accept and do whatever you have to and do it well." Our pastor showed up moments later—he too was just a block away—and shooed the family out to hear my last confession and give me the last rites. He was an older and more experienced man, from a Polish Catholic background. As he finished his prayers, he patted me on the head, and said to me with a confident smile, "Relax. I don't think you're dying." I wondered, "What did I confess that made him say that?"

Soon, the ambulance had arrived and the medics took over. During my ride to the hospital, I remember very well a weird feeling of relief and saying to myself: "My life is over. This is it—for better or worse. There is nothing more I can do. Whatever happens is out of my hands. It's in God's hands now." It was as if I had been released from all my responsibilities, worries, and frustrations. My mind was saying, "relax and enjoy the show," and I easily did. The paralysis in my hands and feet had grown severe by now, and I had no sensation in them at all. I was convinced that my death was definitely imminent.

"People reach conclusions when they get tired of thinking"—Mark Twain

He also said, "The reports of my death are greatly exaggerated." So it was, and so was mine. After several days of in-hospital care and testing and the extreme attention that only families blessed with resident physicians can experience, it was determined that my anomalies would not be fatal. I had experienced a bout of severe hyperventilation, which had caused excessive oxygen levels in my blood. This in turn caused my blood to turn a bit alkaline, which was the source of the paralysis in my extremities. The bottom line: I was over breathing. That sounded like an embarrassing diagnosis to me, and I remember being pretty down about it. (Idiot! You can't even get the dying right!) The doctors were kind enough to attribute my drama to an adverse reaction to my annual foray with antihistamine drugs for summer allergies. They were considerate enough not to call it an overdose, but my self-flagellation was calling it a self-induced trip. It was embarrassing. It added to my debilitating self-image.

A prolonged session with my personal physician ensued. He surmised that the simultaneous demands of fathering my large family, my incessant Ford career ambition, and the ongoing night school efforts toward a master's degree were combining to cause a level of stress in my life that I simply couldn't handle. His advice was blunt: "Keep doing what you're doing, Tom, and not too far down the road I'll be removing half your stomach. Or, you could change your attitude and things could be more normal for you. You need less stress in your life—take care of yourself. No one else can." He gave me much to ponder.

I began a period of serious self-examination. I knew the doctor's advice was probably an accurate assessment, but that only seemed to add to my woes. I was feeling pretty much like a total failure. The goals I had set for myself stemmed from that well-known admonition: "To whom much is given, much will be expected." I knew that I had certainly been given much, but I could not see that I had produced much. Everywhere I looked, I saw only mediocrity. That was my conviction. I was mediocre at best and I didn't like it, but I also didn't know what I could do about it. I envisioned that my "lukewarm" image, while maybe not causing the Lord to vomit, was probably inducing at least a little nausea. I suspect that it is a common affliction of the ordinary. I didn't realize then as I do now, that just doing what's right in front of you, and doing it to the best of your ability, is all that's required—that, and perhaps trying to discern the voice of the Holy Spirit.

The more I reflected, the worse I felt. I realized even my marriage was less than I had planned and was deteriorating. Our total sexual abstention had produced its own ambience of tension and distant detachment. What had at least been the family cave was fast becoming a family of caves with single occupants. What else can I do? Maybe I should simply pray about it. Just turn it over to Jesus. I marvel now how God's grace sometimes comes just in "the nick of time."

Once more in my life, I turned to prayer in a special way. There was no particular formula. I didn't have any such proclivities or inspiration. It was just some very intense conversation on my part. I didn't hear any answers, but I was willing to wait and see how things played out. I knew God heard me. I just wanted to know what to do. I'm not sure what I expected, or even if I expected anything, but I knew that prayer is often a solution to problems in its own right. It helps because it alters that self-focus obsession into which we often stumble. I've learned also, that He often places the solution to your problems right in front of you where it's often hard to recognize. They are hard to recognize because they appear so ordinary. God is a master at camouflage. However, this time there was little camouflage. He went a step beyond for me.

It was not too long into this low period, after I started my prayer approach, when it happened. Most folks would say I experienced a self-induced delusion, or just a dream. Yet the image and affectation has stayed with me for more than fifty years now. I can remember it like it happened last night. It was a dream. However, it was intensely vivid, unlike any other dream I'd ever had—before or since. In my dream, I found myself kneeling, alone in a darkened chapel. I was in the last pew in the left-hand corner farthest from the main altar. There seemed to be a side altar directly ahead of me, a place usually reserved for a statue of the Blessed Mother. However, there was no statue. I suddenly saw a brilliant light shining just to the right of this side altar. It was dazzling and I sensed a numinous quality, which seemed to emit an irresistible attraction. I could not make out any particular form—just this beautiful intense white light and an insistent beckoning. I got up from my kneeling and went straight toward the light. As I approached it, I was overcome, swept toward the light by an indescribably intense wave of emotion and attraction. I felt a sudden sense of joy. Then I began to weep uncontrollably as I collapsed to my knees in a heap. I knew instantly that standing in the center of this light was Jesus. I was kneeling before Jesus! I dared not look up at His face. I could only kneel there, bent over at His feet, sobbing in a happy feeling of liberation. Then it happened. He put His hand on my shoulder, and spoke to me, softly, with an exquisite gentleness that radiated His enveloping love. He said, "It's all right Tom. You are doing just fine." Again: "Everything is all right. You are doing just fine."

I will never forget the loving gentleness of those simple words and the touch of His hand—the immense feeling of relief, a sensation of such intense love and compassion. The emotional experience and sheer joy was unlike anything in the conscious world. Nothing can dim the reality of that encounter long ago. The gentleness, the love—Jesus gave me a special gift that night that I will never forget and for which I will always be so very grateful. It has been a life-long gift that is a source of consistent comfort.

I woke abruptly from my dream and I found my face wet from the tears that were apparently very real, and not just a dream. The tremendous sense of relief remained, as if some terrible burden had been lifted from me, and I knew that God had answered my prayers in a very spectacular way. I wondered at such a gift. I could not understand it, but I was completely convinced of the fact that it was a special grace just for me and it came at a very needy time in my life. I made some adjustments. I gave up the master's program and I think I stepped out of my cave long enough to see if I could get my wife to come back in with me. My conversations with Jesus in the Eucharist on the following Sundays were quite intense and one sided for a long time after that.

It was the second of my personal extraordinary spiritual gifts. It branded my faith with an indelible impression, one which I still cherish today. My perspective now is an unforgettable image of God's love. It is amazing—indescribably gentle, wonderful, and always available. Few of us comprehend it and it is obviously unconditional. This experience has lasted a lifetime and it is one that has consistently lifted me up in the worst of times. It has affected my faith journey immensely. It is impossible to forget the love that I experienced that night; the gentle, loving Jesus, accepting you just as you are.

Chapter 4

A Good Boy?

"Goodness is the only investment that never fails"
—HENRY DAVID THOREAU

The faith of childhood has an innocence often lost in adulthood. When Jesus advised that we become "as little children," He set one more standard that is difficult to meet. It is a standard I have found as compelling contemplation on frequent occasions.

It was evening and time for him to go to bed. The young boy knelt beside his bed to say his night prayers as he had been taught. He had seen his father do the same many times, and he was not even Catholic. Prayer was a given at those assigned times of the day—morning and night, before meals, and of course at Mass. He always wanted to be a "good boy," and he'd decided it really wasn't that hard. As a matter of fact, all the fuss he'd always heard about being good seemed to be a much-exaggerated thing. Being good was easy. It wasn't hard. Why did adults constantly say that doing what was right was so difficult? Maybe he was missing something. Yes, the problem was, being a good boy seemed too easy. His parents frequently told him he was a good boy and he'd even over-heard his mom telling other folks what a good boy he was. Actually, he felt a little ashamed about it. It just seemed that he couldn't take any credit for something that was so easy. It was with this convic-tion that he decided he'd ask Jesus to send him something hard to do. Then he would still do the right thing and prove that he really was a good boy and would always be good no matter what. He was sure it would finally make him feel proud that he had actually done something worthwhile. So that night, as he knelt beside his bed, he asked Jesus to send him some serious temptation or test so that he could prove that he definitely was a "good boy."

Tom's First Communion, 1937

I still remember that incident. I don't remember if I had learned the "Our Father" at that point, but if I had, I surely didn't comprehend the petition "lead us not into temptation." Praying by rote is a lesson commonly infused in early childhood, and is a habit that some of us retain throughout life. Often we parse the words but not the thought. It's a little like hearing but not listening. As that child, I knew I did all my chores with little prodding. Make your bed every morning, help with the dishes, and scrub the kitchen floor, the downstairs bathroom, the fireplace, and the front foyer once a week. Mow the lawn or clean up the garage. Some chores I'd share with my two brothers, but some were specific to each of us. We all had our assignments and it was a routine you never questioned or thought at all severe. Mom always paid us a generous allowance at the end of the week, and it felt good to contribute to the household routine. It never struck me as anything hard. Obey Mom and Dad, do your chores, study hard, and pray regularly. That's how to be good, and it was just too easy. Thus "lead me into temptation" was my naive prayer. Years later, my prayer was answered and my petition granted. I found being a "good boy" was much harder than I'd bargained for.

Life is a universal continuing education. It's like a school that never lets out that we all have to attend, like it or not. We graduate only when life ends and very few of us graduate with honors. My own education seemed to accelerate after I married and began to raise a family.

The hyperventilation episode and the ensuing consultation with my doctor set off some new concepts in my mind. "Take care of yourself," he'd said. "No one else can." Coupled with my unique religious experience that convinced me I was really an OK guy doing a decent job, and with the reinforcement of a contemporary culture that seemed to focus on the primacy of self-interest, I had rationalized that it was time to start taking a little better care of number one. I began to think that life was more about me and maybe I ought to bend my rigid code a little to my own wants and needs more often. I now recognize that such a conclusion was one of the most serious errors I would make in my lifetime. It was a decision I would come to regret.

As a young engineer at Ford Motor Company in those days, I found myself in another virtually all-male environment, not unlike my U.S. Navy experience. I had the advantage of being recognized as a graduate of a big name school, Notre Dame, and as a former naval officer, I enjoyed some further unwarranted advantages. It was a condition I liked, but one that left me feeling a little uncomfortable. I felt motivated to succeed, of course, and was determined to advance up the ranks of management as far as I could, but I was determined to do it on real merit. It had to stem from personal performance, not some phony image-oriented perception. I wanted an automotive career and I had elected to stake it on Ford Motor Company. The primary reason that I chose Ford was that my dad held a high position at General Motors. Had I chosen GM, I would have definitely enjoyed some distinct advantages by having good connections in the executive ranks. However, this was anathema to me. While General Motors was like family because of my dad and our many GM friends, and arguably should have been my natural first choice, I felt compelled to start some place where I was unknown and totally on my own. Daddy wasn't going to pull any strings for me; I was going to make my own way. Besides, Ford had made me an attractive offer when I'd returned from my tour of active duty in the U.S. Navy.

Despite my two-year experience as a commissioned officer, I was still afflicted with a deterrent dose of self-doubt. Looking back, I recognize that I had definitely been infected early in my life by a severe case of low self-esteem. It explains my strong introversion, despite the occasional trips outside of my cave. It was an issue I struggled with throughout the first half of my life. However, it is probably a common situation. Thankfully, I have conquered that affliction, and have probably fallen to the opposite extreme of the spectrum. I suspect the main source of this infection was the exceptionally strict traditional Catholic educational environment of my early youth. It is difficult to assess accurately. Was it nature or nurture? Nevertheless, clearly, the constant emphasis on our sinful nature and need for forgiveness precipitated a further problem; it made any modicum of self-confidence simply a manifestation of another sin: pride.

Love versus discipline. It's a delicate balance at best. Still, many folks wrestle with low self-esteem, Catholic or not, and like many others, I survived and eventually overcame this handicap.

How much of personality is DNA? What component is due to environment? I am probably not qualified to answer that, except to observe that my children's self-assurance seems greater than my own origins. They were not educated in Catholic schools to the extent that I was. Except for Tracey, whose early childhood suffered some distinct Catholic trauma, my children were largely the product of public schools, which were devoid of the intense parochial school discipline and a dogma-centered focus. While the three oldest of my children had some Catholic high school experience, none of them enjoyed the intense Catholic education that I had had, and by the time they had moved into secondary education, the fear-based approach had diminished in our culture. Perhaps Dr. Spock had started the new trend. At the present time, when I do not feel the stress of personal incompetence and the proverbial wisdom of old age has apparently set in, I realize that low self-esteem is no longer a problem for me. However, I recognize that those earlier years were clearly afflicted with that suppressant. I definitely paid a price for it. In terms of Maslow's hierarchy of needs, in the characteristics of self-esteem, confidence, and achievement, I would have scored quite low. In other areas of his measuring stick, I did not seem to be lacking. Therefore, I suppose I can say that I am lucky. It could have been much worse; overall, my blessings have been abundant.

The construction of my exclusionary cave of self-doubt encountered a momentary delay during this period. It was marked by the birth of my writing passion. When I was about eight years old, at my mom's suggestion, I entered a citywide essay contest. Sponsored by the Michigan Consolidated Gas Company, the task was to write in twenty-five words or less "Why I Like to Use Hot Water and Soap." I was astonished to win first prize, a new red and white Schwinn bicycle. It launched my literary career with wheels. Later, I went on to win first prize in a high school essay contest on "What Was Wrong With the Porter Family." I was a lowly freshman who triumphed over more than a few of my upper classmates. My enjoyment of writing was to last a lifetime and my self-assurance from these awards generated some improvement. However, these self-confidence gains proved to be mere blips in my early valley of desolation.

Tom with bike prize, May 1940

Offsetting my self-doubt was one area in which I was more than confident I could excel. That area was personal integrity. I possessed a well-ingrained Catholic certitude on anything remotely bordering on the subject of morality or ethics. In addition to the nuns, Jesuits, and Holy Cross fathers, my own father had done his job well, too. He had always been very insistent that we boys appreciate and practice ethical behavior at all times. No lapses allowed. He taught us boys many little lessons in ethics—specifics we would not hear in our school religion classes. I remember him telling us once, in a moment of serious discourse, that we should never physically strike a woman, no matter what the provocation or anger. A gentleman always treats a woman with respect and gentleness. It was a gender specific requirement. The day we would ever strike a woman would be the day we lost our manhood—no exceptions.

My dad once told me a story of his early career at General Motors, when, as a young man about to embark on his first business trip for the corporation, his boss told him: "Remember, Mr. Nelson, it's important that you recognize that you're representing General Motors on this trip." Dad said to me that he'd replied to his boss, "Yes sir, but it's more important to me that I will be representing Bert Nelson [himself]." He made it very apparent which standard would be the most demanding. The clear and somber message was that your personal integrity is your most precious asset, and no one can destroy it except you.

That story my father told me was a memory I took with me on many a business trip when Ford Motor Company was paying my expenses and I was on my own, alone or with my male colleagues, some of whom viewed such occasions as a unique opportunity to raise hell. Sadly some did. Promiscuous behavior in that anonymous environment was seen as an acceptable norm by some and frequently acted out. Once, one of my bosses teased me for being too rigid and prudish, when, one night on the road, I had rejected some unsolicited, very obvious advances toward me by the attractive waitress at our dinner table. He just could not understand passing up such a great invitation for a little sexual indulgence. Such opportunities seemed to come quite often, but it was easy for me to resist. I abhorred any thought of infidelity to my wife, no matter how far I was from home or what my colleagues did.

Doctored expense reports were another abuse. This occasionally presented a dilemma. At one well-frequented site over the years, a novel arrangement had somehow developed with one of the lower scale motels near our business site. If you stayed there, the management would charge you a low nightly fee but then, on check-out, give you a receipt for a significantly higher rate to use on your expense report. The difference equated to added income for the guest and served to attract visiting engineers to an otherwise unattractive, downscale motel. It became a popular practice. The problem for me was, I could not do that. I considered it blatantly dishonest. It was simple stealing in my mind, but that meant if I stayed at that same motel as the rest of the crew, and I demanded an accurate receipt, I would be exposing the fraud. I was no activist whistleblower and it seemed an imprudent thing to do, especially since my own boss was often involved. There was a limit to my ethical restraint. It didn't include forcing my views on others. My solution was to stay at a different motel, one of the better ones that didn't offer such dubious amenities. Despite a few of my self-righteous dinnertime lectures about personal integrity, I was probably categorized as some kind of quirky religious fanatic who in reality probably just valued the added luxury of the expensive but nonparticipating motels more than the added income. My self-anointed moral superiority became a source of a little arrogance perhaps, but it was also something of an obstacle. I was sometimes left out of the social jaunts on those trips, and it raised the specter in my mind that I was becoming an oddball loner.

Still, these were my close friends, and the people I worked with day in and day out. They were good people caught up in a culture that was essentially self-focused and laissez faire. Yes I was different, but they hadn't had the advantages I'd had. They did not have the cherished Catholic education that defined my strict codes and surely, no one could have had parents as competent, ethical, and loving as mine were. That was how I understood my position, but unfortunately, this attitude also reinforced my natural introversion and continued to enhance the comfort of my personal cave dwelling.

My code of ethics frequently seemed to me to be a hindrance. However, one particularly difficult incident had very surprising consequences. One day, an executive who was far above my lowly entry-level engineering position, called my boss and told him: "I want to see Tom Nelson in my office. I have a personal assignment for him." That got my immediate boss's attention more than a little, as well as my own. He was impressed at this sudden summons from above and it certainly puzzled me. I remembered how my dad had warned me: "You'll never know who is watching you or when. Always do the right thing." I quickly hurried up to the executive's office. It was on "Mahogany Row," and was my first encounter with one of these dark, plush and polished sacred chambers. I was duly impressed. An ambience of power seemed to emanate from the dark paneled walls, like an unseen cloud of insidious intoxication. It was designed to intimidate and I was. "What the heck does he want me for?" I wondered. I was more than a little nervous as I sat in the outer office awaiting the secretary's approval to enter the inner sanctum. Finally, I was ushered into the awesome chamber and this boss of bosses invited me to sit down. He sat behind one of the biggest solid mahogany desks I'd ever seen. It had a spotless glass top, which was sparsely adorned with a small intercom unit off to the left, and a golden twin pen set, with a black marble base, placed in the center of the desk. Nothing else cluttered the vast surface. Opposite the desk hung a large portrait of the company founder, Henry Ford I. It gave the entire scene an unmistakable aura of authority. As I sat down, I began to relax and managed a perfunctory, "Good morning sir. You sent for me?" I'd decided that maybe this first high-level encounter was just possibly an advancement opportunity. I had no inkling of what was to come.

"Tom, I'm told you're doing a great job in the Truck Engine Group. It's good to hear. I've asked you here because I have a little job I'd like you to handle. I want you to come in this coming Saturday. Can you do that?" "Yes sir!" was my immediate response. "Good" he said. "Now what I want you to do is pick up a stake truck at the garage, and take it to engine buildup and contact Mr. Oswald. He'll load you up with a couple of special V-8 engines I've had put together for my boat. I want you to deliver them to the boatyard, where I've arranged for their delivery. Can you do that?" "Holy cats!" I thought to myself. "This guy wants me to steal for him!"

I'd heard rumors about these unapproved perks in the upper echelons. I was speechless for a moment as my mind raced to come up with some reply. "Well? What about it? Can you do that for me?" he repeated. "Uh, I'm sorry, sir." I stammered. "I don't think I can do that." I spoke softly as I envisioned my career potential falling into a mortal collapse.

"What do you mean you can't do that? Why not?" he persisted.

"Well, I just can't do it. I don't think it would be right, sir," I replied. His demeanor shifted from authoritarian to a friendly smile. "OK," he said, "I understand. It's all right. I'll get someone else. Thank you Tom." He waved me off, and I left his office shaking my head in a state of total disbelief. I proceeded to take my delusions into my mental cave for a little brooding. I was sure I'd just shot my career chances in both feet.

It seemed that the exact opposite ensued. That same executive began to single me out for legitimate and very desirable assignments. He asked me to report directly to him on such occasions, and I found myself developing an unlikely friendship with him. He would often enlist me to ghostwrite important letters for him. Eventually he became my mentor and helped me achieve a succession of promotions into management that might otherwise never have occurred. It was only many years later when I began to wonder if the boat engine incident hadn't been simply an intentional ploy—a simple test of my integrity. Apparently I had passed. While promotions finally ensued, more tests were to come and not necessarily at work, but I'd graduated to the next grade level.

Recalling this period of my career, I believe that I had begun to progress into a more secure stage of maturity. My self-esteem had increased, but not always to the benefit of career advancement. It was something of a dichotomy. On the one hand, my self-confidence was improving, but my introversion stubbornly persisted. It hampered developing friendships with management level people. Perhaps introversion is often simply a by-product of excessive self-focus.

Following my promotion to management, I resisted eating lunch in the executive dining room and ate with the common folks in the main cafeteria. I just did not feel comfortable mingling with the upper echelon. I could not conceive of myself as "one of them." I wanted to stay connected with the lower echelon. This resulted in a version of independence that was not always helpful for my career. Too often, I told upper management what they did not want to hear, and in a manner that was probably often too blunt. It did not matter that I was right. If you the ruffle the feathers of your boss, you can expect consequences.

I remember an incident illustrative of that adage. Our chief engineer had arrived at a large meeting at which my presentation was to be the highlight of the agenda. It involved reporting the testing results on a new line of engines that was the chief's pet project. The results were disappointing and not what he wanted to hear. I naively gave him the unvarnished facts. Midway into my presentation, when the negative aspects of the report became clear, the chief rose from his chair and loudly proclaimed to the whole audience, "This is a f—g waste of time," and stormed out of the conference room. I was left standing in front of the audience, stopped mid-sentence, mouth agape, feeling humiliated and looking at my immediate boss for some kind of support. There was none. Later in the privacy of his office, my boss told me: "Tom sometimes it's better, I guess, to muddle the facts." Some would call it discretion, perhaps, but discretion in my eyes did not include muddling facts. Nobody was going to usurp my standards of veracity. My certitude was unshakeable, and it followed my career from beginning to end. Later, when I was demoted, I think that the perception of not being a "team player" was a factor in such a dubious distinction. Once again, my cave was beckoning.

Still, I have no regrets. Ford Motor Company later decided they sorely needed some rigid fact-telling shortly after my official retirement, when they called me back to help them to achieve a more competitive level of quality. I "called them as I saw them" during that period, and there were more than a few toes bruised. I supervised a team of engineers whose task was to visit manufacturing plants and dealerships in order to ascertain the nature and root cause of product quality issues. Folks soon found out that, during our plant visitation quality surveys, the facts held supreme over any local plant politics. The engineering community also discovered that they would receive no special treatment from their alumnus. I held no restraining camaraderie in reporting engineering design deficiencies. It was fun, a source of particular enjoyment, as I felt beholden to no one and had the full support of the vice president for product quality. I was accorded a rare level of respect that I had not experienced before, devoid of any fear or risk. It proved to be a personal educational thing, and I have often lamented that I did not discover such confidence-breeding freedom earlier in my career. I had no realization at the time, but in a subtle way, it had a circuitous impact on my faith, as a newfound self-confidence prepared me for some future critical thinking about my faith. It was more than a subtle part of my faith evolution; it was a significant step in my transition to adulthood.

Chapter 5

A Family

"Life is like college and the situations that life throws at you are those classes that you have to master and move on with knowledge to even harder classes. Discovery of yourself is endless"
—ANONYMOUS

"A nd lead us not into temptation…" When, as an adult, I recalled my youthful naiveté in asking the Lord for the contrary—to send me some serious temptation so that I could prove my worthiness—I would often shake my head and smile. Childhood innocence often has a comical streak to it. I had long since switched to the conventional plea to escape all unwelcome temptation events. There were some welcome ones, which were perhaps unwitting, but our unwitting mistakes can often be some of the most serious and I often wonder about culpability. Yet despite human ineptitude, our mistakes, whether welcome or not, and regardless of culpability, often result in major learning.

My Ford career was progressing nicely, having been promoted to the position of engineering manager, a coveted position in the first ranks of the private salary roll. I could now look forward to substantial annual bonuses and other perquisites. I had attained a new modicum of self-confidence and began exerting my personal convictions on a variety of issues, both professional and social, at home and at work.

It was midlife. My children were into the teen years and the challenges of raising six children were peaking. I began to encounter some completely unanticipated adversities. Coming from a family of three boys was probably not the best preparation for raising my five daughters, but having at least one son offset any distress in this area. He seemed to me to be a special bonus, an attitude that I tried to conceal from my daughters. Yet, while I may have doted over my son, my daughters were not deprived, and any deficiencies of mine were more than offset by my wife's innate parenting skills.

The Tom Nelson Family 1966

My wife, Trish, had two sisters, one brother, and a loving father and mother. The latter was a major spousal qualification in my view. More than that, though, Trish possessed a fine intellect and a sensitive, loving nature that seemed boundless when it came to parenting. No girls ever enjoyed a better mother under any circumstances. It would be accurate to say that, while I held a rather narcissistic self-image of my "exceptional" parenting skills, Trish truly did excel. She had majored in psychology, which was probably a valuable asset for parenting. She had a boundless parental love and patience, both of which were abundant and freely dispensed. She combined it all with an intuition that often left my daughters awed and amazed. It has been observed that parenting is probably the most important job in the world, but it's generally assigned to people who are completely untrained and often more ill equipped than not. Trish was mostly an exception. She had innate skills that I definitely lacked. I didn't realize my own inadequacies in those parenting skills. I tended toward a rather Victorian concept, an arrogant view that I was well qualified, the "prefect of discipline," and "head of the family." More accurately, I was really more like the average poke, mostly learning as I went along. I was deficient in knowing how to balance discipline with love, and in the early years of my family, my deficiency was exacerbated by our parish pastor, who often thundered from the pulpit that if you "spare the rod, you'll spoil the child." I was lucky, though; I had a spouse who was naturally gifted at parenting to offset me.

I recall one particularly educational experience in my journey of learning the limits of certitude. It was a humorous hint of the need for more critical thinking.

The challenges resulting from the turmoil of typical teenage behavior had risen into a din of disorganization. Father, the prefect of discipline, the captain of the ship, had decided to instill a little naval-bred plan of orderly control. It consisted of a carefully designed, naval-styled "plan of the day," establishing some very precise planning to every normal daily task for all hands. Each event was assigned a time slot and requirements were noted for any deviation from the plan. The plan was to be posted in the upstairs hallway just outside the children's bedrooms. Good order was the goal and Daddy's naval experience was the solution. When the captain first posted this order of the day and called a morning muster to launch his new weapon of parental control, all stood at attention for the solemn announcement.

But good grief! Something seemed awry. Daddy looked out only to a sea of women! He was the only male present. Mark had already left for early morning swim-team practice and the captain faced six puzzled feminine faces. Nevertheless, carry-on he must, and the commander-in-chief proceeded to carefully explain how the "plan of the day" would be posted daily and all hands must conform their schedules and actions to the plan. Expecting some complimentary reactions for such a great idea with its careful planning and diligent detail, he looked out to the sea of femininity, and saw only a unity of big smiles. Then, worse! They all began laughing! Even mother was laughing. "Damn it! I'm serious. We're all going to follow the plan of the day—even me!" The laughter only increased and a unanimous cry went up. "You've got to be kidding, Dad!" They all walked away laughing and my wife came up to me to offer some solace. Putting her arm around me she gently said, "Honey, this isn't the navy and besides, you're dealing with girls."

I surrendered. The plan of the day was scrapped. It is always helpful to recognize defeat whenever it occurs. It is an essential part of the learning process and the quicker you acknowledge your loss, the sooner the embarrassment subsides. In retrospect, I came to realize that the plan of the day defeat was definitely an important incident in the education of father.

Among the many learning experiences of raising six children was the gradual realization of the unique qualities each one of them possessed. The concept of individual diversity was not something that had occurred to me in the beginning. Daddy had his plan. Conformity to his plan and ideals was part of it. While their physical appearance might reflect the commonality of DNA, each of my children possessed a diversity of persona that impressed me more and more with the passage of time. It was a slow process for me to discover this. Now in their adult years, I sometimes marvel that they all came from the same parents. They are such unique people. Their individual stories, each in his and her own way, had profound influences on my life. Learning this was an important lesson in my curriculum.

My daughters have taught me so much about the feminine. I now feel certain that this world would be much better off if women were more in charge. Patriarchy is our fate, but matriarchy I suspect would be better. Women intuitively have achieved a better sense of love. Who would argue that it is the greatest of all virtues? Still, it is probably true that my son, male though he is, accomplished the greatest impact on all of us. He certainly has had the greatest impact on my life.

When Mark was a child growing up, he reminded me a great deal of my recollections of my own childhood. He was certainly the "good boy" type. I remember seldom occasions in his childhood when he would provoke his mother and me in even minor ways. He had a gentleness and sensitivity at an early age that was atypical for most children. I remember one summer Saturday afternoon as typical. He had gone insect hunting. Taking a small jar with a metal lid into which he had punctured several holes, he then proceeded to the adjacent vacant lot, where he managed to capture two or three grasshoppers. In a short time, he came into the house to show me proudly his accomplishment. I praised him for his great hunting skills and asked him what he was going to do with his prize. His immediate reply was, "I have to let them go now, Dad. They might die if I keep them too long." Release them he did. He watched them smilingly as they flew away to their freedom. This was my son. He seemed almost too perfect. He was definitely that familiar "good boy" that I remembered from my own youth. I marveled at this precious gift that God had given Trish and me.

Mark and I grew very close over those early years. We did many father-and-son things together. During a camping trip with the local Boy Scouts troop one summer, we won the father-and-son log-sawing contest, a triumph that elated us both. What the other competitors did not know was that Mark and I had substantial prior experience using a two-man saw cutting firewood up north. Boating, swimming, and in later years, tennis and skiing were things that we constantly shared with enthusiasm. All of these things served as strong bonding experiences for the two of us. I definitely appreciated having a son who was so exceptional. Mark was a joy to both of his parents, but for me, as the only male contingent among a household of six women, he enjoyed special status. At the time, I was unaware that he would become my greatest teacher, and that I was a student in the most urgent need. He was definitely destined to provide a much-needed expansion of my curriculum.

My attention to my son was not an exclusionary focus. Trish and I did many things with our kids as we all matured together. In the winter months, it was sledding and ice-skating. Later, when the older kids were teenagers, we left the younger ones behind and vacationed several times at ski resorts in northern Michigan. Skiing was a passion that both Trish and I had enjoyed since our earliest courtship, prior to my tour of active naval service. Mark was the only one to inherit our interest, and he became so hooked on it that he eventually became a professional ski instructor. It has been the source of some occasional parental angst with his jaunts into mountain skiing.

However, the greatest family passion was boating. It was initially my obsession, one launched in my own youth, but it soon became a family affair. All my children loved the water and family vacations in the summer were always on some body of water, usually the Great Lakes. We purchased our first boat, an eighteen-foot aluminum bow-rider with a used forty horsepower outboard engine. We named it the *Tristy I*, a contraction of Trish and Tom. It served us well, as all the children soon learned to water ski. We took it everywhere, even to Mackinaw Island in Michigan's upper peninsula. It soon became evident, however, that we needed a potty to accommodate Mother Nature. This resulted in *Tristy II*, a twenty-one-foot outdrive-powered runabout equipped with a port-a-potty in the cuddy cabin up forward. *Tristy II* was a great ski boat, but we had begun to yearn for even more comfortable cruising accommodations with a more realistic overnight capability.

The Nelsons, Circa 1975

Reading the newspaper one Sunday, I spied a want ad for a used thirty-one-foot Marinette for sale. It was of welded aluminum construction, with a fly bridge and twin engines, an express cruiser at an affordable price of $8,500. While that was an appreciable amount of money in those days, it had become such a family passion that Trish and I both thought we should make the sacrifice and find the means to indulge it. Our conviction was that investing in family fun was money well spent. It was a decision that we often applauded in later years and never regretted. The *Tristy III* was born.

The idea of our family owning a cruiser of this size seemed an unlikely dream. The boat had been stored indoors at a marina in Marine City on the St. Clair River, and had been in storage for nearly three years. That seemed promising, since it meant that the boat had not been used much. What I couldn't know was that because of its long storage period, the engines had rusted through disuse. After the purchase, Mark and I took the long drive to the marina to ascertain more thoroughly the condition of the boat and the engines. The boat seemed to be in excellent condition but after a careful inspection of the engines, we soon found them badly rusted from their long storage period. They were Ford engines, which were models I was quite familiar with, and I concluded a major overhaul would be needed. It was a task I felt I could manage as a do-it-yourself project. Over the following weeks, every Saturday, Mark and I would travel the long drive to the marina where we disassembled the engines, removed the rusted parts for repair, and then reassembled both engines. It turned out to be another bonding experience for father and son. We would leave early Saturday morning, stop for breakfast on the way up, and then work on the boat throughout the day. We would head back home at dusk, tired from our task, but still full of conversation.

After two months of this, it was late spring, and we announced to the family that launch time would be the following weekend. Excitement stirred and we all looked forward to a much-anticipated adventure. We arrived at the marina right after mass on the next Sunday. We had been told by marina personnel that our launch time was scheduled for eleven. Unfortunately, however, the boat scheduled for launching prior to ours was a wooden boat, which leaked so badly that it had to be held in the marina's only launch sling for a protracted period in order for the seams to swell sufficiently and seal. This delayed our own launching until well into twilight. By the time we were in the water, it was nighttime and darkness had fallen. Our father-and-son-rebuilt engines started right up and ran perfectly. My family of eight embarked on our first serious cruise in a real cruiser, the *Tristy III*. It was at the onset of a dark moonless night, a challenge we had not planned on.

I had never navigated the St. Clair River before, even in daylight, and the darkness of night added another challenging dimension. We were all excited at the new adventure. Trish had prepared a German potato salad supper for us to eat during the trip. While she fed the family, I focused on the navigation down the river, feeling buoyed with confidence at the smooth transition to my new sea command. It proved fairly easy. One simply had to stay in the mid channel and watch for the marker buoys. We also had good river charts to guide us. As we motored slowly in the darkness and finally reached the open waters of Lake St. Clair, a new surprise challenged my growing confidence rather abruptly. A little wave of panic interrupted my serenity, as gazing ahead, I saw only a myriad sea of lights in the distant shoreline. They all looked the same. Where was Blue Lagoon, our home marina, in all that confusion? Apprehension quickly set in. My concern was evident to my wife and she soon came to my rescue. She said, "Honey, I remember from the boating course; the instructor told us that there is a flashing green and white light tower located at Selfridge Airfield." Our marina, the Blue Lagoon, was at the southeast end of Selfridge and I knew that if we could find that light-marker we would be home free. Trish and I both scanned the horizon and soon spotted the prominent flashing green and white light. Its discovery spawned a new respect for my first mate's navigational skills, and we set course for it. In a little over an hour, we were docking at our berth in Blue Lagoon. It was now nearly eleven o'clock, and we were all pretty tired and anxious to get home—enough boating for one day.

However, the drama wasn't over. As Trish was stepping onto the dock, her purse tipped open and the car keys fell out into ten feet of water. Disaster! The other set was at home, over an hour away by car. The only possible solution was for me to go for a swim and find the keys. I quickly changed into my swimsuit and dove in. The water was cold and pitch-dark; it was deep. I dove to the bottom and had to equalize the pressure on my ears to compensate for the depth. I had always loved to swim under water as a kid, and other than the depth-induced ear pain, I felt no discomfort or apprehension at my unlikely task. The bottom surface was covered with a six-inch layer of soft muck and sloped quickly to even deeper depths. Trish had pointed out clearly where the keys had gone in, and I began a methodical feeling search for the treasured keys. After several prolonged dives, after which I would reemerge, gasping for air, I found the keys, pretty much where Trish said they should be. When I surfaced with them clutched in my hand, a rousing cheer went up from the kids. I was a hero! I dressed, and by the time we got home, it was after one o'clock in the morning.

This initial experience with serious cruising was one of many times to come when boating proved to be stressful as well as fun. We began to learn a new respect for the big waters of the Great Lakes, and I tried to accommodate this new source of unexpected stress in my life. Such stress is a normal burden of life that everyone endures and we often add to it unwittingly. Yet, it is all essential to the learning process.

My passion for boating was, in some ways, an affliction for my wife. She did not share my obsession to an equal degree, but she certainly did her best to accommodate her husband. Sometimes, the demands approached the heroic. I recall our first long family cruise in our new cruiser, the *Tristy III*. We were on a two-week vacation and had cruised over five hundred miles from Lake St. Clair up through Lake Huron, across the top of the "Michigan mitt," west into Lake Michigan, then southward down to Charlevoix, Michigan. After two days of cruising to Charlevoix, we docked overnight Sunday in the shelter of a marina on Round Lake, a small body of water located on the edge of the city. It was just a short distance from the big waters of Lake Michigan. Up to that point, we had had a mostly uneventful and pleasant trip, and the kids along with Mom and Dad were enjoying the new experience of our first extended cruising on the open waters of the Great Lakes. We were scheduled to meet up with both sets of our parents, who had traveled together by car to Portage Point Inn on Portage Lake, some ninety-five miles to the south. We planned to cruise to that area the following day, and the weather had definitely been cooperating.

We awoke early the following morning to a beautiful, clear sunny day and planned that our cruise to Portage Lake would take a little over four hours. There seemed to be a light breeze blowing and we elected to walk into town for breakfast prior to our departure. As we savored our hot breakfast, we all enjoyed an air of excitement and the anticipation of the trip ahead. The kids were enthusiastic at the prospect of soon seeing their grandparents at our destination. What I did not know was that the "light breeze" in our sheltered marina was actually building to near-gale-force winds out on the big lake. Despite the clear sky, the wind was blowing out of the south-southwest with gusts exceeding forty-five knots. We soon got underway and the cruise through the narrow channel out to Lake Michigan was deceptively smooth. Once out on the lake, however, I was immediately startled at the strength of the wind and the height of the waves. While I had had good seamanship training in the navy supplemented by my power squadron education, I had never experienced boating on the Great Lakes in heavy seas. It was to be a new and scary learning experience.

As we traversed further out into the lake, all the kids were riding out on the bow, clinging to the safety railing with their bare feet dangling over the side. They were screaming in delight at the thrill from the wild rising and slamming of the bow into the oncoming sea, with solid water smashing into their merriment. They thought it was all great fun, but I quickly realized that this was definitely not going to be fun. It was a serious mistake. I was amazed at the sea condition. In all my boating days, I had never seen such huge waves before. Trish looked at me, pale with obvious fear, and plaintively asked, "Are we going to be all right?" "Of course," I replied with a false confidence hiding my own suppressed terror, "but I think you better get the kids off the bow and into the cabin." Soon all the kids were safe inside, disgruntled at the abrupt end of their fun, but no longer in danger of being swept overboard.

Before long, the huge waves, began converging in a confused pattern as, approaching the mouth of Grand Traverse Bay, they began colliding from the south and southeast. Because of the longer reach up the bay, they were increasing significantly in height as well. We were now several miles out and the sea was running twelve to fourteen feet. This was far beyond anything I had ever experienced or even imagined, and I struggled to keep the boat headed into the waves. There seemed to be no discernible direction to the sea and controlling the helm required constant spinning of the wheel back and forth to maintain a course. It was a wild scene and anything but pleasurable. My only thought now was to avoid the disaster of having my whole family cast into the cold deep waters of Lake Michigan

The waves on the fresh waters of the Great Lakes are different from the ocean. Because the fresh water is lighter than salt-laden seawater, the wave periods are much shorter, resulting in steeper wave fronts and more rapid wave succession. It can be an extremely destructive sea condition. It was just such adversity that sank the legendary *Edmund Fitzgerald* on Lake Superior. Great Lakes seamanship can be most demanding.

I was shocked when the water soon began lifting our little cruiser high on the crest of a wave followed by a terrifying plunge downward toward the trough below. At the peak of each wave, the screws on the stern would come out of the water and the unloaded engines screamed in an over speed protest. Between continued and frantic manipulation of the throttles and the helm, I was one busy sailor. This new learning experience with the heavy weather on the open waters of the Great Lakes, found me scared as hell, when suddenly Trish screamed out above the din, "I think we should go back!" Without hesitation, I shouted back, "Yes, I agree!"

However, that would be easier said than done. At this point, we encountered another new threat. Solid water had been passing over the top of the boat as we plunged forward into the waves and I had not noticed that this water was filling up our little eight-foot dinghy, which hung from davits across the stern of the boat. The stress of several thousand pounds of water in the dinghy was overstressing the entire stern structure, and I could see that a major structural failure was imminent if I did not quickly remedy the condition. I shouted to Trish to take the helm and went back to release the dinghy. At this point, my oldest daughter, Lisa, popped her head out of the cabin door and announced, "Things are really a mess down here, and there's water coming in through the windows!" Trish later confided that she was near panic at that point. She said that if she had not been so occupied at the helm struggling for control and that if Lisa had screamed in panic, she swore she would have jumped overboard. After considerable struggle, I was able to attach a towline to the dinghy and managed to push it off without going overboard with it. I was unaware that it would prove to be a hidden blessing, as the swamped dinghy in tow acted as an efficient drogue, serving to enhance our stability and control. It was an effective sea anchor, something, I had learned about previously in my land-based boating education. It definitely helped prevent the stern from swinging forward into a broaching position during our return trip downwind. It was a classic rough weather seamanship aid. I should have quickly thought of it but the stress of the moment afforded zero time for mental focus beyond the immediate demands for survival. My guardian angel overcame my mental lapse and took care of it amidst our plight.

With Trish still at the helm, I then went below to see where water was entering into the cabin. It turned out that the wash of the water passing over the boat was overloading the drain scuppers for the sliding windows on either side of the cabin. I decided it was not a major threat to our security, but the cosmetic effect, I was going to hear about from my first mate. The cabin interior was a complete mess, as all port and starboard cupboard doors had popped open. The entire contents within had been cast about, causing a jumbled and frightening scene. I returned to the helm to relieve Trish and told her to get life jackets on all of the kids and herself.

I now faced the task of turning about in this horrendous sea without being capsized by a broad siding wave. It was a scary and challenging maneuver. I carefully took time to study the sea, picking a spot between waves, and made a sudden, rapid turn under full throttle. We came about successfully, only to confront a new condition. The sea had now become a following one. This would greatly exacerbate the difficult and frightening task of maintaining directional control.

This new more challenging threat involved the danger of a wave lifting the stern, tilting the boat steeply downward. The added thrust from the onrushing sea in the rear would magnify the absurd downward angle, and the bow would plunge deeply in to the water below, halting our forward motion. The stern would quickly swing around and the boat would now be broadside to the oncoming sea. Capsizing would inevitably ensue. It is imperative under such conditions to maintain a position on the backside of the wave, always keeping the stern lower than the bow. Any failure to accomplish this task risks a classic failure in seamanship. It is called, *broaching*. It is one of the greatest risks of disaster in small-boat seamanship.

I knew what broaching was about, because when I was about fifteen years old, it had happened to me on a small inland lake. I had been riding the heavy wake of a large powerboat in the outboard-powered family skiff. I was enjoying the thrill of the accelerated downhill ride on the front-side of the wake generated wave when, at one point, the bow caught the water too steeply and dug in. In an instant, I was in the water peering at my skiff upside down with the outboard prop pointing skyward. It was an effective lesson about the phenomenon of broaching—one that I survived with only a little damaged pride and a water-soaked engine.

This was different. It was Lake Michigan and my whole family was being threatened. I am now convinced in retrospect that our inadvertent dinghy-drogue sea anchor was a life-saving event, another unsolicited gift. It was one of those serendipitous coincidences. I believe such fortuitous incidents must come from beyond the normal The sequence of the sea filling the dinghy and the subsequent necessity to release and tow it had definitely protected us from broaching far more than any seamanship on my part. Had we turned around sooner to return to safety, there would have been no reason to release the dinghy. The task to avoid broaching would probably have been insurmountable under such conditions. I have often recalled it as an unmistakable faith-reinforcing experience—a portrait portion of my lifetime landscape.

The trip back to Charlevoix was agonizingly slow and fraught with terror. We had traveled outbound for little more than thirty to forty minutes, but the necessity to stay on the backside of the waves to minimize the risk of broaching dictated a zigzag pattern for our return course. It was about two and a half hours after our decision to return when we finally arrived back at our slip on Round Lake. We were thoroughly exhausted, soaked wet, and emotionally drained.

Trish came to me as the kids were making fast our dock lines and retrieving our dinghy, and through tears of relief, she shouted out: "You can keep your damn boat! I'm taking a bus home."

I knew exactly how she felt, and even wondered how we could all take a bus home. It wasn't a moment later when the skipper of the boat docked next to us, overhearing my wife's outburst, came up to Trish and put his arm around her and said, "Relax, honey. What you need is a couple of aspirin or maybe a good stiff drink of scotch." Trish quickly responded, "I'll take both!" The gentleman was quick to supply the prescription, and then addressed us both with some somber words of wisdom. He said, "Now look, guys, you know, you don't *have* to go out in that kind of stuff." It was good advice and I placed it in my mental logbook of nautical lessons learned. We left for Portage Point the following day in an incongruously calm sea, eventually returning home with no more trauma. We did however introduce a new and diligent daily monitoring of the NOAA weather channel on our ship-to-shore radio.

Reflecting back on that time, I now recognize that this was one more time in my life in which I seemed to have received special protection. That wild sea ride could very easily have ended in a terrible tragedy. I do not recall whether I said a prayer of thanksgiving to my guardian angel at the time, but it would have been appropriate and typical for me to do so. I try to be aware of graces received and express my thanks immediately. Awareness of graces received is something I have tried to cultivate over the years, and I think it has helped me recognize the Holy Spirit many times.

Aside from graces received, I also realize the burdens I unwittingly inflicted on Trish over the years. She was a patient, giving woman. While boating was more my passion than hers, she accepted my indulgence with a typical feminine generosity. I am sure there must have been times when she felt that her investment in our marriage was a gross mistake. I was a demanding fellow and in retrospect, she was doing much giving without much getting. I especially regret my cigarette smoking over the years, and my inconsiderate pollution of her environment. She was a nonsmoker and her tolerance of my vice was something I often wince at in recollection. In later years, after overcoming the addiction, I became very aware of others who were then afflicting me in a similar manner. I placed plenty such hurdles for her love to surmount, but I was lucky. She was a loving woman who taught me so much about that virtue. Unfortunately, it was a lengthy process.

An appropriate sequel to that memorable Lake Michigan event occurred, years later in 1985 when Trish finally declared an ultimatum: "Enough. We've done it your way—boating for more than twenty years. Now it's my turn. We're going to cruise *on land*." We did. We sold our boat and bought a thirty-three foot house trailer. It marked the birth of our RV experiences and another phase of happy family entertainment, one that we mutually enjoyed to the end of her life some twenty years later. They were years of a much more relaxing cruising mode.

My children's teen years occurred in the 1970s. In many ways, it was a tumultuous time for our country. The sexual revolution coupled with the maturation of the baby boom generation had firmly altered the nation's culture in major ways. Our Catholic faith proved to be a welcome retreat from society's often-shocking affronts, even while the Church was undergoing its own revolution from the reforms of Vatican II. While it sometimes proved an added burden through the unchanged dogmatic stances of historical precedent, on the whole, our Church-driven faith proved more refuge than burden. Both Trish and I participated in Church lay affairs frequently during those years. The Christian Family Movement was a favorite for us. Lectoring, teaching CCD, ushering, choir membership, and other church-sponsored activities all became a part of our family life. Parish picnics were a favorite with the kids as was church-sponsored summer camp.

The crises that come to most every family with teenagers did not bypass ours, but our faith-based environment definitely provided welcome succor during those challenges. As a father, when prioritizing career distractions with family demands, I had neither hesitation nor difficulty placing my family first. It proved to be the better investment. It was simply a part of my Catholic faith. Yet while maturity began to surface, I still had a long road to travel toward an adult faith. Evolution is always a gradual process. Sometimes cataclysmic events can hasten the process. Our comfortable ordinary Catholic family's quiet life was moving toward just such an event.—a period that would definitely prove to be a life-changing epoch.

Chapter 6

The Feminine Factor

*"I can see as clear as a daylight that the hour is coming when
women will lead humanity to a higher evolution"*
—HAZRAT INAYAT KHAN, CIRCA 1916 [3]

Four of my five daughters have left the Catholic Church. In
many ways, their journey has mirrored my own, but I am
reluctant to leave. Why have they stayed while I persist? Did
they simply choose a different cure for the same affliction? If the
Church has hurt me through its paucity of loving and the persistent and official demeaning of my gay son, it has certainly hurt
them just as much for the same reasons, but perhaps there is the
added aggravation of the perceived denigration of anything feminine. I sense this is the difference. Their experiences and reactions to the official Church have contributed uniquely to my own
conclusions, and critique. I admire the flower of feminism they all
display and the feminine element they have infused in my life. It
has had no small impact on my journey. Considering that affect, I

---

3   Inayat Khan (July 5, 1882–February 5, 1927) was a follower of Universal
Sufism and the founder of the Sufi Order in the West in 1914

am struck by their dramatic solution, so different from mine. Why? Did Trish and I somehow short-change them, or was it simply the central focus on *loving* that we tried so hard to instill which made their departure inevitable? I'm not sure, even now, but I do know, that for most of them the Church assault began early and mom and dad were only observers.

Much of what I write about in this book relates in one way or another to my son, Mark. He gets a lot of attention mainly because his sexual orientation caused such a revolution in my thinking and my life. His being gay, how Trish and I handled that revelation and our ensuing activism in the gay community had a major impact, not just on Trish, me, and our faith, but also on our whole family. Yet, even while it's probably natural for a father to dote on his only son in the midst of six women, and despite his unique influence, it doesn't diminish the profound impact of my girls. They are an amazing crew and have been the source of so many blessings; what they have taught me, contributed to my activism and evolving faith in major ways. What they gave me was different from their brother, but no less essential to my spiritual progress. Along with their mother, as they have taught me about the feminine, they endured a lengthy and challenging educational effort, as I was an ill prepared student, with an all male upbringing, who had little preparation, yet great need. I had no inkling how they would affect my faith.

It all started in early 1956 at a small hospital in Garden City, Michigan. Trish and I lived in nearby Redford Township on the outskirts of Detroit. We had been married some eleven months before and our first child was about to arrive. When Trish's labor began, I nervously drove the twenty-minute ride to the small osteopathic hospital, which was housed in an ancient structure on the main street of that small city. The doctor was waiting for us when we arrived. After placing Trish in a wheelchair and taking her away, he came back to the waiting room and advised me to go to the nearest bar just down the road and come back in two or three hours. He said, "I think Trish is going to be a while." I took his advice, as those were the days prior to when the husband could be by his wife's side throughout her ordeal. It was a Monday evening and I was feeling very insignificant and a bit bewildered at this new experience. I was wondering very much what my role should be in the next few hours, and how I could best handle it. I felt a little relieved at the prospect of moving from the sterile waiting room to the comfort of a local bar scene. Besides, I was following the doctor's orders. After about an hour and a half of nursing two scotch and sodas and realizing that my anxiety was not about to abate, I returned to the waiting room. I was determined to spend my time in purgatory like a man, for however long it took. The next four hours were consumed contemplating the imminent changes that were about to occur in my life. Suddenly, the doctor bumped through the swinging door of the inner sanctum carrying a little bundle in his arms. He announced rather perfunctorily, "Tom, you have a baby girl." I came to over to take a look at the little one he was holding. My initial reaction was fright. She looked so tiny and fragile. I wondered at the portent for such a tiny little being to survive. The prospect seemed precarious. I probably muttered something profound, like "Wow!" or some other such inane reaction. That was it. The doctor turned and left with my daughter, and I think I was feeling a bit relieved that he had not handed her over for me to hold, if only briefly. I was once again a scared little boy.

Baptized Mary Elizabeth, it soon became Lisa. She was definitely my mother's favorite, probably because she was our first child. Also, as a girl it was a bonus that my mom had been denied. Grandma eventually would become an active influence in Lisa's life. She definitely contributed a version of her own self-confidence and tenacity to our daughter.

Lisa has been a leader all of her life and carries a lot of her mother's determination. Never a quitter, she is the only one of my children who is still firmly Catholic. The rest of my girls have ditched their Catholic upbringing as, in their words, "Dad, if the Church doesn't want our brother, we don't want them." Notwithstanding Lisa's Catholic commitment, she has been known on occasion to walk out of a packed Church on a Sunday morning in the midst of an antigay homily she might be perceiving. Later on, the homilist will get a stern lecture. You just don't mess with Lisa. She remains to this day the leader of my children, one who always seems to be promoting togetherness and looking out for all of us. She is the family organizer who consistently seems to keep us on an even keel, and like her mother is typically focused on the unheard or overlooked among us. Perhaps the greatest lesson I have learned from Lisa is perseverance. Lisa has always exhibited an iron will coupled with an integrity that never sags. You know she is always giving her best. Whatever life throws at her, Lisa responds with an unwavering determination to accept, adapt, and carry on. It seems to be always accomplished with philosophical good humor. I have often been inspired in my latter day activism by the example of Lisa's perseverance. It's also one of the thoughts that keeps me in the Church.

It was just thirteen months, almost to the day, when my second daughter entered this world. We arrived in the usual rush at the new Garden City hospital when Trish first encountered regular labor contractions. I was a little more relaxed this time, and I was allowed to be with her in the labor room for an initial period. This did not last too long before I was peremptorily ushered out to the regular waiting room. I was not disappointed at this dictum, as I did not enjoy seeing my wife undergoing her painful ordeal. I think I personally winced at her every contraction. However, it was just the beginning of an unanticipated agony for Daddy. I had a quiet confidence born of my prior experience, and after perusing the waiting room library, sat down to read the first of many magazines provided for the non-contributors to the birthing process. After several hours with no word, I began stretching and started the proverbial pacing of expectant fathers. Somewhere around ten hours into my ordeal, I began to worry seriously. "What the hell was happening?" Nobody had come to reassure me. I finally hailed a nurse who was willing to look into it and report back to me. A bit later she returned with a condescending smile and said, "Everything's going fine, Mr. Nelson. It will be a while yet." A while? Hell! That "while" turned into more than ten additional hours! I think Trish broke all hospital records for labor longevity at that time, and I felt every single second of it. I don't know who was more exhausted, Trish or me. (Yes I do.) Poor Trish. Her labor lasted nearly twenty-three hours! I think our Theresa Jane was not convinced she really wanted to enter this vale of tears. Things were just fine where she was.

From the very outset, Theresa Jane was different. It soon became evident that she had a visual problem. One eye was severely crossed so that it gave her a unique quizzical appearance that definitely said "I'm different." The doctor assured us that she was perfectly normal in all other respects and that her eyes would probably soon return to a normal position without any medical interference. "Don't worry," he said. "Don't worry? You've got to be kidding," I thought. We were both damn worried. But he was right. Theresa's eye soon returned to its correct position, yet the attention she got from it all did not abate. From the very beginning, I sensed a unique independence in this seemingly harmless little infant.

Understand, at that point in my educational process, I considered my main role as a father to be the chief disciplinarian—to provide a stable environment for the family. I viewed myself as the pinnacle of authority. I would brook no challenges. Theresa would prove to play no small part in collapsing that parental myth. She really had a mind of her own, even at that very early time in her life. In an indefinable way, she projected, what seemed to me, a vague challenge to my authority. Her mother did not share my attitude and seemed immune to responding to Theresa's demands with anything other than her unremitting, unconditional, parental love. This little bundle of energy would cry without stopping. When you thought you had exhausted all the possibilities for her wants and decided to "let her just cry it out," you would soon find out that it was futile. You simply could not outwait her. After you finally figured out the need and she finally got her way, you'd swear she was grinning at you from her wet little tear-streaked face as if to say, "I won that one." Then, all would be well. To me, it definitely seemed like a contest of wills. My reaction was a testimony to the paucity of my parenting skills, especially for girls. I could swear that little grin I perceived was saying, "Don't fight with me mister, you will lose." It was a battle I was definitely destined to lose. Yet, it was a loss that eventually was a win, as it wound up teaching me very much. I was to learn about a marvelous feminine tenacity cloaked in a deceiving meekness and sensitivity that still awes me. Like her sister, Theresa Jane became Tracey in her later years. She marked the dawn of a new realm for her Daddy as I began my discovery of feminism. This discovery and appreciation of feminism has provided some very effective nourishment to my spiritual growth.

Tracey was a flower child when she was a teenager. Her independent nature morphed into an early rebellion to most authority. In retrospect, her rebellion was surely exacerbated from an early traumatic confrontation between her independent nature and the Church. It was a dilemma combining parental authority reinforced by Church authority, when we enrolled her in the local Catholic grade school. Early in this environment, an incident occurred which absolutely started her experience with the Catholic Church off on the wrong foot. One day during her first grade class, my very meek but determined little daughter discovered that Catholic school was definitely not going to be like her prior experience with public school kindergarten. Hello discipline unbridled! The nun was asking the class some questions. The little boy in front of Terry could not answer when he was called upon. My sensitive little daughter whispered the answer to him. Immediately, the nun marched down the aisle (she sat well in the back) picked Terry up bodily from her desk, and shook her in the air, telling her, "Don't you *ever* give someone help when I am asking them a question or speak when you are not called upon." With such a startling admonishment, my frightened little girl got so scared and was so caught off guard that Mother Nature lost control. Poor little Terry wet her pants. Her gentle meekness prevented any disclosure. She didn't tell anyone at the time, and tried to hide it in the bathroom. Somehow, the nun discovered this little tragedy, and Tracey would say years later, "I think the nun felt bad afterwards. I remember her trying to help me wash my hands in the bathroom and being aware of her feeling sorry." Yet, I suspect that the pitiful public embarrassment she experienced at that time began a series of unfortunate occurrences that inflicted long-lasting scars. Those scars eventually resulted in a permanent negative image of the Church.

Over the years, there were two other perhaps unwitting but inexcusable and stupid misuses of authority by Church clergy. One of them occurred during the early phases of Vatican II. Our local parish had already adopted some of the new reforms emanating from Vatican II, including reception of the Eucharist in the hand. One Sunday, while on family vacation, we attended Mass at a small parish in northern Michigan that had not yet incorporated this change. The pastor at this church had not been so progressive, and when eight-year-old Terry held out her hands to receive the host as she had been taught, the priest cried out in a loud voice for the whole congregation to hear, "Stick out your tongue!" I heard the reprimand clearly, even from my place in the rear of the church. When Terry returned to our pew, she was weeping. I knew that this very public embarrassment could not have happened to someone less equipped to handle it. I was furious, and later gave the pastor an emotional dumping of my mental bucket. Yet the damage had been done.

There was one other inexcusable and public embarrassment inflicted by the clergy in those early years. In retrospect, it still causes me to shake my head in disbelief and lingering anger. It was an astounding abuse of clerical authority. During confession one Saturday afternoon, the visiting confessor raged at my seven-year-old daughter in the confessional for some perceived fault or improper procedure. It was done in such a ridiculously loud manner that his verbal attack was clearly broadcast throughout the church for every waiting penitent to hear. I was dumbfounded. My daughter rushed from the confessional in tears.

The scars inflicted on my daughter by a few mindless clerics were impossible for Mom and Dad to assuage fully. Tracey would marry in a church but that was it. She has rarely set foot in it since then.

The callous insensitivity Tracey experienced reflects, in my opinion, one more deficit endemic to the celibate environment. Any man who is a father would be highly unlikely to inflict such a cruel mental and emotional assault on such a very young child. The harm done might have been unwitting, but even I, who might have been deficient in parenting skills, knew better. Does unwitting behavior dismiss culpability? I don't think so. Witnessing these episodes enraged me at the time, but I felt helpless to respond in any manner. I was ensnared in my own bonds—the bonds of Church doctrine, which placed all clergy on a pedestal of flawlessness. Tracey didn't know it, but it was the beginning of my own serious discontent with the Church. It was definite signpost on the road of my evolving faith—the first time in my life I began to discern flaws in my hitherto flawless Church.

We had moved to Allen Park, Michigan, during Tracey's early childhood, and it was then that I began a lengthy process of understanding my child as a uniquely sensitive and loving creation. I did not understand it at the outset. It was a sensitivity that was rather beyond my comprehension at the time. Raised in a family of boys, my father was always "ribbing" us or teasing us. It was an earmark of his parenting technique. Through criticism masked with humor, he intended to establish masculine toughness as part of the lesson. It was an approach designed to equip us boys not to be easily upset and to handle the challenging world out there. Teasing was not a good way to approach a very sensitive, childlike Tracey. She took every criticism, however slight, casual, or couched in humor, very deeply. The rest of my children would, more often than not, just shrug off most fatherly admonitions, regardless of their perceptions. Paradoxically, Tracey became an early favorite of my dad, who seemed to develop a special relationship and affection for her. Yet, I recognized very early that I was mostly baffled. I simply did not know how to handle her unique personality. Today, one would say I could not think outside of the box.

Nevertheless, Tracey was going to teach me, and together we managed to survive a series of confrontations beginning in her early teen years. She had firmly latched onto the "flower-girl" image of that time, and often, if it was opposed to convention, Tracey applauded it. What she applauded, I opposed. Her mother provided her much compensation through love and affection. Yet I mostly didn't have a clue how to understand this little feminine bundle of energy, or how to be a really loving father to her. I did not lose every attempt at it, but my learning curve was steep. Tracey's unique personality, especially through her teen years, taught me much about sensitivity, humility, and meekness. I later recognized how Jesus-specific these attributes of love are. My evolution of faith continued to mature with every child.

It was so with Julie as well.

One morning,
Without warning,
When I was walking by the sea,
The rhythm of the waves reached out to me.
I forgot my reasons,
Forgot my goals,
Committed treason to my mind,
Left my searching far behind.
Gentle sighing wind,
Swept my sorrow away.
Good-bye dreadful dying day.
The simple song from the sea,
Has set my sinning soul free—
For a decade in a minute—
A million thoughts combined,
Nothing left to find,
I found myself free—
With only me to be.

That little poem, written by Julie in her teen years, still resonates with me. Nicknamed by my mom "Merry Sunshine," she seemed to have a perpetual grin on her face. She was always disarming you with her sense of humor, and it was unavoidable

One day when I was engaged in some stern correction of her behavior, I found myself becoming increasingly frustrated. Despite my rising tenor, I looked across the room to where she was seated, and saw only a grin on her face. She obviously wasn't getting my message. Seated some ten some ten feet apart in our family room, she suddenly decided to demonstrate her contrary view to what I had been pontificating. Julie took off her shoe and threw it right at me. Fortunately, I had sufficient reaction to duck, and the shoe missed, but not the message. I was momentarily dumbfounded, but I quickly overcame my astonishment and impulsively started to laugh. We both continued just to sit there looking at each other and laughing. I think Julie was probably secretly relieved at my atypical response, but I had learned something from it all. It was a lesson I'd build on in the future. It is simple. There are many things in life that we would do better to laugh at, rather than fuss about. It is true in matters spiritual as well. My existence in the universe is sufficiently insignificant, as to present a comical element, a fact which should logically evoke at least a little smile.

Julie's struggle with the Catholic Church lasted well into adulthood. She clung to her faith for years, but finally dumped the institution when she refused to ignore the anti-gay atmosphere she sensed at the small rural church she was attending. She had been an active member of her parish, and got on well with the pastor in all other areas, but the continuing homophobia was not something she could ignore. My girls are not the silent type.

It's been said that after parents have produced four children, anything more is gravy. You just can't get any busier or more harried. You should just relax and learn to enjoy all the commotion. Well Nancy Ann, the fifth of my six children, proved that dictum. Gravy she was. Nancy and Julie were born only one year and one month apart, and Nancy like her sister has always been just as upbeat. Perhaps because of their similar disposition and blond hair, we nicknamed the two of them "the gold dust twins." They have been just that: especially close to one another over the years. If I phone one of them today, I can count on also getting an update about the other. Nancy was born on a Wednesday in the new Garden City hospital like her siblings. From the very outset, she too displayed a smiling persona, coupled with a solid, immovable, and quiet little stubbornness, a bit similar to Tracey. No matter what you attempted, when you tried to change her view or behavior, it would prove futile if Nancy had made up her mind otherwise. Even corporal punishment was useless. She'd simply respond with her little grin as if to say, "That didn't hurt me a bit." By the time she came along, I had already made some progress in my education on the limitations of fatherly control and some degree of comprehending the feminine.

Nancy was, in many respects, a part of my graduate curriculum in the education of father. When, as young children I tried to instill in them an appreciation for neatness, the gold standard for which was a neat and orderly bedroom, I would conduct a naval-bred captain's inspection. Everything in their room had to be in its place—no clutter. When they got wind of an imminent inspection, there often ensued a hurried solution. They would scoop up all visible debris, stuff it quickly into the dresser drawers, and close them up tight. Dad would come in and looking about, presumably see immediately that all was obviously spotless as the girls stood by at attention. But the darn old geezer had been around this block, it seemed. Dad would go directly to the dresser, open each drawer, and finding any whose contents were not carefully folded and neatly stowed would cause a disaster. He would pull the drawer all the way out and fling the contents about the room. He would then sternly command: "Now, do it right." Nancy's common response to this performance would invariably be a deep sigh, and the resigned observation, "Oh Dad, you didn't have to do that." I did not let on, but she effectively sowed some seeds of doubt in Daddy's mind. Maybe there was a better way.

Today, Nancy sells health insurance on a part-time basis. She has been doing this now for several years. Drop any hint on the state of the nation's health care system, and you will receive a lengthy dissertation on the many faults and failures of it. She once said to me, "Dad; I have seen firsthand the terrible abuses of our nation's insurance-driven health care. It cries out for reform. The injustice and harm are a disgrace. Most people just don't know."

Nancy too has a gift of written expression. She wrote a poem during her own teenage years, which is on display next to Julie's in my den. It captures that spirit of our family's love, something I consider the essence of the best of my family and reveals something about the blessings in life that I have enjoyed. It says:

> The Greatest Gift on Earth,
> God—how blessed we are
> It fills my heart with mirth,
> Shines brighter than the brightest star
> It is pure
> It is strong

It can cure
And forgive all my wrong
It is perennial as the mountain snow
If only all the world could know
Even in eternity it will not vanish.
If gone, it has only fled
To relinquish even stronger on my soul to tread.
IT is the love which unites and flows within our family
Evermore.
If upon our unique quests
We drift from the feeling,
It could be only for a while,
Till it returns to bring a complacent smile,
Which by its mirth may trickle
Among and submerge
All human beings we meet.

Nancy married her husband, Tim, a geologist, in the picturesque garden area of a rural inn. It was one of her first confrontations with the Catholic "rules." Her love affair with the outdoors
was matched by Tim's and they wanted to be married in an outdoor setting. However, the Catholic Church would not hear about
marriage in any non–church environment. No problem. Good-bye
Catholic Church. Her Presbyterian husband's church welcomed
their desire for an outdoor setting and graciously accommodated
them. The ceremony was performed in a formal garden some
forty miles west of Detroit. While Nancy never had any fears that
God might not approve, she began to wonder a little when the
weather preceding the wedding was a steady rain for almost a
week. However, Divine approval reinforced her convictions when
the rain stopped two days before the scheduled event, and the
wedding day was sunny, clear, and seventy-two degrees. Today,
Nancy is no longer Catholic because, she says, "my father taught
me to think for myself." Actually, I believe Nancy was *born* thinking for herself. As an independent thinker, no one is going to set
the rules for her relationship to the Almighty, not the Catholic
Church, not any church, not even Mom and Dad. Her upbeat view

and a persistent grin, has taught me to have calmness in the midst of adversity by her own unique way of doing just that. I will always hear her whispering to me: "Oh Dad, it's OK. Everything will be just fine." I've decided it's definitely a characteristic of the feminine. Her unflappable nature has often helped me in my frustrations and reactions to the perceived failings of my Church.

Finally, number six, Kathleen Cecille, was born New Year's Eve, 1963. Her arrival was especially welcome for me, as she was my last-minute IRS deduction. She made it just in time, arriving a few hours before midnight on the thirty-first of December, and instantly provided her joyful daddy with the dual gift of herself and the welcome tax break. She was our caboose, who seemed to incorporate the best characteristics found in all my children. From the very beginning, she was easy. Always good-natured, an infant who almost never cried, her personality was definitely enhanced by the doting attention and affection showered on her by all of her siblings. She definitely mirrored the "good boy" image I had conjured early in my life. Kathleen was a "good girl," for sure. She has mostly retained her Kathleen baptismal name, but to her siblings, she is often just "Kat." While she definitely enjoyed much attention from all of her siblings, she and her brother Mark developed a special bond that persists to this day. Of all my children, they were the only two who assumed Mom and Dad's passion for tennis. Trish and I had a long love affair with the game. We had even won some local doubles tournaments together. Today, at family reunions, Mark and Kathleen will break away from the rest of us at least once for their own private tennis tournament. Kathleen began her tennis in earnest when she joined the tennis team in high school. It was the beginning of an athletic slant for her future career.

All of my girls are very attractive women who tend to reflect either their father's Swedish or their mother' Irish ancestries. Kathleen definitely tends toward the Swedish with her naturally very blonde hair. She has a classic beauty that is rare. I remember during my working days, I had placed a photo of her on my desk at the office. It was a recent picture of her in her early twenties. One day, when one of my fellow employees came into my office

to discuss some business issue, I noticed he seemed to be continuously gazing off, not at me, but to the side toward my desk.
When he finally got up to leave, he stopped, and pointed toward
Kathleen's picture and asked, "Who's that?" I replied, "That's my
youngest daughter, Kathleen." He then said, "My god! She's the
most beautiful woman I've ever seen!" I enjoy reminding Kathleen
of that story, especially whenever she might be feeling a bit down.
When I retell it, it never fails to bring a grin to her face.

One day, about the time near her graduation from college,
when Trish and I were going through our marital separation
trauma, (See Chapter 8) the three of us were walking off the tennis courts at the end of a three-way workout. I decided to bring
Kathleen up to date on her parents' marital status. I told her that
it looked like Mom and Dad were going to divorce. She fell silent,
put her head down, and began weeping. Then, she ran over and
grabbed both Trish and me, pulled us together. While the three of
us embraced, she sobbed. It was a wakeup call for me. Life was not
just about me. Kathleen is that way with everyone. You can't miss
her love and, most of all, her gentleness.

Kathleen very nearly majored in music at Michigan State. She
had been studying piano for years and had achieved a high degree
of competence at it. That she chose another path did not detract
from her skill, as she still plays often. She can make me cry at any
time with her performance of Beethoven's *Pathetique,* which was
her mother's favorite classical piece. Kathleen married her husband, Paul, in a beautiful formal Church wedding in Chicago,
where they currently live. Paul is in the higher echelons of the
banking business, while Kathleen pursues her athletic bent as a
personal trainer. They have two young boys who are amazingly
"good," like their mother, and are definitely two of their grandpa's
favorites.

Kathleen taught me about gentleness. It is a quality of the spirit
I have found essential to a balanced view of my faith challenges.
Gentleness—it is not a common virtue, especially in the male spe-
cies. But, the image I see most often in my mind's eye is Kathleen
leading her four sisters and her mother in a session of kickboxing
on the road behind our place on Lake Michigan. She is a constant

reminder to "stay in shape, Dad." Her association with the Church seems to be vacillating affair. Her faith in God may be strong, but her acceptance of the Catholic certitude is tenuous. Her unique closeness to her gay brother is probably an agitating and conflicting influence.

My six daughters, without exception, fully supported Mark when he first divulged his homosexuality to us all. They definitely handled it more casually than Mom and Dad did. However, they all must have been affected in their stance toward the Catholic Church by the demeaning of their brother. I have concluded that the Church's homophobic rhetoric coupled with the second-class status of women in the Church has caused all but Lisa to turn to other faith dimensions for their own spiritual succor. I take no personal arrogation for their individual conclusions. I've always urged all my children to think for themselves and to pursue critical thinking in every endeavor. I am proud of that. The Church's effective denigration of women is also not a minor issue for them. It is another certainty in my observation of their faith journeys.

However, my greatest pride in my children is their unwavering love for each other, and their unique, unremitting commitment to goodness. Without exception, they are always trying to do the right thing, regardless of the cost to themselves. They all seem to know how to love, and the joy experienced in doing so. Despite the focus of much attention I give in this writing to my son Mark, the impact of my five daughters on this man's journey of faith has been great. Perhaps most of all, I have learned from them about the true beauty of the feminine. It has been a most treasured lesson, which differentiates in a major way my current faith perspective from the past. I yearn to impart a little of the feminine to my clerical brethren. The Church suffers from a great void in this respect. If one wants to learn or teach about love, look to women.

> "*Man's love is of man's life a thing apart,*
> *'Tis woman's whole existence*"[4].

---

4   Lord Byron, British poet, circa 1819

Chapter 7

Mark

"There is neither Jew nor Gentile, neither slave nor free, nor is there male and female, for you are all one in Christ Jesus"
—GALATIANS 3:28

The person who has had the greatest impact on my journey of faith and my understanding of God has undoubtedly been my gay son. While it all began around 1980, a significant incident occurred early in the year 2000. I had received a call from Kerry Temple, the editor of the *Notre Dame* magazine, a quarterly publication for the University of Notre Dame alumni. Kerry had heard about me from a talk I had recently given at an on-campus university alumni gathering. I had spoken of my experiences of being the father of a gay son and the impact on my faith. It had gone well and Kerry was calling to see if I would write an article for a forthcoming issue of the magazine. The magazine was planning to devote an entire edition to the topic of homosexuality. I was quite surprised, as I regarded my alma mater as distinctly conservative and expected such a topic to be taboo. I quickly assured him that I would be delighted to submit an article for consideration, and wished him well on the project he had planned. I also cautioned him that I was an engineer, not a journalist, and that engineers are notoriously poor writers. He said to just tell my story and that the magazine would "work with" me.

A few months later, I submitted my initial draft, and shortly thereafter, Kerry called and said that the editors liked what I had written. "It needs a little work, but it's a very good story. We'll submit it to the editorial board for approval and get back to you soon," he said. He then added that the editorial review board was something new that the university had inflicted on the magazine, but he didn't expect any problems. A couple of months went by and I had heard nothing. Then one morning I received a call from Kerry. He said that he had to regretfully tell me that the editorial review board had not approved my story. They felt it was "too controversial." He said that the magazine would not be doing an issue devoted to homosexuality, either. I was very disappointed and after his phone call, I immediately sat down and wrote Kerry an emotional letter expressing my frustration. I wrote:

Dear Kerry,   September 21, 2000

> I want to thank you for your recent efforts on behalf of my story, "A Father's Journey." I was not surprised at the verdict, but obviously, it was disappointing. I felt that perhaps a bit of pragmatism was involved in the board's decision. But to you, sir, I can only express my heartfelt thanks for your significant efforts on my behalf. I've known a little of your perspective even before I began my labors over the article, so I felt certain of a fair chance. Your awesome 1996 article "One Night in Gulfport" remains one of the best I've ever read in ND Magazine. You will always rank near the top of my hierarchy of ND people.
>
> Your critique of my writing is appreciated. It will be helpful if I choose to pursue my story in other venues. Frankly, I felt considerable constraints writing what I did and your description of the board's comments confirmed

my assessment. Anything considered remotely critical of the Church these days appears to be an anathema to some. And it seems these same folks are the ones in control of things. That may be a cynical view, but as I've related in my story, I have a problem with those who feel the Church is beyond criticism and that it possesses all the answers.

You may be interested to know that my current efforts as a retiree find me on the board of directors of PFLAG [5] [Parents, Family, and Friends of Lesbians and Gays] Detroit. What began as a personal balm has evolved into an active ministry for the LGBT community that has made me aware of the issues and the often-tragic family stories artfully hidden from the public view. In some cases, the tragedy is almost unbelievable. The adverse consequences that society inflicts on the individual homosexual person are familiar to many, as I'm sure they are to you. Less familiar, perhaps, is that good families are being ravaged to an extent that seems surreal in an age of information. At monthly PFLAG meetings, I hear firsthand accounts from gay young people and parents devastated by a condition not of their making—tales of suicide, even by parents—wrenching tales of family tragedy, most of which have religious fundamentalism at their roots. I've listened to the young victims and their mourning parents and I can't understand the silence on this issue. There is a running feud between the Christian fundamentalists and the GLBT community, both of whom seem to want to purge society of the other. But the rest of us are mostly silent. Silence for me is an accessory to a crime.

I realize you probably know all this. Your consideration of my article says as much. But while I can empathize

---

5   PFLAG is Parents, Families and Friends of Lesbians and Gays. It is a national support, education, and advocacy organization for lesbian, gay, bisexual and transgender (LGBT) people, their families, friends and allies. With 200,000 members and supporters, and local affiliates in more than 350 communities across the U.S. and abroad, PFLAG is the largest grassroots-based family organization of its kind. PFLAG is a non-profit organization and is not affiliated with any religious or political institutions. - PFLAG, "Frequently Asked Questions," 2012, http://community.pflag.org/page.aspx?pid=191.

with the advisory board members who think I blamed the Church too much (I've been there), I'm compelled to say that I think they are "out of the loop." Being unaware of the misery that exists all around us sometimes seems inexcusable. If only they could attend a couple of local PFLAG meetings and just listen, I think they would find that religion *is* at the core of the problem. At the very least, perhaps they could ask themselves the question I still ask myself: "But what if I'm wrong?"

Finally, I agree. The topic would make some folks uncomfortable, and yes, it's a challenging issue. There are risks involved. It might even cost some money. But I'm sure you recall: there is a recent, historical precedent for a silence that we now lament. Fifteen thousand gays preceded the Jews in the Holocaust. The silence of that era also seems to have been a product of pragmatism. It is my earnest hope that *Notre Dame* magazine will not be too silent. Perhaps the magazine could engage a professional writer in the future to accomplish what I couldn't. If not *Notre Dame*, then who?

Which is the reason for this long-winded reply to your message. I know you share much of my concerns, Kerry, and I can appreciate the environment you must operate under. Thanks for listening to me again, and my thanks to Carol and the advisory board. It was a thrill just to have you folks consider my effort. It has given me more motivation to continue my Journey. I wish you every success and *Notre Dame* magazine a continuation of its tradition of excellence. Someday, I'd like nothing better than to meet you and share a little conversation...over a cup of brew or such.

Sincerely,
Tom Nelson, '53

At this point, I put the matter behind me and concluded the whole affair was finished. I was wrong. Nearly three years later, the phone rang, and my wife answered. She called out to me, "Honey, it's Kerry Temple on the phone. He said he'd like to speak with you." I was puzzled. What could he want? When I came to the phone, I listened as Kerry said, "That letter you wrote after the board of review squelched our gay edition really made the rounds out here. I think it affected a few folks. Bottom line is, we're back on. Let's have another go at your story. OK?" "Of course," I replied. "I'll get right on it."

I was delightfully dumbfounded. I rewrote the story and it was published in the Summer 2004 issue of the magazine with the magazine's theme entitled "The Love That Dare Not Speak Its Name." There were six articles including mine, "God Gave Me a Gay Son and I Did Not Always Think it a Blessing." That issue of the *Notre Dame* magazine won several literary awards. It also received more feedback than any previous issue. My own story was cited for an additional award and was subsequently republished in the anthology *The Best Catholic Writing 2005*.[6] I still can't believe that outcome. The story I wrote:

God Gave Me A Gay Son

...And I did not always think it a blessing.
—*Notre Dame Magazine*, Summer 2004

Mark gazed out the small window of his dorm room. It was Saturday morning and the bitter cold bleakness outside matched his mood. He may have made a mistake going to school so far north and so far from home, but he had chosen this school in northern Michigan because he loved the natural environment of the North Country where he could ski, hike in the woods and enjoy the serenity of this sparsely populated place. Mark also had thought college would bring people into his life who wanted a good educational experience, people with whom he could be open and find companionship. But the dream turned into a nightmare.

His anguish—realizing that he was attracted to some of the young men around him and the conviction that those feelings

---

6   Brian Doyle, ed., *The Best Catholic Writing 2005* (Chicago: Loyola Press, 2005). Doyle is the award-winning author, essayist, and editor of the University of Portland's *Portland* magazine.

would disgust people—fed his terrible feeling of isolation and left him feeling numb. He didn't think it was his fault; he wondered if God had made him that way. But it wasn't a problem he could talk about, not to family, not to friends. No one could help him. Even God didn't answer.

So on this Saturday morning Mark realized nothing really mattered anymore. It could only get worse. And while it frightened him —having considered it for quite a long time—he also knew how he could fix it. The only way to confront this demon was to end it all. Nobody would understand it anyway. He didn't understand it. But he knew he was gay, and he knew being gay was an abomination. So he would put an end to his agony. Suicide, he had decided, would be less painful to his family than revealing to them who he really was.

So Mark sat down at the small table at the end of his bed. He picked up his pen and wrote: *The fog thickens . . .*

I try to see through it at my paper and pen.
Through them to the world.
The fog thickens . . .
They pound and laugh all around me,
Their laughter a testimony to my despair
"All that you need is wine and good company."
I can be like them,
I am not alone.
I can be like them,
I will find happiness.
I cannot be like them,
I am alone.
Why not just rest and forget about it?
Rest and forget about it.
Outside the wind howls.
Inside the silence howls.
It has been snowing for some time now,
And my soul is buried in a drift.
The wind blows too hard for the plows to clear the roads.
I am destined to die in a snow drift.

Then Mark went to the window and gazed at the gray blur of the winter storm. He thought: It will be easy. Just take that bottle of prescription pain killers. No more anguish. No more self-hatred. No more struggling. The hell with it then. God forgive me.

And the thought became the act.

The pills went down easily, and he lay down on the bed to die.

* * *

It was a sunny afternoon in San Francisco. My wife, Trish, and I had just arrived at our room in the Mark Hopkins Hotel for a business conference. It had been a long and tiring trip from Michigan. "Tom, look," Trish said, "these flowers are from Tracey." She was holding a mixed bouquet sent by our daughter, with a card that read: "Welcome to San Francisco. Call me when we can get together. Love, Tracey." My wife sighed as she collapsed into the plush leather chair. "Aren't our kids wonderful?"

"They sure are," I replied. "I guess we're pretty lucky." As I gazed out the window savoring sights I hadn't seen for 30 years, I thought how lucky we really were. Our six wonderful children all seemed so perfect. The company was paying our travel expenses, and tonight we were going to have dinner with Tracey. We hadn't seen her in over a year. Her older sister was back home at work, and the rest of the kids, including our son Mark, were safely away in college. My life was going pretty much according to the script I thought I had authored.

* * *

Raised in a traditional Catholic family during the 1930s and 40s, I enjoyed a thoroughly Catholic education, from elementary school through college. The Church was a central part of my loving family. My two brothers and I were expected to excel in everything, but our grades in religion classes got special scrutiny.

After graduating from Notre Dame, I had a certitude about religion and morality. My understanding of the contemporary culture was defined by a black-and-white perspective on most issues. I felt comfortable expressing my views on those things, and often did. I was solidly Roman Catholic, more than proud of it and ready to defend it to anyone. My parents seemed reasonably satisfied with the product of their labors, as we had survived the Depression and the Great War, and we were all healthy, college-educated offspring. It was the '50s, and I was a young man ready for career, marriage and family.

Trish came to our marriage as cloaked in traditional Catholicism as I did. She, too, had enjoyed 16 years of Catholic education, though she wasn't the cocksure moralist that I was. Typical of that time, our children came early and often. Having five girls and one boy in the first eight years of marriage was part of our education. We felt blessed with such healthy children, and I often bragged about how we were growing up with our kids." Life confronted us with the usual mundane hurdles all families experience, and we handled them as best we could.

Soon the children were entering the teen years; the Church was adjusting to Vatican II; women were being liberated; the United States at war in Vietnam; the moon was the latest frontier for human progress. Hippies were in vogue; a president was assassinated; immorality seemed rampant. Just about every norm that appeared certain was being assailed. The world was going to hell and outer space at the same time.

Our best efforts couldn't totally shelter our family from the dangers and challenges of those days. However, armed with self-assurance and the absolute truth endowed to us by our Catholic background, we confronted each issue with confidence. We sought opportunities to promote family discussions, and our dinner hours evolved into a ritual of stimulating conversation. We would discuss any topics that any family member wanted to explore.

I indulged in a lot of preaching during those family sessions. Often, I simply pronounced the official Church teaching as the final word on various issues. I cautioned my children to beware of all the false propaganda that bombarded them from virtually every source. When they were confronted with a difficult choice, I urged them to consider the right thing to do. I would stress: Use your intellect. Decide for yourself. What does the data say? I wanted these as family mottoes. Of course, Vatican II challenged some of my long-held convictions. Still, my immutable Catholic dogma continued to fortify my comfort. In hindsight, I now realize I was suffering from an intellectual coma. My brain was in hibernation.

* * *

As we returned to our room after our first day of the seminar, we saw the red message light on the phone blinking urgently. My wife checked in with the operator while I mixed a couple of drinks. As I handed a glass to her, she looked puzzled and alarmed. The message was from my doctor. Some tests I'd taken just before leaving for San Francisco indicated a serious cardiac condition. I was to avoid any strenuous activity and see him as soon as I got home.

* * *

Eventually, at a few of these dinnertime discussions, the subject of homosexuality was ever so timidly broached. "What do you think, Dad?"

I don't remember who asked the question, but it wouldn't have been Mark. It had to be one of the girls. They liked to challenge Dads agenda. While I'd have preferred to avoid anything relating to sexuality, my answer was fairly easy, and it came quickly. I knew the words of the magisterium: *"An abomination. Sex is reserved for marriage. Love the sinner, hate the sin. Natural law. Et cetera."* Concluding with a short lecture on the virtue of chastity, I clearly conveyed, "End of discussion . . . next topic."

It was a well-intentioned automatic response, but one that avoided open dialogue of a difficult topic. Little did I realize the struggle my son was undergoing at the time. My brilliant pontificating was stifling his attempts to communicate and secretly causing him to question the worth of his very existence.

* * *

Taking a stroll in San Francisco two days later, Trish gently posed a question that was to impact my life far more than the doctor's report that I'd been dwelling on. "I've been worrying about

Mark," she said. "He's been seeing a lot of one young man and hasn't been dating girls. The thought of it scares me. Does it scare you?"

My initial reaction was a quick little laugh. Then, a bit sarcastically, I said, "Relax. There's nothing to worry about." But a wave of panic swept through me. *"My God! No. It couldn't be."* The seeds of doubt took root. Dreading the prospect, I resolved to confront my son as soon as we returned.

* * *

Mark defied all the popular stereotypes I believed about what being gay means. I was sure I could recognize a gay person a mile off. But my son was just too masculine. He never displayed the effeminate traits that I was certain a homosexual male would exhibit.

I recalled as typical of his masculine toughness an incident when he was about 8 years old. One day, when he was to play in an important junior hockey game, he had a dental appointment to have five teeth pulled. His mother insisted that the hockey game was second priority. So, after a little nitrous oxide, the five teeth were extracted. Getting out of the dental chair after this ordeal, Mark proceeded to the restroom where he promptly vomited. Then he calmly returned to his mother and said: "Now, can I please go to the hockey game?" She took him, and he played. This was my homosexual child? No way.

Nothing during Mark's childhood indicated any sign of homosexuality. There was none of the verbal violence many young gay people endure from earliest childhood; no derisive jeering, no faggot or queer talk. He was seemingly happy, well-adjusted and straight.

Of course, there was that time in high school. Late afternoon one pleasant spring day, we received a phone call from Mark's after-school employer. Mark had not shown up for work. His employer said he was concerned because Mark is never late. "He's my most reliable employee." We didn't know where he might be, and a series of frantic telephone calls came to no avail.

Eventually, we discovered that our son had withdrawn all his savings from the bank, and he and two friends had taken a bus to Florida. While he soon telephoned to assure us of his safety, he had apparently resolved not to return. We were dumbfounded. Fortunately, economics soon intervened. When his money had nearly run out, Mark was relieved to learn we would not only welcome him back, but we were ready to wire him the return plane fare as well.

This incident was definitely disturbing to us, so we decided Mark needed professional counseling. The counselor came highly recommended and with all the appropriate credentials. His evaluation quickly assured us that Marks Florida escapade was little more than 'a lark, a healthy, youthful rebellion.' His prompt conclusion: "Your son is a very normal, well-adjusted and intelligent young person. It would be a waste of your money and my time to proceed any further." Without hesitation, my wife and I accepted his reassurance and breathed a sigh of relief.

* * *

My wife and I, like most parents, had hopes and dreams for each of our children. These entailed the usual trappings of health, education, spiritual welfare, material success and all the nuances these include. We wanted their lives to be happy and fulfilled. However, again like most parents, we unwittingly tried to fit our children into preconceived molds. Now, older and perhaps a little wiser, I marvel when I observe how different each of my adult children is. They are like startling reflections of the incomprehensible diversity of God's creation. Nevertheless, back then, this father certainly had some definite assumptions about his son's future. The possibility of homosexuality was a dim and distant issue about which I knew and cared little.

It has been said that possession of the absolute truth is the end of learning. While I understood there were many things that I didn't know, moral issues were not among them. I knew the rules, and I knew the reasons. The possibility of a gay son was not part of my plan. Not only was I unaware, but my pontificating moral certitude had actually been adding to his anguish. I was unwittingly encouraging my son toward suicide. I did not know then that the suicide rate for young gay persons is three times that for other teens. Their struggle to accept their sexuality is too often a lonely battle devoid of family support, not unlike my son's. I fear that, like me, too many parents suffer from rigid moral convictions. Unfortunately, the result can be the ultimate of tragedies - the loss of a child.

* * *

Mark's act of ultimate despair was overcome only through courage and God's amazing grace. Years later, when I learned of his suicide attempt, Mark would tell me that as he waited for death to release him, he went through what he could only describe as a unique religious experience in which God spoke to him in a special way. Somehow, he abruptly realized that God had created him just as he was, and so there must be some good reason for being who he was. And that God surely accepted him as he had created him, and so Mark should do likewise. He ran to the bathroom and forced himself to vomit the painkillers he had taken. Had he reacted soon enough? The next 36 hours proved to be a benumbed and desperate struggle as he dragged through a drugged twilight, not daring to allow himself any sleep for fear there would be no morning.

My son did survive his trauma. Mine was still to come.

* * *

My wife and I had returned from San Francisco. I was with Mark. We were alone in the car, returning home from the University for his Semester Break. Freeway traffic was light, and I had decided it was time to take the plunge. There was no prologue, no warning. I was abrupt and blunt. "Mark, are you gay?" He looked startled. After a long pause, he quietly said, "I don't want to talk about it." I thought a moment and said, "I guess you've just answered my question." To which he responded, again very quietly, "I guess so."

With those three little words, the world came crashing down for me. Despite my mental preparation for this moment, I was speechless. We were almost home, and neither of us spoke another word for the rest of the trip. I was still in shock when we walked into the house. My wife looked at me and knew instantly that I had asked the question and, what the answer had been.

* * *

My son's disclosure was a personal trauma. Initially, I didn't think about the implications for him. My immediate reaction was mostly self-focused. What had I done wrong? What will family and friends think? Could he change? What should I do? What *can* I do? My heartache alternated between anger and fear. This son of mine, who moments ago seemed so perfect, was now a torment. Of course, I loved him still. But how could *my* son be gay? He wasn't like *that*. It simply wasn't plausible. I just had to fix it. Yet what could I do?

I realize today how little I knew. My level of understanding homosexuality encompassed little more than a now defunct Freudian theory that a homosexual child is the result of a weak father and a domineering mother. As part of my selfishness, it gave me some immediate solace to place the blame for this tragedy on my wife. *Of course, it's her fault. A dominant woman!* I thought. But I quickly found this strategy neither right nor helpful. It simply added stress to our marriage. Still, there was this weak *father* thing. I just couldn't accept that idea. Maybe there was something I could do. I realized I needed more information.

I began by reading every book or article available in the Detroit libraries. I had an insatiable need to learn everything I could about homosexuality. Gradually the myths began to dissolve. I learned that some 5 to 10 percent of the population is estimated to be homosexual. Such estimates tend to be understated, as many gay people are hidden from view by their closeted life. In many cases, even close family members don't know their true identity. Homosexuality is probably not the result of environmental conditions but more likely genetic in origin. It is the general professional consensus that it cannot be changed and that attempts to do so can be distinctly harmful. The best minds in the fields of medicine, psychiatry, psychology and biology generally agree that homosexuality is a normal variant of the human condition and certainly not some disorder that requires treatment. Even during that period, without the Internet, there was plenty of data that homosexuality was a normal condition.

Following this phase of my education, I began to realize that this issue was about my son and not so much about me. My spell of self-indulgence was fairly brief, but I still feel sad that I wasn't more help to Mark, immediately and without any equivocation. He needed it. He deserved it. My intellect began to awaken from its hibernation. I felt more empathy, a virtue too rare in my past. My predilection for expectations of the conventional gave way to a frightening vision of my son's future. What was he going to face? It was not pleasant to contemplate.

The risks of violence, discrimination, harassment and ostracism are all too common for the gay community. The chances of my son being accepted as a normal member of society seemed to be slim to none. Otherwise decent people often oppose, with self-righteous moralistic railing, some of the most fundamental human rights for gays that the rest of us take for granted.

Homosexuality is not a condition I would have chosen for my son. So why now celebrate the gift of a gay son?

Since that disclosure many years ago, because of Mark, I have come to know many gay persons. We have dined together, walked together, traveled together, worshiped together, and laughed and cried together. I have some new stereotypes as a result. Almost without exception, I have found my gay friends to be likeable, loveable people of high integrity. More than that, most seem to have a resilience, a forbearance for life's burdens. I have been deeply moved by their tales of adversity overcome. I have seen them subjected to insults and abuse by their government, their churches, their neighbors, some even by their families, then seen them respond with a patience I envy. They have taught me how a quiet tenacity can achieve success in the face of the most discouraging odds. I have watched gay people, young and old, routinely living lives of often heroic charity toward others, done without fanfare. It is a charity most of us professing Christians would find difficult to match, and it is too often accomplished while deprived of the nurture of organized religious groups that seem focused only on condemning them. By their example, they have shown me how to truly love my neighbor.

These experiences forced me to confront the fallacy of my former arrogant certitude. I realized that I had been given the opportunity to learn from everyone I meet in life, but that I had been passing up many potential professors. I resolved to attend all my classes in the future. Through my involvement in PFLAG (Parents, Family, and Friends of Lesbians and Gays), I have come to know many other parents of gay children. I have learned about the anguish and abuse society irrationally inflicts on their families. It has been a journey to a new perspective that has enabled me to understand my own failings and the world around me better. My struggle to be more fair-minded and less judgmental has been made easier.

I also have watched my children gain a unique appreciation of others. And I've found that not having all the answers has resulted in a closer, more trusting relationship with my God. It has been a bonus to watch Mark mature into the successful, happy adult that he is today.

Yes, Mark does experience more than the normal challenges of our culture than straight folks endure, despite the fact that being gay is only one small part of who he is. Yet he now seems to shrug off most of those gay-related burdens. He prefers to think of them as society's problems, not his. His goal to lead a normal and happy life has been largely successful, but that other reality is always lurking in the background.

Mark, Circa 2003

There is one challenge that gives me, his father, much anguish. It is his feeling of utter rejection by the Catholic Church. After his long struggle to find a place in it for himself, it seems that too many official proclamations only remind him that he is considered depraved, disordered and intrinsically evil. He has given up on it. I am at a loss as to how to convince him otherwise. I've discovered that when I apply my newfound empathy, I've had a tough time not reacting as he has. I can only continue to pray and wonder about what it all means. I try not to let it destroy my own love for the Church. Sometimes I'm not too successful at it.

I know that many of my Christian fellows and others would take grave issue with some of my views. They would argue with sincerity the same positions I once so adamantly held. I am well aware of the popular biblical arguments that are used to condemn homosexuality. I am also glad that some of the best biblical scholars have given us new insight into those popular literal interpretations touted by many to support their castigation of homosexuality. Sadly, too, I regret the promiscuous immorality displayed by some in the gay community. Yet I doubt that any segment of our society has a monopoly on immorality; heterosexuals are certainly just as accomplished at this. I also share a deep concern for the welfare of what some describe as the endangered American family, but heterosexuals have done their share to break up marriages and threaten the health of the American family. And how can we justify the dishonest labeling as "special rights" those basic civil, legal and human rights the rest of us take for granted? Much of our Christian rhetoric is anything but Christian. I have personally seen the tragic human consequences of intransigent, righteous moralizing. I nearly destroyed my own son with such "loving" dogmatic proclamations.

Now, late in my journey, I find myself with more questions than when I started. Answers that I once was so sure of have fallen far short. Some have proven to be false. I have found many answers in unlikely places and from unlikely people. Most of the answers have given me joy; a few have made me sad. Many of my unanswered questions, my beloved Church will not even address, acting as if "the data" were irrelevant. Like me, the Church, too, has feet of clay. I realize now that the absolute truth is a far-off goal, attainable only in the hereafter. Perhaps now, though, I have a better understanding of humanity's common struggle. For a Christian, I think, the task is to try to comprehend and apply the truth and the full implications of Christ's final plea: *"Love one another as I have loved you."*

For me, discovering the complex meaning of this message has been a lengthy journey that continues to this day. It has been a difficult lesson for me, and one that might never have happened. But, fortunately, God gave me a gay son.

Yes, God gave me a gay son - a fact I celebrate today - a son who has had a most profound effect on my life. While it was obviously not his intention, Mark, just being who he is, has taught me more about myself, about the nature of the Creator, his unfathomable love, and the diversity of his creation, than perhaps all of the academic and social experiences of my past. I believe most parents would agree that they learn from their children, probably as much as they teach. I have certainly enjoyed this reward of parenting from all of my six children. Being the unique individuals they are, they have all taught me - all in their own special way. But Mark had the advantage of being gay.

I have told this story many times before groups large and small. It is usually told to groups of other parents who have gay children and who are new to the challenge of the discovery that they have a gay child. On every occasion, I have a difficult time when I relate Mark's attempted suicide. It is very hard for me to recall his struggle, and how I was not a source of support for him when he needed me the most. It is a personal failure that has been hard to recall and admit to. I think, however, in relating it to others, I have helped other parents come to a better understanding of the overriding importance of parental love. It is my constant desire to help them come to this truth sooner than I did. Our gay children are the same treasures as our straight ones, perhaps even more so.

Chapter 8

Consequences

"Do nothing out of selfish ambition or vain conceit. Rather, in humility value others above yourselves"
— PHILIPPIANS 2:3

The years following the discovery that I had a gay son were a period of intense learning for both Trish and me. It was also a period that exacerbated the stress in our marital relationship. I probably held some vague subconscious feelings that somehow my wife was to blame for this trauma. While it wasn't the tragedy I thought it was at the time, I was still into the blame game and trying to vindicate my self-perceived failures. Our marriage had declined into an ever-increasing darkness. I now realize with clarity that our marital problems were mostly a product of my continuing drift into self-focus that had begun years earlier. That selfishness was evident in my initial response to Mark when I first heard his admission of being gay. I wasn't immediately concerned about the implications for Mark; I was wondering how it all would affect *me*. As a result, before Trish and I became involved with PFLAG and while my own education in this area was slowly progressing, we ran into serious marital troubles. It was the culmination of the compounding stress of unresolved issues and my festering self-centered attitude. It had nothing to do with my son being gay. My self-focus had made a solution to our problems a very difficult hurdle. In fact, I very nearly destroyed our marriage.

In retrospect, I had experienced a pretty spoiled upbringing, in that I'd always seemed to receive the best that life had to offer. My wife had less of the material gifts than I had historically enjoyed, but she was a gem. (It's probably accurate to say that, following her death, I have sincerely canonized her in my lamentation.) She had maternal gifts second to none. It was one of the things that had attracted me to her. I knew that I wanted a loving mother for my offspring. Among other convictions, it was part of my Catholic mantra. I had other old-fashioned ideas born of a somewhat Victorian upbringing. I went into marriage with the conviction that Trish was my princess, and there was nothing I would not do for her. I assumed she had complementary views, though she never quite articulated them as such. She had not enjoyed the marvelous loving atmosphere of exceptional parental harmony that I had. Her parents had a more contentious relationship and her mother suffered the worst of it. I think this latter issue established a defensive mindset for Trish that probably infested our relationship from the outset. But for me, Trish had only to make her wishes known to me. I envisioned myself as some latter-day Sir Walter Raleigh, ever ready to shed my coat for her to cross the errant stream. Unfortunately, that resolve to "take care of number one" that I'd made somewhere in the early 1960s had infested that better goal. It had become a crucial turning point in our relationship. Like some malignant growth, it metastasized over the years, and the consequences eventually became the central focus of my relationship philosophy. It was about me. My focus was about being loved, not loving.

It was in the mid-1980s when my employer, facing the periodic economic downturns that have become too common in our country, decided that executive cutbacks were in order. The ax was broad and swift. First, I was demoted, and then the grade to which I had been demoted was eliminated carte blanche throughout the company. All of management was taking hard hits. There were serious concerns about the survival of the company. The next crisis for me was an offer of early retirement. The caveat was that I had sixty days to make my decision as to whether to accept the company's "generous" offer. It was, to say the least, a difficult time for me. I was only fifty-seven years old, unaccustomed to this kind of adversity, and had certainly not considered retiring at such an early age.

I thought about it for several days when I decided to take some accumulated vacation days to think things over. Mistakenly, still being a cave dweller, I had not mentioned anything of my potential retirement to Trish. We drove to Florida and spent a few days on the beach, but I was off in my own world wondering what the heck I was going to do. I was leaning toward accepting the company's offer, since it was a generous one that I found difficult to decline. Finally, on the drive home I took the plunge: "Honey, the company has offered me special early retirement, and I think I'm going to take it," I announced. "How about that?"

Trish was stunned. There was a long silence and finally, "How long have you known about this?" she asked. I mumbled quietly, "Oh, a couple of weeks or so." I could see her anger and frustration building. After a long silence, Trish blurted out, "Wonderful! But I'm not sure I can stand you around all day!"

In retrospect, I think her response was probably aimed at easing the tension with a little humor, and I realize now that it was stupid of me to conceal the issue from Trish for so long a period. But I was in my cave. I didn't get it. Because of my unrelenting self-focus, her words cut far deeper than Trish had any reason to suspect. This was her reaction to such a momentous event in my life? I'd thought being with her full time would be the fulfillment of a dream—a delightful one. I was hearing only that she doesn't want me! Over our nearly thirty years of marriage, I harbored a constant fear of not being really loved by her; a festering factor that had gradually grown to distorted levels. There had been many nights over past years when I'd lie awake next to her in bed, agonizing over just such a conviction for hours, while she slept soundly, totally unaware of my angst-produced insomnia. Marital communication is so important, and we were both deficient. My cave dwelling and self-focus were much to blame, but her abrupt and thoughtless response, despite her subtle humor, as a first reaction was devastating for me. She seemed unaware of the impact.

My response to her fear of my daily presence around the clock, seven days a week, was of course to crawl further into my cave and pull the stone into the opening behind me, there to lick my perceived wounds. The boiling brew was measured and stirred, and as I dwelt in the darkness of my retreat, masculine instincts gave off their destructive vapor. I was angry, and I concluded some kind of drastic action was called for. "I'm no wimp," I thought. "You'll see!" Communication was not an option. We were both incapable of that. I took my macho action. In two weeks, we were separated. The company had given me a three-month extension before my retirement decision, and assigned me to a new position. I abruptly moved out of our family home into a one-bedroom apartment close to my work.

Trish and I had not experienced the normal type of interaction associated with courtship that most couples enjoy prior to marriage. There was very little face-to-face dating when we could both be together. After our first real encounter on a normal date, I had been called to active duty in the navy for a two-year tour. During that ensuing period, Trish and I exchanged over three hundred letters. While we learned much about each other, and definitely fell in love, there were many of the ordinary aspects of courtship that we were denied. Those deficiencies were not minor. I tended to be more demonstrative in showing affection and she was much less so. There were probably other characteristics that a more physical type of dating would have exposed, but we felt we were very compatible in the important areas, and in many ways, we were. One of these was being Catholic, and our concern for being good, loving parents was a primary goal. We were naive, but in love, and we were married in 1955, five months before my tour of active duty expired. I was probably a rather "frightened little boy" type of groom, and Trish was the bride equivalent.

Our early years together were largely harmonious. When differences occurred, we dealt with them in effective and in sometimes-humorous ways that we both laughed about in later years when reminiscing. The greatest challenge of course was the arrival of six children in eight years. While it was educational in some ways, the serious toll on Trish's physical health became an impossible burden for her. After her eight pregnancies and the doctor's warning against further pregnancies, she was forced to undergo an unrelated major surgery to correct a congenital anomaly that had become life threatening. Another pregnancy was simply out of the question.

I was really worried for her health and was desperate for some solution. Our adherence to the Church's inane rhythm system had subtly, but seriously aggravated the conflicts in our relationship. Intimacy was systematically denied us when natural attraction was at its peak. Trish would curse "this male invented torture" as anything but *natural,* and it had frustratingly resulted in two "rhythm pregnancies." The ensuing total abstinence solution had taken an ever increasing toll on our relationship, and while it was a reluctant choice, it was the only option we saw as moral. It was another sad example of the fantasy world created by the magisterium's dogma-distorted concept of reality. It was also an example of the consequences of blind obedience and letting someone else do your thinking. It's not a good formula for marital success. We went to marriage counseling, but it didn't resolve our issues and proved of little help. The negative scenario that we had cultivated so unwittingly grew over the months and years. Clearly, the deferral of our intimacy through abstinence, aggravated the "you don't love me" syndrome, which dominated my thoughts. While my deluding self-focus and our inability to communicate were basic to our dilemma, we certainly found no refuge or help from the institutional Church. We were both first-class victims of a rigid reality-deficient dogma, and our unflinching acquiescence to it. Ironically, our Church commitment, rather than helping us, accomplished just the opposite. It nourished a distinctly negative environment that nearly destroyed our marriage. I now wince at our devastating ignorance during that period

Our separation lasted nearly a year. During that period, in my anger, I compounded my mistakes by resolving to date other women. I urged Trish to do likewise. I conveyed my conviction that our relationship was at an end. I had concluded that divorce was certain and that I was already tantamount to being single. Shortly after openly declaring this attitude to Trish, I became seriously involved with another woman who was also going through a divorce at the time. It was a vulnerable time for me and for her, but it proved to be a stupid rationale for which we all paid a heavy emotional price. About midway into this new relationship, I began to doubt seriously the wisdom of my drastic "masculine" solution. It seemed disaster lurked everywhere I looked. I was finding the idea of leaving Trish impossible, and I now found myself with the added task of severing this new bond I had slipped into as well as dealing with my marriage and finding some way to retrieve my relationship with Trish. I had thought that I wanted to divorce and all the baggage that entailed. Yet the more I contemplated the path that I was on, the more I kept hearing a little voice from the past that kept rousing into my consciousness. "Are you being a good boy?" was the nagging question. My code of ethics had always held that divorce was a cardinal failure. Yet, here I was, seriously considering it. It forced me into deeper thought. Gradually I began to realize a startling thing: Divorce was an impossibility for me. The more I actualized my intentions, the more I realized that I still loved my wife and there was simply no way I could abandon her. It was inescapable and an amazing revelation for me. It flipped my mental deck of cards into the air and my resolve was scattered in disarray. I began to understand that there existed a permanent bond between Trish and me that no contrived dissolution of our marriage could break. Nothing I could do would change that. When I finally began to recognize this mystic bond, it dawned on me that my love for her was unconditional and unending. It didn't matter whether she loved me according to my narcissistic needs and wants. I wanted only to be with her and love her, and to hell with anything else. This realization precipitated a definite desperation. I'd made a mess of things, and the situation was now probably irretrievable.

Once more, I finally began to turn to some intense prayer. The whole situation and my own feelings were something that I didn't really comprehend at the time, but I was slowly coming to the realization that there was simply no way I could leave Trish and also split up my precious family. Yet, I saw no solution. Eventually, as my desperation escalated, and perhaps as a response to my prayer, I was moved to approach her and see if we could reconcile. Hesitatingly, Trish accepted my plea to explore such options over a dinner date, the first in a long time. After lengthy conversation and the beginnings of some newborn communication achievements, we agreed that we would sell our home of eighteen years and that she would move in with me into a new three-bedroom apartment in the same complex where I had been dwelling alone.

Our troubles weren't over, however. I realized that essentially nothing had really changed, even though I had severed my new relationship. Old issues had not been resolved. Still stuck in the past, meditating on former grievances, things now seemed possibly worse—worse, because by introducing the third-party complication, I now perceived myself as an unfaithful spouse. I saw myself guilty of a status I had always abhorred in others who had failed at fidelity. Trish had dated casually a couple of times, but nothing serious. Despite my rationalization that our separation was merely the prelude to divorce, I was now convinced that I had lost my precious integrity. I could not ignore the serious nature of my excursion with someone else. No "good boy" me! I was a complete failure and had messed up big time. I retreated into a deep depression. In retrospect, it was the worst period of my life. I did a lot of crying and began to have serious suicidal thoughts. The problem with that solution, though, was that besides being permanent, I believed the Church's teaching that suicide was the only unforgivable sin. (Jesus was carrying me again. He'd answered my prayers, but I didn't know it yet. It was a period of unique growth in my journey of faith. From major failure, I was achieving major spiritual learning.)

Finally, I concluded that there was no solution to my dilemma. I believed there was no way Trish could possibly love me now or accept me. I knew that I had compounded our estrangement by turning to someone else, and yet I knew that I could never stop loving Trish. I couldn't envision now how she could ever fully take me back. I wanted real reconciliation and I wanted it badly. I wanted to put the past behind us, and begin our relationship anew. Would Trish agree? Could she forgive my stupidity and infidelity? No, that was impossible, I concluded—impossible. It was too late for that.

After considerable thought, and desperately wanting some prompt resolution, I concluded that the only route open to me was to cause an end to my life in a way that wouldn't be suicide. I would run—run until I collapsed—run myself to death, hopefully. I was asking God to take me. I wouldn't commit suicide. I would simply exert myself unrelentingly to a life ending finality, and thus produce the relief I sought. I knew I had been diagnosed with heart disease previously, and figured it would be easy to precipitate a cardiac trauma. It was a silly idea, but it illustrated well my muddled thinking and self-focus at the time. Thus one evening, in a light rain, I began the attempt. I ran around the broad court-yard outside of our apartment complex. I ran and ran, round and round the courtyard, for over an hour nonstop, weeping all the way. But this stupid body of mine wasn't cooperating. Why doesn't it quit? I'm not going to stop until it does, I thought, not until something happens. I was desperate—determined.

Then, something did happen. Trish looked out the second floor window of our adjacent apartment and saw her idiotic hus-band running in the rain. She immediately came down and ran to him, stopping his endless marathon abruptly. She embraced him tightly and said, "Come inside, you big dummy! You'll catch a death of cold!" I was immediately overcome by her spontaneous affection. My weeping subsided, and I felt strangely relieved. As I reflected further on my wife's action, I recognized clearly her unsolicited act of love. Was it possible? Was it possible that we could reconcile? Would Trish have me back? Of course she would. She loved me. I just didn't understand.

Luckily, Trish wanted reconciliation, too. She never wanted the stupid separation in the beginning. This wife of mine whom I'd feared didn't love me actually loved me way beyond anything I had understood or had any right to expect. Her little act of affection was a turning point. A major grace had been bestowed. Somehow, the Holy Spirit managed to gain my attention. I had been suffering from a mental and spiritual blindness, but gradually, I began see, to understand. My renaissance had begun. I knew I had hurt Trish deeply. It wasn't the first time, as my excessive self-focus had caused past hurt as well, but I had simply been unaware, or too self-focused to care.

At the outset of our reconciliation, I experienced an even more important grace; it was a grace of an enlightenment that was long overdue. Mysterious grace is the only explanation. I somehow firmly and consciously resolved that the quality of our new relationship was to be *my* responsibility, and that if happiness were possible, my own actions for achieving it were going to be primary, and total if necessary. In retrospect, I think that my turning to someone else had an unlikely positive effect. The resulting vivid self-awareness of my failure became a strong catalyst in finally achieving a modicum of unselfishness. Whatever the cause, it was good-bye egoism, hello empathy. When it came to our renewed relationship, if Trish had anything new to add, well, fine, but the ball was in my court. In essence, I had scrapped my previous philosophy of looking out for number one, adopted so many years before. My future focus was going to be on my spouse, and nowhere else. My focus became: *How can I make her happy?*

This new approach immediately began to pay amazing dividends. It opened a whole new perception of Trish for me. I began to recognize some of her little sensitivities and subtleties, and a uniqueness that I'd overlooked over the years. I began to realize that we were two different people who could engage our individuality and actually become more than compatible. I began to accept Trish just as she was, not as I fantasized. My need for affection was supplanted by a determination to give it rather than get it. My introduction to empathy was a startling revelation, and the "you don't love me" syndrome was effectively destroyed and buried.

More than all this, I experienced at some point an additional gift of a special grace from the Holy Spirit—at least I interpreted it that way. I don't remember any special occasion or incident when this occurred. I only remember a very clear message developing in my thoughts at some point. The message was simply that God was constantly speaking to me through my wife. It really got my attention, and I started to listen. What I heard through her, often dumbfounded me because of the coincidental accuracy of what I was thinking and feeling at the time. This new approach revealed a lot about my own faults. I heard solutions to issues that I hadn't considered before. My own unreasonable demands and hurts became a clear and embarrassing awareness for me. I began to see more about what it meant to love my wife, and not be just some caveman dwelling in the same vicinity. It was amazing how much our relationship quickly improved. It was also amazing how much more aware I became of my love for her and hers for me; it was probably the first time in my life I had *authentically* loved. I eventually came to a firm conviction that she could do no wrong, and that I was the luckiest of men to have her as my wife. I began to see things, that in the past had seemed so important and so offensive, now appeared trivial. Without any doubt, the last eighteen years of our marriage were happy beyond anything either of us could have imagined. We could not have hoped for such marital joy at any time in our prior relationship. We'd had happy times in the past, but nothing compared to this. I had begun to learn how to love. It began a personal process that has been unending. I have come to understand that the virtue of love is an amazing thing. It is the pinnacle of human experience. I also observed that divorce is a terribly painful thing. It is sad that it is so prevalent in our culture and it says much about much human unhappiness. My own experience suggests that it is nearly always the wrong choice.

In retrospect, when I consider my behavior and recovery, I am struck how the Spirit led me out of disaster and back to a path where Jesus, who was obviously carrying me, could set me down. I was finally able to navigate my journey on my own once more. The Holy Spirit's abundant grace is particularly evident in the drastic change of scrapping my philosophy of taking care of number one and shifting my focus to simply loving my wife. That idea definitely came from outside me. It was not something anyone suggested. It was simply a grace received. Selfishness couldn't have produced that selfless insight. My resolve to hear the Spirit's voice, as articulated through my wife, was definitely another inspirational grace. I simply cannot ignore the obvious help that I received during that period. It has alerted me to the continuing need to listen—listen for the muffled voice of the Spirit. I suspect that as another grace, I've since been awarded a spiritual hearing aid for this task, and I have it turned to full volume.

It gives me much confidence and serenity to see such Divine love showered on me. When I think how I tout the five exceptional "religious or spiritual experiences," the semi–paranormal events in my life that I relate in this story, I realize that the other, less spectacular graces are equally important, maybe even more so. Perhaps they are the most important. They have certainly had a profound influence on my thinking and actions. It is these more subtle graces that often get us through the tragedies of life. Most of us seldom recognize them. One might term them mundane manifestations of Divine love, but they are amazing things.

Following retirement from Ford, the company subsequently called me back for an additional seven years of work, but they were happy years for both of us, and when I finally opted to end it, I was sixty-five years old. For Trish and me, happy times became even happier. Not only did my wife not mind having her husband around 24/7, she actually seemed to love it, and she did not even express any surprise or remembrance of her previously fearful forecast. We bought a fifth-wheel trailer and began a few years of travel adventure, eventually winding up in a trailer resort in Central Florida close to Cape Canaveral. I began to become less of an introvert and was seldom off to my cave. When those rare occasions did occur, my stay was very brief and I'd recognize quickly that I'd reverted to some stupid tactic.

During this period, as our marital relationship grew to surpass the dream we'd both started out with, and in between travel and Florida stays, we began to become active in the gay community. We'd both more or less gone into the closet when we found out Mark was gay. We didn't discuss it and tried not to think about it. Mark seemed to be doing well and he understood clearly that we loved and accepted him without qualification. It was one day late in the fall that Trish ran across an Ann Landers column in the local press in which she advised the parents of a gay child who had written her, to get in contact with the local PFLAG chapter. We had never heard of PFLAG and in short order we were off to our first meeting with PFLAG Detroit. Trish pretty much had to drag me there, as I felt it threatened my privacy and lingering introversion.

That first Sunday meeting at PFLAG Detroit was an awakening experience for both of us. For the first time, we heard heart-wrenching stories from other parents of gay children, some of whom hadn't handled the event as well as Trish and I had. It is impossible not be to be affected when listening to such emotional family drama if one has any sense of empathy. It was a life-changing experience for both of us, and it quickly became evident that we were feeling a strong call to become active in the group. Soon we were elected to the board of directors, and within a couple of years, Trish became the organization's president. It was a fulfilling time and a fun time. We made many new and loving friends and participated in what for us were unlikely activities. We estimated that more than 60 percent of our new PFLAG friends also shared our Catholic faith. It seemed that Catholics had a special problem in dealing with the discovery that their child is gay. Most of them, like Trish and I, did not find a ready source of support in their Church. Most often the only message heard was the denigrating, homophobic Church doctrine that homosexuality is "intrinsically evil and disordered." Despite our new and intense involvement with the gay community, in the non-gay community, among our straight friends, we were still "in the closet."

Then came the Matthew Shepard[7] murder, a gay killing by two homophobic men in Laramie, Wyoming, wherein the young gay man was severely tortured, beaten, and then hung on a fence in crucifixion fashion, there to die. A short time later, our local gay community, including PFLAG Detroit, decided to hold a candle-light service in Matt's memory. The service was to be held outside an antigay group's political rally at a local public hall. The political group that was the target of the protest was national in scope and readily associated with blatant proclamations that homosexu-

---

7   "Matthew Wayne Shepard (December 1, 1976–October 12, 1998) a gay man, was a student at the University of Wyoming. He was tortured and murdered near Laramie, Wyoming, in October 1998. The two men accused of the crime were later convicted and are serving lifetime prison sentences.

als were an "abomination" and a sign of America's "moral decay." Our candlelight rally caught the attention of the local media as well as local law enforcement. Possible violence was anticipated, as emotions on both sides were intense. Media and police turned out in force. The rally was well attended and lasted more than an hour, as we all marched in circular procession carrying our lighted candles and signs about the entrance to the hall. Near the end of this protest/memorial, suddenly Trish and I found a microphone thrust in our faces backed up by a looming TV camera. "Excuse me," said the reporter holding the microphone. "Would you mind being interviewed for Channel 7 News?" Trish and I looked at each other a little bewildered but we recognized an unspoken mutual consent. I shrugged and responded, "Why not." The reporter quickly proceeded with the interview in a professional and direct manner. We were questioned about why we were participating in such a protest and then about our gay child. We both spoke. Trish's contribution was far more effective for our cause than mine. I was probably too emotional and strident. It all lasted no more than fifteen minutes. When it was over, I asked, "Will we be on TV?" The reporter responded: "Oh yes. You'll be the lead story on the eleven o'clock news tonight." We blew out our candles and returned to our car for the drive home. Trish turned to me and said; "I think we just came out of the closet." "Yup. I think you're right," I responded—and indeed, we were.

When we got home, we immediately turned on the TV and waited for the Channel 7 eleven o'clock news program. Leadoff we were. "This unlikely couple from Farmington Hills…" it began. The reporter had done a thorough and detailed job of telling who we were, why we were there, and the fact that we had a gay son named Mark. Even years later, as far away as Florida, on a few occasions when meeting someone new, the person would say something like, "Oh yes, the Nelsons. Didn't I see you folks on TV news one night a couple of years ago back in Michigan?" We were definitely out of the closet. It also occurred to us that not only had we come out of the closet, but we had unthinkingly dragged our son into the limelight, too. Mark later expressed his chagrin, but the deed was done.

It turned out to be an energizing experience. We became more active than ever, and our lives would never be the same. The consequences of having a gay son continued to heap unlikely rewards upon us both.

Looking back on that phase of my life, perhaps it is worthwhile to analyze the decline and separation that Trish and I endured in our marriage and our ensuing recovery. It was the worst period of my entire life, but it lead to the best of times. I often ask myself how it happened. I have already described that I regard my own failings and selfishness as the primary cause. Yet, while that is true, I would also lay some blame on the Church's mindless doctrine regarding contraception.

And there is another accusation of Church failing that I see as contributing factor in our troubles. The central focus of Jesus's life, as I now understand it, was love. The Church has somehow lost that focus. When it comes to relationships, there is too much concern with the sexual. It has constructed a set of rules and regulations, a dogma essentially devoid of love; it is one of crime and punishment. Arguably, one could find exceptions to this conviction, but broadly speaking, the critical concept of love as a primary goal in life is effectively well concealed. The central theme is that our sexual nature is infused with potential sinfulness. We tell people mostly what not to do. The how-to aspects of moral living might as well be incomprehensible. The prohibitions seem endless, little more than an expansion of the Ten Commandments.

Beyond the proscriptions, any Church help in the practical aspects of everyday living are all too rare. Because of the obsessive concern for doctrine, the Church seems incapable of comprehending everyday married life or understanding and teaching love. Could this stem from Church authority not knowing how to love? I observe that I have come to understand a little bit about loving, mostly because of the intimate relationship I've had with another human being. Church clergy who are supposed to lead the rest of us are denied this gift.

A related criticism is the lack of effective preaching by Sunday homilists. It is embarrassingly evident in most any parish on any given Sunday. The norm is an inane presentation that seldom relates in any way to the real issues of everyday living. The exceptions are refreshing, but tragically rare. Find a good homilist, and chances are you'll also find packed pews. In my own parish, a unique solution has been devised. The celebrants for the specific coming Masses on each Sunday are not published in the weekly bulletin, but carefully concealed from the congregation, in order to avoid empty pews when an empty homily could be expected, based on past performances. I don't blame the individual priests for this as much as I do the out-of-touch directions from on high. Priests are apparently advised to formulate their homilies on the day's scriptural readings. This most often results in essentially a second presentation of the prior readings, but in perhaps, a more vernacular mode, virtually all of which the congregation already knows by heart. It is the cause of much dozing in the pews. Any relevance to real living people and contemporary issues is absent.

This mantra reflects a malignant lack of awareness. There is no relationship to real life. Is this because our celibate clergy do not experience human relationships? Can one effectively speak to life issues if one is removed from it? How can bishops, archbishops, cardinals, and popes, from their opulent castles and darkened chauffeur-driven limousines, speak to ordinary folks from across such a yawning divide? Catholic marriages can expect little support from such an enigma. Trish and I survived our own marital trauma not because of help from our Church. We actually survived *despite* the Church. Their proffered assistance consisted mainly in unnecessary hurdles they placed in our path. Indeed, I recall one priest-counselor who tried to help us who was summarily dismissed by my wife. Her rationale: "This guy just doesn't get it." This counselor had been recommended to us as an expert Catholic marriage counselor. That experience and the other lessons we learned in our journey toward an adult faith are among the chief reasons for this book.

Chapter 9

Grief 101

"Blessed are those who mourn, for they will be comforted"
—*Matthew 5:4*

It was a beautiful sunny day at The Great Outdoors, our trailer park resort in Florida. Trish and I were playing golf together on the resort golf course and we were both striking the ball well. Riding close next to me on the golf cart, Trish suddenly turned to me, grabbed my hand for a little squeeze, and exclaimed earnestly with a loving smile, "Oh honey, life doesn't get any better that this! Does it?" I gave her a little hug and agreed that we were exceedingly blessed. I urged her to put her next shot on the green.

But things were about to change drastically. A little more than a month later, I began writing a personal journal of the e-mail and letters I sent to our friends. It tells the story of my most profound tragedy—a grief I could not have imagined. It also tells about the amazing and loving person that Trish was. She impacted everyone around her and her husband most of all. Her life was a constant effort to practice love, and it evoked a loving response in those around her.

I want to tell this story because of the profound influence it has had on my own faith journey, and the ultimate understanding of the essence of human love her death imparted. Her death was beautiful reflection of her life, and it presented me with an opportunity to love beyond anything I had yet experienced. Death is truly one of life's greatest learning experiences. I will be forever indebted to this woman for the gift of her love. What she taught me through that love is immeasurable. I want to share it with you. I wrote in my journal:

March 29, 2004
This nightmare began a month ago. I remember it like it was last night. I remember the date all too well. It was February 27, my mother's birthday. I think I will try to write this all down, as the experience, while traumatic, is very much of a learning experience for us both. Perhaps it's worth passing on—to my dear family, so you all can remember our ordeal and maybe learn a little about life along with Mom and me.

That night is still too terrifying to recall. No effort of mine can come close to describing the utter horror of that moment in the middle of the night on February 27, 2004. I was awakened by her crying out—loudly—trying to call my name but unable to say it clearly. Her speech was garbled and she was shaking violently. I thought it was a nightmare, but it seemed more than that; she was in some kind of trouble. I put my hand on her to try to calm her, but she didn't awaken, or so I thought. She just continued to shake and cry out. I quickly realized this was no nightmare. I knew she was awake and aware and I couldn't do anything to help her. I was scared—terribly. I held her and tried to calm her. It couldn't have lasted more than two or three minutes, but it seemed much longer at the time. She tried to call out to me to get an aspirin. She thought she was having a stroke and that was what we should do. When it ended, she was perfectly normal, and we both almost simultaneously exclaimed, "What the hell was that?" I said, "I think we should go to emergency." She agreed, and we dressed quickly and drove off to Parrish Medical Center in Titusville. The real nightmare had begun.

The emergency people took us in quickly—without the usual wait. I think they knew this was something more serious than Trish or I had considered. Soon she had undergone a CAT scan. I remember the doctor coming in, looking somber, and gently putting his hand on Mom's shoulder, he said softly, "You have a mass on your brain."

The following days were a blur for us both. She was admitted. More tests were run. They wanted to establish whether this tumor was primary to the brain or had metastasized from somewhere else in her body. I was in a state of numbed shock from which I have yet to recover. The care at Parrish was loving and professional. Trish's primary care physician, Dr. Ricardo Rivera, became a friend to us both and after tests showed the tumor to be a primary brain mass, he felt that prompt action was imperative, and wanted to transfer her to Orlando for immediate surgery. But we opted to return home to be with family.

It was three days later when, still at Parrish, she was medicated for the return trip and released. Daughters Julie and Kathleen had flown down from up north to be with us and help us cope, while Mark had made plane reservations for us to return. We gathered a few things and left The Great Outdoors Resort, a place of many great times, friends, and memories, not knowing when or if we would ever return.

It was a Monday morning at neurosurgeon Dr. Daniel Pieper's office at Providence Hospital in Detroit. I listened half-dazed as I heard him describe the unthinkable, the bewildering challenges and frightening risks of the surgery ahead. Neither Trish nor I could comprehend yet what was happening to us. Our life seemed to have suddenly halted. This must be a bad dream from which we would soon awaken. Decisions had to be made. A second opinion? Henry Ford Hospital would be the source for that. Should we investigate the Boulder Colorado Radiation Clinic? What else should we be doing? Where to turn next? Explore the Internet—yes. There was too much to do, too little time. I don't think we could have survived it without the guidance and complete dedication of my oldest daughter,

Lisa. She put her life on hold to take care of us. She was everywhere and everything whenever it was needed. She knew what to do, who to talk to, and where to go. We scheduled surgery for March 12 while we sought second opinions. However, fate intervened again. Trish had another seizure Monday morning on March 8. We could wait no longer and she went into surgery Tuesday morning, March 9, 2004.

What followed was physically devastating to Trish, and mentally a terrible torment for me. I was on automatic pilot and I guess I still am. As the cards, phones calls, and e-mails began to arrive, I undertook to respond to some of them. I formed a list of e-mail addresses to keep friends informed and I've decided that the easiest way to record this journey is to post copies of those e-mails here. It forms something of a chronology of our path.

March 3, 2004
Dear friends at The Great Outdoors: We just got back from the neurosurgeon and the news is mixed. We won't know until surgery whether the tumor is operable or not. The problem is the proximity of the motor function in the brain, and if the tumor is too close or in that portion, then surgical excision is impossible. The good news is that the surgeon thinks that it is only moderately aggressive and relatively small. He said in any event that Trish would require chemo and radiation for follow-up. Please continue to keep her in your prayers. Thanks for all your concern; we'll keep you posted. We love you guys.
Tom

March 10, 2004
Dear friends: Trish was operated on yesterday morning. The surgery had been moved up as she had another seizure Monday morning. The news is very good! The doctor feels he got the entire tumor without affecting her motor skills. He feels there is a good chance for the tumor to be low-grade or even non-malignant. A full recovery is expected. Your prayers have sponsored a miracle! Indeed, those were Trish's first and only words

she kept repeating in recovery after the op, "Miracle! Miracle! Miracle!" She has a long way to go, but we are much relieved.

My second-oldest daughter, Tracey, has come in from San Diego. She is a lifesaver...so calm and steady, taking the watch more than she should. Dad is lucky to have such support. Nancy is coming from Colorado soon. More help. Family is so great. I go home to an empty house. It's like a tomb. I remember past times. We didn't realize how it could all end so suddenly. I think of the future. I cry a lot. I have to live only the present moment. I don't feel much like eating, and sleep never comes, it seems. Again, to you all—thank you, thank you, and thank you. We love you guys!

Tom

March 11, 2004

Dear friends: The latest on Trish: While the news on her surgery and the follow-up MRI has been good, her recovery has been tenuous at best. After forty-eight-plus hours post-surgery, she remains paralyzed on the left side and is unable to speak. Communication with her is mostly via sign language. The surgeon feels this is all temporary, but I remain terrified!

The cards and flowers pour into our house for Trish. It's obvious she is one popular lady. The e-mails continue to inundate my mailbox, too. One letter that she received from a minister at Beaumont Hospital she had met through her PFLAG work was particularly moving. It expressed so well how much she means to all of us and especially for me, what this tragedy means to the two of us. He said:

"Because you are a part of Mark's [Mark Mason, my oldest daughter Lisa's husband] family, you are a part of mine...From the moment we met, I have felt a special bond—of your gentle understanding and sincere friendship. Your daughter shares some of your very special "spirit" too! I just wanted to write you a note and tell you that you are in my heart right now, and I am praying while all the energy of spring is near and all the blessed power of Easter is close by, you will be touched as well. Please be assured of my prayers and support for you. If I can do anything, let me know. You always bring light and love wherever you go—now may you receive the same from everyone God places near to you until this shadow is behind us and the journey is bright again. I pray for nothing less than your complete healing and restoration to your world and to your family Why ask for anything less from a God who can do all things? I also pray God makes of this not an ordeal but an adventure in faith and life. Again, I am praying; when the night is long or the way is dark, know that you are being lifted up in love and faith."

Thanks for your prayers and your friendship. I'll try to keep you posted.

Tom

March 12, 2004

Dear friends: The news is better. Trish is improving and is able to speak a little. Her spirits are remarkable and her personality is as good as ever! I am not so terrified. I think God has been inundated by all your prayers. My cup runneth over. Thank you my beloved friends. I will continue to keep you posted.

Nancy arrived today. Thank God—Tracey will get a little relief now. Nancy is so upbeat—and hospital people beware—Nancy gets what Nancy wants. Don't any of you nurses neglect her mom. She is everywhere attending to everything. It's not so lonely at the condo now, with Tracey and Nan. My dear grandchildren Anna and Alex help me remember that there is much left to life for me yet.

Tom

March 14, 2004

Dear friends: I think Trish has turned the corner! She is eating by mouth for the first time, and is speaking a little. She is still paralyzed on the left side of her body, but the doctors expect a near full recovery. I am beginning to feel like we both might survive this nightmare. The next big hurtle is the pathologist's report, which we will hear Monday. God has given me one

miracle and now I want one more. His will be done. Thank you all for your outpouring of sympathy and prayers. You have given us so much comfort and support.
Tom

March 15, 2004
Dear friends: We received the pathologist's report on Trish's tumor today. It was found to be malignant— a grade-three astrocytoma, which means moderately aggressive. This is not great news, nor the worst news. She will require both radiation treatment and chemo. God's plan for us is unknowable but we accept, with trust in Him, whatever it holds for us. Your prayers and support have helped us accept the future with a hopeful and trusting spirit. I have much to learn. Again, thank you for your comforting response. I will keep you all posted, but my next update may not be real soon, as I have so much to do.
Tom

March 22, 2004
Dear friends: The news on Trish is encouraging to us. She is now in rehabilitation at Providence Hospital and we expect she will be there for some time. She has regained some movement in her left leg, is speaking better, and is in good spirits. Thankfully, she is in no physical pain. She is remarkably courageous about this whole thing. I marvel at her fortitude. It's better than mine is. I think women are the stronger sex. I am doing better also. I have a little time on my hands now, as they limit how much time I can spend with her now and I am catching up on home chores. I want to tell you all just a little of this experience we're undergoing. This abrupt turn in our life has been a cataclysmic event to us of course, but it's the little things that seem to have come into an amazing new focus that surprise me. You have been a part of this process. In this regard, I want to tell you how much we have both been overwhelmed by the outpouring of prayers and affection from you all. Your cards, letters, and e-mails have touched us both to a degree you can't

imagine. In the past, when Trish and I had sent greeting cards or get-well notes to friends, I didn't think it was a big deal, and frankly, I thought it probably didn't matter that much. Now, on the receiving end of this phenomenon, I have learned that it matters distinctly. You have made a difficult time for us bearable; you all feel like family. I can never express adequately the gratitude and affection we both have for you all. Thank you, my dear friends. The future looks good!
Tom

March 27, 2004
Friends: I continue these updates despite not wanting to sadden your day in anyway, but wanting to tell you of our journey and share our experience with you all. We remain upbeat. We got some bad news when we received the Armed Forces Institute pathology report this week (a second opinion requested by our surgeon). They're supposed to be the gold standard on pathology. They said Trish's cancer is a stage four—the most aggressive. I found this pretty devastating, but our surgeon said it didn't matter that much. The treatment remains the same: radiation and chemo. The outlook is...who knows? We just need a bigger miracle, I guess. In the meantime, Trish's progress continues. She is now regaining the use of her left leg and today we both cried when she moved her left arm for the first time. It was a great event for us. While Trish tires very easily, she seems so very determined that it amazes me. It must be her Irish ancestry!

One of our friends, who is a chaplain at Beaumont Hospital here in Detroit, wrote Trish a letter. In it, he told us that God has put us on a path of adventure in life and in faith. It is an amazingly accurate description of what we have both been experiencing. We couldn't agree more. There have been so many little signs and amazing coincidences in which He seems to be saying: "I am here. I hear you. I am with you. Have faith and be at peace. Come see. Follow me!" Another piece of good news we received today: The Realtor from Florida called, and said they have a buyer for not only our lot down there, but also our trailer. We couldn't believe it. They even met our asking price. Before this trauma began, Trish and I had decided that it was time to give up our Florida lot and the trailer. I had just about forgotten about such material concerns amid the confusion and demands of these past days, but the joy we both experienced at the news that this little issue will soon be behind us was more than welcome. When I told Trish that not only was the lot sold, but the trailer too, we both cried and laughed at the same time. The emotions were mixed, because while the sale is welcome, the thought of leaving our friends at The Great Outdoors grieves us. Those of you from TGO, please try to understand.

My personal education seems to intensify each day. It is an unlikely, yet indescribably satisfying experience that seems to make the trauma of this all somehow bearable and even acceptable. You all have been a part of that and I suspect you are not even aware of what you've done by sharing your concern, prayers, and affection. You have been a channel through which He has poured His grace upon us. How can I ever thank you all?

I am optimistic, feeling better about all this, and pretty much OK. I know the future will have some more "speed bumps," but that's OK. The journey continues. I'll keep you posted.

My love and affection to you all,
Tom.

July 9, 2004

Dear friends: Trish's progress has slowed to a nearly imperceptible rate of recovery, and it seems every week brings a visit to yet another doctor with a new problem to be diagnosed and treated. Her left-side paralysis persists, mostly confined to her left forearm and hand. Still, she remains dogged and upbeat. Her courage is amazing to me and it keeps my tear ducts flushed. Sometimes, when she gets frustrated at her handicap, she gets testy toward me, the nearest venue to vent her emotions, and when I sometimes respond in kind, our little spat most often erupts into laughter as we both release the stored tension that is part of this scenario. It has been and continues to be an educational experience. There is good in it! We are planning a family reunion in northern Michigan later this month. Trish, having finished radiation, is now on a chemo schedule where she is on five days at triple dose, then off for twenty-eight. Our reunion is scheduled for the latter part of an "off" period so that she will be feeling her best. We are all looking forward to it and the whole family plans to be there. At this point, Trish walks a little unassisted. (Though I try always to be near enough to prevent any falls.) She even made it to an adaptive golf clinic for the handicapped recently. She stood at the tee, with a therapist behind her to help in her balance, and hit about fifty balls using only her right arm. I estimate she only miss-hit two of the fifty! She hit seventy to eighty yards right down the middle, and did so well that the PGA pros and assistants who were present to instruct, all came to her tee to watch "this amazing lady." We both had fun and a lot of laughs. I plan to take her out on the course when we go north. Your cards and phone calls have continued to brighten the shadows in our life these days. Thank you all.

Tom

October 28, 2004

Dear friends: It's been awhile since I last wrote you. We learned in August that Trish's tumor has returned. There is nothing more to be done but await the inevitable. Some of you have e-mailed me inquiring about her status. This will update you and also give me the opportunity to share with you some of the unique experiences God is giving Trish and me and our family. I want to share it with you because you have been a part of it through your prayers and messages of kindness. You have given us both something beyond support, something that we both treasure deeply.

Ours days are cloaked with a shroud of sadness as Trish declines toward her journey's end. She is virtually bedridden now and mostly helpless. She suffered another seizure a little more than a week ago, which is an expected part of her decline. She sleeps more now and experiences little pain or discomfort. Her greatest burden seems to be the frustration of her paralysis. Yet even there her calm resignation is an inspiration. The other night as we were both retiring, and I was going through the ritual of attaching the night splint to her afflicted left hand, she looked up at me, smiled and said, "I suppose it's pointless to continue this, isn't it?" She realized that the imminence of death was now the focus.

Her humor and courage are unrelenting and she is able to communicate well when awake. Even at this stage of her decline, Trish seems focused on others. Despite the fact that the surgery was supposed to destroy her emotional center, she still manages to spread cheer. The other day, commenting on my attentiveness to her and how I catered to her every whim, she looked at me and smilingly said, "You're my Saint Thomas Fetch-it." It surely touched my heart. No way. It wasn't true—they didn't destroy her love.

Her appetite is great and we joke about how she can now eat all the forbidden fruits she chose to avoid back when a chief concern was the waistline. She's even become a fan of dark chocolate, an affliction I've laid on her these past weeks. Of course, we continue to enjoy each other's company, savoring every moment we have left. We've evolved into a routine of a video in the evening before bedtime, usually some silly romantic comedy, and then we laugh more when Trish, after falling asleep during a greater part of the movie, insists that I relate to her in fullest detail what happened in the movie. The trivia of life seems unabated in many ways. Yet, we both talk openly of her impending death. Her faith strengthens my own and I have little fear because her future will soon be most happy. The hospice care workers tell us that it is very unlikely that Trish will survive until Christmas. The Thanksgiving holiday will be a challenge, perhaps. Realizing that next February would have brought us to our fiftieth wedding anniversary, and that I will be without her then, is a great distress to me. Things past and the thoughts of the future are part of my cloak. For Trish, her focus continues to be on others. She laments not what she will miss, nor her own death, but what will happen to her grandchildren and me—missing the "thank you" to all her friends, the letters she can no longer write, the help she can no longer give. I have yet to see her complain. She is an amazing woman. I've learned so much more about her in these past months and all only to multiply the love I feel for her. I realize now more than ever how blessed I have been to have her in my life.

This dying thing has been described to us as at once sad and yet beautiful. It is that. I have personally come to a vivid realization of the depth of our love for each other. I thought I knew what love was all about, but I've found that this experience has transcended all my past understanding. A very special and bizarre experience occurred to me one evening these past days: I have been blessed— to glimpse ever so briefly, in a fleeting and indescribable way, her soul. I had been simply sitting next to her, meditating about our life together and things spiritual. Then, suddenly, while looking at her frail, failing body, an overwhelming vision floods my mind and sight. I don't see her ailing body. It fades away suddenly to an irrelevant blur and I see Trish in another realm. She now appears surrealistically beautiful, dressed in a long, white robe standing before me surrounded by what seems to be a numinous luminescence. She looks taller than in life, but it is her, I know it; I recognize her face. Her beauty is overwhelming, and a tremendous tidal wave of utter awe stuns me! I quickly realize I am seeing—a soul! Yes! This is her soul I am seeing—I am sensing! I can't convey the awesomeness and reality of it. The result left me quite numb and rather dumbfounded. I have concluded how insignificant these bodies we inhabit really are. It has been a great gift to shore up my faith and comfort me for what is to come.

When I described this experience later to Trish, in her typically Irish way, she just nods, pats my hand, and simply smiles. I get the feeling she's mostly skeptical and writes it off as my emotions playing tricks with me. I don't think so. It was very vivid, intense, and spiritual.

This was third of what I have termed extraordinary spiritual experiences in my life. Uniquely, this experience occurred when I was fully awake. It was not a dream. My journal continues:

The hospice people are wonderful beyond description. Their sole focus and action is Trish's comfort and my own. Their career of dedication to the dying has given them unique abilities and experiences. Our lead nurse, Martha, is now like family to us. Her talent to cheer us and her eagerness to tend to our needs is priceless. She has related some amazing spiritual episodes that she has witnessed in past patients, tales that would leave even the most skeptical shaking their head in wonder. She says that "spiritual events" are typically part of the dying process more often than not. Just last week, she related to us how, during the prior week, one of her male patients, dying of Lou Gehrig's disease, had been in a coma for several days. She was sitting nearby, when the man's wife entered the room and stood at the bed next to her comatose husband. As she was gazing down at him, he suddenly opened his eyes, sat upright, took her hand, and exclaimed, "I have seen the other side! It is beautiful! I have seen the brilliant light of the Holy Spirit! I am so happy!" He then fell back, closed his eyes, and died. Wow! Martha has told us other similar stories she has witnessed.

For our part, we had a strange experience on a recent trip to Chicago. We had flown there for the Labor Day holiday because Trish wanted one last good-bye visit with her youngest grandkids and our daughter. We returned on Saturday via Northwest Airlines and because of the light passenger load, they bumped us up to first class. We were seated in the first row on the plane when we landed in Detroit and were waiting for all the other passengers to deplane so that Trish's wheelchair could be brought up without any disruption. All of the other passengers had to pass our seat when they left. The last person off, an African American, stopped at our seat and he bent over, put his hand on Trish's shoulder and said to her, "Jesus told me to tell you you're not going to die." Then he looked at me and said, "She's going to be healed. Jesus told me to tell you.

It won't look like she's getting well, but she will be healed!" Bizarre! We'd never met this man in our life. He had been sitting near the rear of the plane during the trip— nowhere near us. As events have since transpired, I am convinced his message was legitimate, only our interpretation was off. Trish is being healed—into a new life. We both agree. There have been a couple of other strange occurrences which tend to support the latter. It has been very faith nourishing and comforting. Joy can happen at the most unexpected times. It is an amazing journey. I talk too much. We miss you all. God bless you for all your kindness and prayers. May He bless you as much as He has us!

Tom

November 18, 2004
Dear friends: I am sad to tell you that my beloved Trish is gone. She died in my arms about 7:00 a.m. this morning. She is with the angels now. I can write no more now. Much is needed from me at this time.
God bless you all.

Tom

November 25, 2004
Dear friends: My Trish is gone. Our dear friend is at peace. I am very sad, but she died a beautiful death and we both have much to be thankful for. We had many blessings in life, and these past ten years of retirement were exceptionally wonderful. The day Trish suffered her first seizure, we were playing golf on a beautiful sunny day at The Great Outdoors. As we rode down the fairway she turned to me and said, "Honey, it doesn't get any better than this!" "Yes, yes," I agreed. There were many days like that, and we both were thankful for the Lord blessing us with such enjoyment of life. If you've followed my e-mails, you know that God continued to bless us. The blessings were not those that perhaps I anticipated, or wanted, but we both accepted that His way is ultimately for our good and what we both wanted.

As I look back, I realize that her lack of any pain, her time to say good-bye, her lucidness to the end, her humor to the end, the presence of all her family at the end—all these were God's blessings, compensation not only to her for an early end to her life, but to me also for my terrible loss. It is the most painful experience of my life. Yet Trish continues to comfort me in amazing ways. She very quickly let me know that she was OK. It has been and continues to be a very spiritual experience. I feel a need to tell you a little of the end days so you will perhaps better understand this woman we all knew as our friend. Not long after the tumor returned and Trish was confined to a wheelchair, the trips to the bathroom became ordeals that challenged us both. On one of the first occasions of this adventure, my oldest daughter, Lisa, was with us and insisted that she assist in the operation. As we shoehorned the wheelchair and the three of us into our very small powder room on the first floor, I suddenly realized it wasn't going to work. There was simply not enough room. I announced that, "Somebody has to get out." Immediately, Trish raised her good hand and announced in a firm manner, "I'll go!" That's the way she was—to the very end, always good-humored.

I remember too, when she was first confined to bed, I set up an intercom system so that she could easily reach me no matter where I might be in the house. Shortly after I had first set it up, I was away in the basement or somewhere out of reach, when the intercom I was carrying began beeping with an obvious urgency. I quickly ran to her bed, and breathlessly asked, "What's wrong, honey? Are you OK? What do you want?" Trish replied with a grin, "Oh nothing, I just wanted to see you come."

Despite her obvious frustrations with her affliction, she never complained. She continued to focus solely on others to a degree that will always cause me to marvel. She had this amazing empathy; it continues to challenge me. In the days shortly before she died, Trish, as predicted, entered a coma. Despite this, we were told that she could probably hear us as we stood at her bedside and said our farewells. Once, when I was doubting the accuracy of this hearing thing, as she seemed so comatose, I spoke to her, not expecting any answer, and said, "Well honey, it looks like I finally get to have the last word." Amazingly, she opened her eyes, looked directly at me, and very clearly spoke in her husky, afflicted voice, "Don't bank on it!" and she grinned. I could only laugh and nod my head in agreement.

Trish died about 6:45 a.m. Thursday morning, November 18. I was sleeping in the bed next to hers on the first floor. We had set up a second bed there so that I could be near her throughout the nights. About 5:30 a.m. Thursday morning, I could tell from the change in her breathing that the end must be near. I got up and knelt at her bed, cradled her head in my arms, and spoke softly to her. I told her I loved her and reminisced of times past. Finally, I held her close, and said, "It's OK, honey. Be at peace. You can go now." Immediately, she let out a loud groan, and within minutes breathed her last. It is a moment burned into my soul. I know that she is happy now, even though my own misery weighs so very heavy. The evening after her death, I went to bed to try to sleep in our own bed for the first time in many weeks. After a little weeping, I turned out the light, sat back, and wondered how I could ever sleep there again. Suddenly, I felt Trish's presence in a very real way. I sensed her saying to me, "Relax dear. You have much to do in the next few days. You will need your sleep. Lie down now and go to sleep. I will be right here next to you tonight." I suddenly felt amazingly relaxed and within five minutes, I fell peacefully asleep. She has touched my shoulder several times since and brought me comfort when it seemed most impossible. I'm sure this all must sound like the hallucinations or emotions of a bereaved husband.

Perhaps. But let me tell you of one last incident that has amazed all of us. Trish and I had planted a maple tree directly behind our condo. It failed the first planting two years ago, but last fall, we planted anew and it took very well. It survived the winter and throughout this past summer, it thrived with dense green foliage. When fall came, and all the other trees in the sub changed color, our tree remained a vivid green. When Trish saw it, she complained, "How come it's not turning color? It's supposed to turn crimson! Did we get gypped?" I shrugged, not knowing what to say. Soon, all the other trees were stripped of all their leaves in a gale-force November windstorm, but our tree only bent in the wind and refused to part with a single leaf. Not long after this, our green friend finally did its thing. While the rest of the neighborhood trees were long since barren, our tree stood alone, cloaked in brilliant red, like some odd monument. When Trish saw it, she exclaimed, "Oh, it's beautiful. Finally!" Jokingly, I said to her, "Looks like it was just late—like you've always been." This crimson phenomenon continued about ten days—through Wednesday, November 17. I saw it every day, as it was just outside our living room window near Trish's bed. When morning dawned that next day, and she was gone, I was stumbling through my terrible gloom and finally opened the blinds on that window. There was our tree. It had dropped all its leaves! It was damp and foggy outside. There had not been the slightest breeze to precipitate this bizarre event. I stood there and stared. That tree was in full-color bloom yesterday. Not even a dry curl to its leaves. Yet now it was bare! It was as if that tree had known and shed its tears in the only way possible, its weeping matching my own.

Trish's funeral was what you might expect. She was buried next to my father's grave after a funeral Mass on Monday, November 22. I saddled my girls and Mark with the task of writing most of the nearly three hundred thank-you notes to those who attended. (It pays sometimes to have a large family.) They have been, as you have these past months, a great comfort to me. I'm a lucky guy. I know that God has plans for the rest of my life and I trust His goodness. I didn't want this change He gave me, yet, as I've told my friends here, when they asked how I was doing, "I'm miserable, but Trish is happy, and that's good. It's better than way than the other way around." I'm told that I will survive this, and that my life will find some peace somewhere in the future. I don't want to think about that right now, except to hope that my future will allow me to see each of you in that future to thank you all for your friendship and help, but also to laugh with you all again, tip a brew or two, and brag about our latest golf myths. I have attached a copy of the eulogy written by my children and read at the close of her funeral Mass. I send it so that you may know a little more of her… and our children. Once again, God's loving blessings on you all.

Tom

MOTHER
November 18, 2004
Mother,
Words will not capture
Your smile, your smell, your sweetness,
All the images and many moments that make up
The essence that was you.
These are too personal,
Too close.
Each of us will hold them in our hearts,
And linger there
Later.
But now,
Now
We can share
Your gifts.
And gifts reveal the giver.
You gave us a love of food.
(We were doomed, inheriting that passion from both sides of the
family)
Not just a meal,
But the sweetness of fresh vegetables,
The kind your father used to grow.
The patience put into the preparation.
The surprise of some new gourmet concoction.

Your gave us the Gift of Gatherings,
Holiday celebrations,
Feasts,
Planned meticulously with
Elaborately set tables,
Centerpieces,
And silver,
And china,
And crystal,
And colors.
Creations that were works of art,

Meant for all of us,
Friends and family.
We sat at your tables,
Joined in conversation there.

You gave us the Gift of Talk.
That came after the meal.
And sometimes, you would say,
Too long.
But then,
There was plenty of time for talk
You were always the last to sit, the last to finish.
Aaah…
Your Gift of Talk,
While preparing meals,
On the phone,
In the car traveling,
On the phone.
On the phone.
You often complained
About how much time you spent on the phone.
But how else were you to keep up with your busy life
And stay in touch with 6 children,
12 grandchildren,
And your many friends.

You gave us the Gift of Listening.
Our referee,
Calming and soothing ruffled feathers,
After heated debates.
Yes.
We admit it,
Our conversations did get overly passionate at times.
But you always called us back,
Listening and pointing out…
Who went unnoticed?
Whose voice needed to be heard?

You gave us your Gift of Family.
Taught us to understand,
The importance of staying close.
We grew up knowing
That you wanted us
To be there for each other.
Not just siblings,
But friends

You gave us the Gift of Leadership,
Although you never saw yourself that way.
You led.
Led us to understand,
That it is our responsibility
To look out for the little guy.
Look out for the underdog.
Like all true leaders,
You led by example
In the home and out in the world.
Speaking up.
Taking action against
What you felt in your heart was unjust.
Even when it wasn't easy to do.

You gave us the Gift of Laughter,
Even in times of adversity.
You never lost your incredible sense of humor,
The Irish wit inherited from your father.
You showed us how to laugh
When laughter was unexpected,
When laughter was needed most.

You gave us the Gift of Playfulness.
Childlike in your pursuit of fun,
Sledding with the grand kids,
On the hill behind your home,
Skiing down,

The most difficult slopes with your son,
Swimming in Lake Michigan,
Even kickboxing,
With your daughters on the beach.
You were never one to sit and watch.
Maybe that's why you were often late,
Always trying to pack
So much into every day.

Your gave us the Gift of Determination
Whether it was
Working on your golf game,
Enlightening your husband,
Directing your children's self-improvement
Or battling childhood illnesses.
You were resolute,
Always a fighter,
Even the to the end.
Most importantly,

You gave the Gift of Love,
Your greatest gift,
Constant,
Never wavering,
You were there for all of us,
Unconditionally, loving, and forgiving

These were,

Your gifts,

Your love,

Your legacy,

Your children: Lisa, Tracey, Mark, Julie, Nancy, Kathleen

Trish: The wake was mostly a blur. I remember talking to so many people. You looked so good, my dearest. Yet you were so frail at the end and you could never appear as you did in life. Sunday night we said the rosary—led by Father Brian. It was done well, of course, but it made me recall so vividly that rosary five nights before. You were in a coma. We all stood around you—most of us in tears—and started the rosary. I stood close to you on your right, and knelt as we began. As we started the first decade, I saw tears forming in the corners of your eyes. I knew you heard and prayed the rosary with us. I dried your tears with a tissue as your children watched, and we finished the prayer. It was a foretaste of the days to come. That Sunday, the last night of the wake, ended with son-in-law Paul saying the most loving farewell to you. He is such a good person. He moved us all greatly. Then, finally, Lisa, always orchestrating us all so well, spoke the closing farewell. I was the last to leave you and told you, "I love you dear. God keep you close, sleep well."

I know you loved your funeral Mass as you watched us from above. Your granddaughter Anna and her violin! She was her magnificent self as she began the whole procession in toward the altar. I couldn't help but remember that day at the hospital when she came to play for you. You remember how all the patients, nurses, visitors, and even the duty doctors emerged like animals from their holes, and listened to her impromptu concert? Déjà vu? No, it was a real joy once again. The boys with their saxophones played their melancholy "Dust, Ashes…," and Colette…her "Ave Maria"! How she managed to sing so beautifully, I'll never understand. As she rushed back to her seat, her emotions must have demanded release. She sang for you, dear. Julie recited the closing eulogy to you. It was so right on. She, with help from all your children, captured your essence in poetic words. I still don't understand how she controlled her emotions so well. It tells of her love for you; she spoke for us all.

The gravesite service was nearly impossible for me. Father Brian prayed over you, as we all did, and as they finally lowered your white casket into the ground, Jonathan played mournfully on his trombone. I cast some earth upon you, my dearest, and my heart went with it, where I fear it remains. The children did the same.

My real nightmare has now begun. These past two weeks have been a flurry of activity. I've cleaned the condo, been to the bank, grocery shopped, visited Julie, spent Thanksgiving at Lisa's, been to Sunday Mass with Mark, paid the bills, done my e-mail—the many mundane distractions. Suddenly it all collapsed on me. I'm not the strong fellow I thought I was—what people wanted of me. Turns out, I'm a weakling. Yesterday I started crying somewhere around noon. It wasn't anything specific. Things just crashed in on me. "Trish is gone. I am nothing without her. What good can life ever be without her? How can I look everywhere and not find her?" Nothing appeals. This pain is worse than any hell could ever be. God has taken from me what He gave—my most precious beloved, Trish, Trish. I love you so, my dearest. Hear me! This terrible pain, this terrible, terrible pain, not even our children can know it. I accept it and offer it as my personal holocaust of thanks to Him for giving me you these fifty years. I'm crying too much. Trish! I miss you so! Will sleep ever return? No more pills. They don't work that well anyway. The booze is temporary but can have its own vengeance. There is no escape. I know I must do only what is right in front of me, and do it as best as I can…as you always did. I know, I know, you would remind me like Scarlet: "Tomorrow is another day." I will write more then perhaps. It helps me.

It's one month today, December 18th. This haunting pall continues unabated. The war between my emotions and my intellect has now been joined by physical pain. (I fell in the bathroom at Lisa's at 3:00 a.m. two nights ago and I must have cracked a couple of ribs.) It's another barrier on my road to sleep. I continue this stupid crying. My emotions seem to win every skirmish. Christmas. The cards addressed to the both of us are the hardest ones. "Merry Christmas to you both…and blessings for the New Year!" Oh yes. *Be Merry. Be Happy.* If only I could fast-forward these next months. I have to answer those cards and tell them Trish is dead.

I finished reading C. S. Lewis' book *A Grief Observed* some days ago. In some ways, it was helpful to read such accurate prose…he is a writer. Someone else has traveled through these dark, shadowed, and lonely valleys, too! Indeed, others travel them even now. Misery's company…it's not a love that satisfies.

Trish! Where are you? Are you really happy? How can that be? I am not there!

Another of God's mysteries. Will I ever understand His ways? I think I will cry now…and then go to Lisa's again for dinner. Why do I write this? Stupid!

* * *

As I write this now, many years later, and reflect on this chapter of my life, I recall more vividly than ever how much God has blessed me over my entire life. I recognize too, more than ever, that this woman Trish, who graced me with nearly fifty years of her life as my wife, has been the channel of so much of that blessing for me. More than anyone else, she taught me to love. I've come to believe, when I consider the pain of her loss, that if hell exists, it consists in the pain of knowing that one has lost the love, and the possibility to love, the most loveable and loving God. The loss of my beloved companion of nearly fifty years had an unimaginable impact on my faith. It continues to do so.

No words of mine can fully express the extent of the wonderful legacy to me and to all whom Trish touched in life, except to say: It is her love. I can say nothing more than that and,

Trish, I love you so…still.

Trish Merry Christmas Family 2003

Chapter 10

A New Beginning

*"And to make an end is to make a beginning. The end is where
we start from"*
—T. S. ELIOT

I had walked through the valley, through the dark, terrible shadows of her death, but the sun is now shining once again; my life has begun anew. My grief over the death of my wife of nearly fifty years was beyond anything I had ever experienced or could ever have imagined. Many times in the past, I had been to the wakes of friends or relatives and offered my condolences, thinking that I understood their grief. I had no clue. No one who has not lost a spouse, or perhaps a child, can comprehend the terrible pain involved. In the two months immediately following Trish's death, I lived with my eldest daughter nearby. Despite her loving care and sensitive kindness, I suffered from a total insomnia born of an unyielding sadness and a saturating grief. Over a period of two months, I doubt that I had slept more than a total of two or three hours. This insomnia began to take a serious toll on my health. I began to need a cane to assist my walking and arthritic pain seemed to assail every part of my body. Finally, recognizing that my grief was mine to alone to manage, I resolved to relieve my daughter of the certain burden I'd become and return to my own home. I must somehow get on with my life. Grief became an enemy to be engaged. I remember it well.

It was a Sunday evening when I walked back into our condo after this protracted period of absence. As soon as I walked in, I knew it was going to be traumatic. Trish was everywhere I looked, but nowhere. I began to cry uncontrollably. After about two hours of continuous weeping, a different emotional wave arose in me. I found an anger welling up and I looked up to the ceiling and cried out, "Trish! How can you be so happy without me when I'm left here so damn miserable?" I received a sudden and unexpected answer. I heard her distinctly say to me in a firm and demanding manner, "Go to bed; go to bed." I did. I mounted the stairs to our bedroom, crawled into bed, and lay back. I again heard her speak to me, "Now listen…listen…listen," she said. (It would be like her to say that. Earlier in our life together, she had often admonished me, "You hear, but you don't listen.") Then she said a most unlikely thing, "Go back to PFLAG. It's more important than I thought." It more than caught my attention.

Years earlier, Trish had been president of PFLAG Detroit for more than three years. It was tantamount to a full-time position into which she poured her heart and energies. Finally, she wore herself out and resigned her position. She said to me at the time, "It's enough. I'm burned out. Besides, the issue is dying out. People are becoming more aware and accepting." She resigned her position as president and we quit attending PFLAG meetings, becoming mostly inactive. Thus, for Trish to say to me from beyond, "Go back to PFLAG. It's more important than I thought," would have been most unlikely. It's certainly not something I would have dreamed up, even out of my subconscious, as I had been in total, enthusiastic agreement about our withdrawal from that activism. Her startling words had a big impact on me. I could imagine her becoming newly aware of realities unseen by those of us on this side of the veil.

The impact of her words was almost frightening to me. I had thought a lot about what PFLAG accomplished to right a topsy-turvy world; the good that it created to offset the injustices against those God created gay. I had heard so many depressing stories of family anguish, and witnessed the healing of injured souls as we ministered to each other at our monthly meetings. I wondered if Trish was saying in effect that we had made a mistake withdrawing our active commitment to this endeavor. I quickly knew I would obey Trish's command, and resolved to attend the next regular meeting of PFLAG Detroit. It had been several years since I had been there.

The next morning I awoke from twelve hours of continuous sleep, a first in several months, which in itself seemed an unlikely and transcendent experience. I felt better and enjoyed a strange feeling of newness and wonderment. What was I going to do next? It all seemed a bit bewildering, but the anticipation was a refreshing change. I showered and dressed rather quickly, as if I were late for some appointment. I came downstairs to have a little breakfast, but suddenly, I felt an urge to pray. I walked to the door wall in the breakfast room and looked up at the bright morning sky and began to meditate. I found myself pleading to be led. "What is left for me in life? What do you want of me? What am I to do? Please let me know." Then, after a few moments of gazing upward in this prayer, feeling completely vulnerable and resigned to whatever the future held, I suddenly felt a strange inspirational wave come over me, and I was moved toward a prayer of earnest commitment. My emotions urging me on, I cried out loud to the Holy Spirit, "OK. From now on I will go anywhere, do anything that God has in mind for me. I will even go to a monastery for the rest of my life, if that is His plan." (I think I heard a little heavenly laughter at this point.) "I only ask that it be made plain to me, in order that I know what I am supposed to do." I said it without any caveats or equivocation—absolutely no mental reservations. It was one of the most sincere and resolute prayers of my life. It was the first time I was ever able to make such an unequivocal resolve, though I had previously tried some rather meager attempts at such a commitment.

I believe it was a beginning of a special relationship with the Holy Spirit for me. Since then, I have often thought back about that time, and in moments of doubt or reticence, when hesitating to do what is directly before me, the thought pops up: "You said you would do anything, go anywhere," and immediately, I remember, and I do whatever it is that I am momentarily reluctant to do. It seems always to turn out well. It frequently leads me on some new path that at first appeared unattractive, but then I find out that the result was really quite nice. I think too, that often I had missed that in the past, as probably most of us do.

I walked into Lutheran Church of the Master on the second Sunday of the month for the regular PFLAG meeting. It was a little before two o'clock, the normal starting time. I was quickly engulfed by many warm greetings from close friends whom I hadn't seen since Trish's funeral and from others I hadn't seen in years. There were many new faces, and I was immediately glad I had come. After the initial rush subsided a bit, a special friend approached me. It was Linda Karle, an attractive women some ten years my junior and a widow of some fifteen years. We were acquainted with one another, but she had been more of a special friend to Trish than to me. Linda had traveled with Trish and me during out-of-state meetings associated with PFLAG, and the two of them seemed to bond in their common maternal dedication to the gay community. In fact, later, during Trish's final illness, Linda was the last of two people outside of family to visit with her shortly before she died. The other was Mary Black, also a close PFLAG friend. Linda was an exceptionally kind and sensitive woman. It was she who had sent me a copy of C. S. Lewis's *A Grief Observed* soon after Trish's death. The book had served me well. I had found it comforting to read of another man's terrible loss in which he so eloquently relates his grief in a journey that seemed so much to mirror my own.

Three hours after I had arrived, the PFLAG meeting ended and Linda approached me and said, "A group of us are going to Dignity Mass at Marygrove. Would you like to join us?" Of course, I accepted. The prospect of being with friends a little longer was far more attractive than another lonely evening at home. Dignity Detroit is a group of Catholic LGBT persons who gather to celebrate Mass every Sunday at Marygrove College. Previously, a few years back, Dignity met every Sunday in downtown Detroit at Holy Trinity Catholic Church. As the conservative trend in the Church metastasized, Cardinal Adam Maida decided that Dignity was unwelcome in the archdiocese. It was a continuation of a pattern of antigay actions by the cardinal that stretched over several years. Employing then-Bishop John C. Nienstedt as his eager hatchet man, Dignity Detroit was told they were essentially persona non grata at Holy Trinity or in any local parish in the archdiocese. It was then that the IHM nuns, who ran Marygrove College and who were not under the control of Cardinal Maida, invited Dignity Detroit to come to Marygrove for their weekly Mass celebration. (This is one more example of how women—even celibate women—seem innately more attuned to love and compassion than men are.) The Holy Trinity edict was the final insult to my son Mark's sense of Christian justice, and he finally left the Church. He wrote me a long letter explaining his decision. He has not been back since. His was only a bit part in a mass exodus of young people from the Catholic Church because of such antiquated bigotry. It continues to this day.

Following Mass at Marygrove that evening, Linda and I decided to go out for dinner together. I don't remember who asked whom. I always recall that Linda invited me, but she remembers it differently. She definitely recalls that I invited her. I've decided that I'd like to take credit for that, but that it was more likely a rather mutual invitation. It didn't matter. It was to prove a bright and major turning point in both of our lives. In the ensuing months, we saw each other with increasing frequency and intensity. When I first recognized the reality of a developing relationship between us, I pondered the sudden and unlikely occurrence. Following Trish's death, I had felt certain that I would never again seek a relationship with a woman. That phase of my life was past. Yet I knew that Linda and I had some unique things in common. We both had gay sons, and we both had survived the trauma of the death of a spouse. I remembered, too, that I had been lovingly counseled by a particular friend whom I respected greatly, a former colleague from Ford who had also lost his wife to cancer. He said to me at Trish's wake, "Remember in the months ahead, Tom, your life is not over; you will have to get on with it. God has plans for you yet." Now, so soon after Trish's death, this was happening.

Was this what Trish really had in mind when she directed me to "Go back to PFLAG"? I smiled at the thought. I only knew that my life was rapidly changing—away from grief toward a new and unknown future. Could happiness lie somewhere ahead for me? It would be like Trish to lead me toward that.

Some time before, immediately following Trish's death, I had begun attending individual grief counseling offered by Angela Hospice. It was at the same hospice that had attended to Trish and my family during Trish's decline. Grief counseling to those who have suffered the loss of a loved one was also a part of their mission. They are the most compassionate, loving people, and highly skilled at what they do. It was about a month after Trish's death and I had been attending counseling at their center in Livonia, Michigan, near my home, once a week. Some time later, after I was finished with my counseling session and was walking out to the parking lot to my car, I started experiencing an urgent and compelling thought, "Call Mark, call Mark." The thought was so vivid that as soon as I got to my car, I called my son at his work place on my cell phone. When he answered, he said immediately, "Dad! Why did you call?" I replied, "I just got this sudden urge to call you. Are you OK?"

"Bizarre," he said. "I was thinking about Mom and I got feeling so bad, I thought I'd leave the office and go find a place somewhere and just sit down and cry. When I got up to leave, the phone rang and it was you. It's amazing." After a short period of trying to comfort him, we both wondered over the amazing coincidence. We concluded that it was Trish, just looking out for her family.

Trish seemed to revel in her newfound powers and there were other incidents when she manifested her continuing love and concern for me. Call them coincidences if you're a skeptic, but I recognize her Irish humor when I see it. One of those incidents occurred some weeks into the New Year following her death. I had been out shopping to purchase a piano for my condo. I wanted to try to change the ambience of my home so that it would be at least a little different from all the constant reminders of Trish. Then, in addition, I wanted a piano so that I could enjoy playing for myself as another distraction from grief. It was a prior enjoment that I had deferred for a long time. I had played the piano for many years before, but when Trish and I had moved into our small condo, we had chosen not to accommodate a piano. As I perused the piano store, I knew that I wanted a small upright, and I soon found two instruments that matched my requirements. I went back and forth between the two, playing briefly on each of them, but I couldn't decide. Finally, sensing my dilemma, the salesman who had been following me, asked, "Have you decided?" I said "No, I just can't make up my mind." Without saying a word, the salesman walked to one of the models, a lovely Kohler & Campbell upright. It was small and had a shiny black finish similar to the other model I was considering. Then it happened.

He sat down at this piano and immediately began to play, in an exceptionally skilled fashion, Beethoven's *Pathetique*. I was astonished. It was Trish's absolute most favorite piece of music. I listened as the salesman finished, tears running down my cheek. When he rose to move to the other piano, I said, "Don't bother. I'll take that one," pointing to the Kohler & Campbell unit he had just played. Then I asked, "Why did you select *Pathetique* to play?" He answered, "I don't know, it just came to me." I smiled as I thought: "Trish you're there, still helping me, even to the point of redecorating our condo!" I still weep every time I hear Beethoven's *Pathetique*. It just seems to capture the essence of Trish.

I continued with my weekly grief counseling and also frequent dinners with Linda. One day, at one of my sessions, I happened to mention to my counselor that I was dating Linda. She immediately said, "Oh Mr. Nelson, it's too early for that." That rather puzzled me, for she had been encouraging me to attend a weekly social gathering of widows and widowers sponsored by hospice. I said I would think about it. Think about it I did.

Linda had been attending the University of Detroit in pursuit of an advanced degree in religious studies. As part of her curriculum, she was required to write a spiritual autobiography. When she told me about it, I persuaded her to let me read her writing task. After reading it, I knew immediately, how I would get my counselor to learn more about my friend Linda. At the next session, I brought a copy, handed it to my counselor, and said, "This is what Linda wrote recently. I thought it would give you an idea of who she is."

I include it here because it illustrates well my continuing blessings, and because it is an eloquent tale, however brief of another's spiritual journey, one that, in important ways has mirrored my own. Linda had written:

Interim Spiritual Autobiography
Am I There Yet?

Since I have lived what for some could be considered a whole lifetime already, it is interesting that I am still wondering where the finish line is in terms of my spiritual journey. For most of my life I have lived as a contented, faithful Catholic. I have always been attracted to prayer and to service in some way. I never considered myself merely a "Sunday Catholic" who left religion at the church door on the weekends. I have looked for the way that would lead me closer to God, at some times with more attention than at other times. That having been said, I find myself in recent years to have encountered questions and struggles that I would not have imagined in earlier years. These struggles derive from circumstances and events in my life that have left me questioning my earlier easy acceptance of my faith and my Church.

I was the wartime child of Catholic parents who themselves grew up during the Depression and had been high school sweethearts. They bore two baby girls, Linda and Denise, during their first years of marriage in the early forties. Their lives were interrupted when my father was sent to the Pacific as a navy seaman. When he returned, a third child, Nancy, was born. The next few years were lean ones for our family and we lived with a series of relatives for a while. This never seemed strange or out of the ordinary to me. It was just the way our family lived. It was during these years that I became aware that my mother was the backbone of our family and my father, for whatever reason (some in the family suggested it was his reaction to his war experience), pulled into the background, unable to play the traditional paternal role. This perception of my father's lack of involvement with our family led me to resent his emotional absence and lack of support for my mother. These feelings were later the cause of much guilt for me.

My early memories of religion in my life were rather uncomfortable ones, for I was not a willing first-grade student at St. Ambrose School. I was insecure and suspicious about the nuns, who appeared very severe and serious. Indeed, they terrified me. I have vivid memories of my mother chasing me around the dining room table prior to my enforced walk to school each day. I don't recall now what, if anything specific, prompted these feelings, but perhaps it is significant that I do not have happy memories of my first encounters with Church "authority." When my family moved to a rural area sometime during that year, I no longer had to face "the nuns" and for two years happily attended a two-room public school, where the teachers were not nuns and were much more approachable.

Once my family moved to what became our permanent family home, an apartment on the naval base on Grosse Ile, Michigan, I was once again sent to a Catholic school, but this time with much happier results. I loved not only the nuns who taught me, but also the priests who served the parish. I learned about "doing penance" for the pagan babies who lived, we were told, in far off places like Africa and China and needed our prayers and sacrifices so that they might be baptized as Christian babies. I loved the Bible history stories, going to Friday Mass with the rest of the students, May crowning, singing holy songs, learning about the saints, and wanting to be like them. I was in love with religion. I began to wonder about what I'd learned about God, not in a questioning way, but in a wondering, exploring way. "Eternity" and "infinity" were words whose meanings I tried to capture, but which remained deliciously intriguing and elusive.

My parents made great financial sacrifices to send their three daughters to Catholic grade school and high school. It meant that my mother worked long and arduous hours as a presser at a local dry cleaner to make enough money to pay the tuition bills. The significance of this was not lost on me... religion was important.

By the time I reached high school I was no longer a "cradle Catholic"; I was a confirmed adolescent Catholic with a firm allegiance to the Ten Commandments, the Spiritual and Corporal Works of Mercy, and the Rosary. I became a member of the Sodality, which meant that I increased my prayer life by a fifteen-minute period of "mental prayer" each day. This prayer was performed according to a prescribed formula. It was to be done in solitude, of course, and on one's knees. This presented problems in our small apartment since one could hardly avoid being interrupted at prayer time by someone wandering in and out of the bedroom which I shared with my two younger sisters. I was never gracious about these interruptions, and I'm sure must have appeared "holier than thou." I considered myself a "good Catholic girl" and was happy with that title. I was not rebellious nor did I question anything I had learned about God, my Church, or my religion. I was a good student and enjoyed my academic and my social successes.

These are very impressionable and sensitive years and I reacted as one might expect when the nuns suggested the possibility of entering the convent. I was flattered to think that I might be considered good enough to serve God in that way. I prayed a lot about it and even made a trip to the IHM Motherhouse in Monroe to observe firsthand the life of a sister. Ultimately, the romance of the nun's life lost its appeal when I pondered not being able to date boys anymore. Apparently, my "vocation" was short-lived.

But I had been indoctrinated by the IHM nuns. Only Marygrove would do for me. My parents made huge sacrifices so that I might be the first in my family to attend college! I had fewer opportunities to date when I entered Marygrove College, but I was so involved with my academic life that I hardly had time to think about my social life. I loved being in the college atmosphere. I loved the authors I was exposed to through my literature classes. I loved the challenge of thinking and arguing about my faith, learning that others thought and believed differently than I had been taught. This was new to me and very exciting. It did nothing to shake my faith in God or the religion into which I had been baptized. On the contrary, I read Thomas Merton and Dorothy Day and claimed them as my heroes. I wanted to emulate them. Social activism became very important to me. I thought of joining the Catholic Worker Movement, which, at that time, was very much alive in Detroit. I also thought about the Peace Corps, but not very seriously, I'm afraid, since it was in my senior year at Marygrove that I met my future husband.

Joe was a member of the Legion of Mary in his parish as was my Uncle Jim, who played Cupid and introduced me to Joe. I was almost immediately in love with this man who seemed to embody so many qualities that were important to me. He was a former seminarian whose spirituality and goodness made me wonder at my good fortune in knowing him. But it wasn't good fortune…it was certainly God's grace which led me to Joe. We were married eleven months after we met and thus began a journey of love and faith together, which lasted for twenty-seven years. Our marriage was blessed with three children.

Those years were filled with so many experiences of Church community. Joe and I were always involved in some way in our local church, first as members of the Legion of Mary, through which we made "house calls" on people in the parish who were identified in some way as removed from the parish; later as members of the Worship Commission as lectors, and, for me, as director of the Preschool Religious Education Program. These were things that we deemed important to our faith lives. We attended weekly Mass regularly and sometimes even made daily Mass in the early years before children. Three children in five years made us truly a family and we were blessed with an extended family which showered us with love and pride in us.

In those early years of our marriage we were faced with some unusual challenges for a young couple: the care of my paternal grandparents fell to us for a period of many months; Joe's sister and her three children moved in with us for a period of time; and my father often stayed with us during his treatment for throat cancer, which progressed to lung and bone cancer and eventually took his life.

We were able to handle those stresses on our lives, I believe, because of the faith that we both had and because of God's constant help. But I had a more difficult time dealing with my father's needs than one would expect from a daughter who professed such a strong faith. I mentioned earlier my resentment of and sometimes anger at my father for what I perceived as his lack of support for my mother in the raising of our family and later in caring for his aged mother, another job which fell to my mother as well. My mother's death at age forty-eight from a cerebral aneurysm was another opportunity for me to blame my father, however unreasonable that might have been. This presented a mental and emotional block for me in caring for him. I knew what I had to do and I did what was expected, but not with an open heart. I'm sure he must have felt my reluctance, but he never expressed any awareness of it. On the contrary, he was always so grateful and pleased to be with Joe and me and his grandchildren. When he died, it was a relief from watching the slow process of the cancer, but not from my guilt at my feelings for him.

Many years later, I had a related experience which I will describe now even though it is chronologically out of order. I was about thirty-three years old when my father died. Nearly two years ago (I was sixty-two) I was making an attempt at "centering prayer." I had read the readings of the day, which spoke about faith as the blessed hope (assurance) of what cannot be seen. I asked myself what I needed to have faith about. What am I afraid of that should be a matter of confidence and hope?

What follows are the words I wrote in my journal about that meditation:

The above was written about thirty minutes ago. Since then I was given an answer to that question. I was attempting the "centering prayer" using the word "Abba." I was feeling much unconnected to God and was just trying to persevere in the prayer time. It occurred to me that perhaps "Abba" was not a good mantra word for me because of how I felt about my dad.

That led to a strong feeling of guilt for that feeling about my dad (not an unusual feeling for me). Then something happened and I knew God was there letting me know I was OK. I felt God's presence, but no words can explain it. It was very emotional. I also knew that the answer to my question, "What do I need to have confidence and hope about?" was to believe that God is here with me even when I don't feel it *and* it's OK about Dad...no more need to be guilty.

There was a great sense of relief and peace. I include this episode here because it marked an important step in my grasp of the extent of God's mercy. I knew that God's mercy had allowed me finally to accept my dad's forgiveness.

Sometime in my late thirties, I found myself looking for "more" in my faith life. I was generally happy and content with my life, but I felt there was something missing in terms of my relationship with God. I was invited to attend a charismatic prayer group meeting at a nearby church. I was impressed with the sincerity of these people who were so open in their praise of God. They were unashamed of their enthusiasm, and my natural inhibition in overtly expressing myself in this way was challenged. I attended these meetings regularly, participating in the songs with upraised arms and swaying body, never feeling quite at home, but longing so for the closer presence of God in my life. I persevered through the "baptism in the Spirit" during which event many were "slain in the Spirit," but this did not happen to me. I longed for that experience for myself, but felt it was not given to me for some reason, perhaps that I was not free enough or that I didn't believe as deeply as the others did. I continued to attend these prayer sessions for some time before I decided it just wasn't comfortable for me, so I took my leave of the group. I think it is important to understand that I was not unhappy; I was just searching for a closer experience of God which I knew was out there for me, but where? I had some time to wait before God began to make some inroads with me.

The way that eventually opened for me was not one I would have expected or chosen.

The greatest upheaval in my life took place with the sudden loss of my husband at age fifty-four. I was forty-nine years old and not prepared at all for life without him. But death doesn't ask permission and I did somehow survive the shock and pain. This event and its aftermath are important in my spiritual journey because it was after Joe's death that I began keeping a journal. In retrospect I *know* that I got through that period of mourning only because God was holding me up. That was when I became consciously aware that God uses people to do God's work here. Friends and family were God's lifeline for me. My comfort came directly through the many people named in my journal. It is overwhelming to look back at the loving things people said and did that held me up and carried me through this dark time, as well as totally affirming that God touches us in the people and events of our lives.

At first, and for a number of years, I addressed the journal entries directly to Joe, speaking to him as in a letter about the various stages of grief I was experiencing. This was a great comfort at the time and a valuable record of my journey through that difficult period. It was a time when I had powerful experiences of Joe's presence over a prolonged period of time... God's way of easing me into being without him.

After a few years the dates of the journal entries grew further apart and life took on a new look for me, one that could encompass more than my loss. I turned to my church community for help with "the next step" in my pursuit of a closer relationship with God. In view of my unsatisfactory experience with the charismatic prayer group years earlier, it is surprising to me now that I began attending the charismatic prayer group at my own parish. Somehow, I was able to react much more positively than before. There were "teachings" each week given by members of the prayer team and I often found them to be inspiring and motivating. One thing I was motivated to do was to set aside a regular prayer time in the morning before going to work. This was not an easy task for one who dislikes the early morning hours, but it seemed to be the right time for me to be looking for God's presence in this way.

It was at this time that I began reading Thomas Keating's [8] books on "centering prayer." I did not expect to experience what happened to me when I began this prayer time. I was hoping for spiritual consolation, a closer relationship with Jesus. What I got initially was a clear picture of my faults and weaknesses! My journal entries of the time indicate that I was, in prayer, discovering who I was, and I wasn't pleased. One such entry, notes from a prayer group meeting reads as follows: "God wants to show us who we *are*, then replace that self with who God calls us to be. When we trust enough, surrender enough, to let God break down our barriers to Him, we become humble and open to God's movement to change us into what we are called to be." This is difficult and certainly remains an ongoing task, but I am now more able to look at my weaknesses and realize that I needn't throw up my hands in despair; that this is a process, not an overnight experience.

Centering prayer is likewise not something I have achieved successfully on a consistent basis. It is an up and down experience for me, one day receiving a warm sense of the presence of God and the next day thinking more about what I have to do that day than repeating a mantra word. But the good days bring me back for more attempts to find that silence in which God can finally reach me and touch me.

We find God in prayer which is true. But I had learned that events and people in our lives are another means of experiencing God. Sometimes these events and people cause questions which are disturbing and make us think hard about what we have always believed. I had a life-changing experience when my son John told me he was gay. I couldn't believe that this was possible in our family. We were the "Ozzie and Harriet generation." I had no tools with which to deal with this news and no one to share it with. So I became a "seeker," as did Judith Bruder in *Convergence* [9]. She speaks of a "hunger, and thirst,

---

8   Father Thomas Keating (born 1923) is a Trappist monk (Order of Cistercians of the Strict Observance).

9   *Convergence, A Reconciliation of Judaism and Christianity in the Life of One Woman,* Judith Bruder, Doubleday 1993

and emptiness, but it began as restlessness." I felt that same restlessness, but it was the awareness, however faint it was at the time, that I was on the brink of something new... not necessarily a welcome thing, but something which I was compelled to learn about because it involved my dear John, who was flesh of my flesh and heart of my heart.

The conflict here began as an "all about me" reaction. What would people think about our family? What about the grandchildren I hoped for from John? What had we done to make John gay? Thankfully, through a long process of reading and learning facts and finding friends who had gone through the same agonies as I had, I finally realized that my John is a precious gift to me. However, my Church was not as enlightened as I had become. The Catholic Church proclaimed that John was "intrinsically disordered" and that acting upon his sexuality was a "serious depravity." This was not confirmed by my experience of John or of so many other gay persons whom I've come to know and respect. In my eyes the Church was mistaken, just as she had been about usury, slavery, and Galileo. This prompted me to look for ways to change the thinking of the Church in this regard. What an ambitious and unrealistic thought! But a little crack in the armor of the Church was found and that was the willingness of some Church people to listen to stories. These stories are the experiences of gays and lesbians and their parents as they explain how they have remained in the Church despite the unwelcome atmosphere in most parishes for gays and lesbians. Their stories tell how they have reconciled their sexuality and their spirituality. They are the foundation of a new generation of thinking about homosexuality in the Church. This change is a long way off, but the stories give me hope.

For me this conflict aroused other questions. I began to question not only this teaching, but also others which I had always taken for granted. These teachings were not necessarily connected to homosexuality in any way, but I began to look more critically at some of the Church's traditional beliefs. For example, when my son-in-law asked me a few years ago if I really believed Jesus was God, I was amazed. I had never thought about the possibility that Jesus Christ was *not* the Second Person of the Trinity, God incarnate, sent by the Father to save us from sin. But here was this very intelligent young man wondering how I could believe that. So I began to wonder myself. Looking for answers, I read Elizabeth Johnson's *Consider Jesus* [10], which looks at the Jesus of tradition as well as at a more contemporary evolving Christology. I read Rahner's *On the Theology of the Incarnation.* [11] I discovered the Jesus Seminar people and read a book by Michael Morwood addressing that very issue. After reading it, I realized that there was a radically different view of Jesus and his life presented there, and it was certainly not the traditional teaching of the Church. This was not a faith crisis for me, but my continuing questions about the nature and mission of Jesus prod me to learn more about these views of Jesus and how they affect other aspects of my faith. It is becoming a more usual experience for me to wonder about the soundness of Church teaching in some areas.

These questions, particularly regarding differing views of homosexuality, have created in some ways a distance between me and the people in my local church community. There is a sense of "otherness" that I am feeling not only during liturgies but also in meetings and at other parish events. It stems from the belief that most other people in my parish believe what the Church says about John and others like him. I am finding it increasingly difficult to be a part of a community which holds my son to be not only different, but also disordered. There are days when I feel totally alienated and am sure I should leave and join a more open and welcoming community. There are other days when I realize that the Church is a very diverse place and that the people here are so good in so many other ways. Perhaps the best thing is to stay here and try to change some of their thinking. I am not sure yet where this conflict will lead

---

10 *Consider Jesus: Waves of Renewal in Christology*, Elizabeth A. Johnson, Crossroad, 1990

11 *Theological Investigations, Vol. IV*, Karl Rahner, translated by Kevin Smyth, Baltimore: Helicon Press, 1966, pp105-120

me, but I look forward to the journey. Though the way may be crooked for a while, God has never yet failed to bring me to Himself through my life experiences.

So I return to the question posed as a title for this piece: "Am I there yet? Have I finally come to a place of contentment and peace in my spiritual journey?" And of course, the answer is "No." How could it be otherwise? As evidence that we are never "there" I offer a quote from an address given by Monsignor Clement Connolly, pastor of Holy Name Parish in South Pasadena, California. It is from an article I clipped from the *National Catholic Reporter* sometime in 2002 and which resides in my journal: "All spirituality is incarnational, which is to say that we pray and we reach out for an experience of God in the place in which we find ourselves and according to the condition in which we live. It is true that we see things as we are, not as they are. It is through the lens of our own experience that the voice of God is heard and the presence of God is seen."

So, just as my own experiences will continue to change, so will my experience of God continue to unfold in ways that are sometimes wonderful and sometimes terrifying. I am always a creation in process and the journey is often surprising.

This story would be incomplete if I did not mention a friend who has made a great difference in the most recent years of my life. This person has been a source of hope, of sound counsel, and of a most gratifying friendship which is very much a part of my current spiritual journey. This sensitive person has consistently recommended readings which respond to my ever-increasing need to "know" about matters of faith. Intense conversations about religion, politics, and culture have energized my mind and my heart. The suggestion for me to continue to learn on a more formal level at UD Mercy was something I may never have considered had my friend not said, "I think you could do it." The experience at this university has been enriching beyond my expectations. For all of these gifts I am most grateful.

* * *

After the long period of silence during her reading of Linda's spiritual autobiography, my counselor, when she had finished, looked up at me and said, slowly and very deliberately: "Mr. Nelson, you are a very lucky man." I replied, "Yes, I know I am." And I thought: My newfound love was not a product of loneliness over the loss of Trish, as much as it was Trish having a distinct hand in it. She was acting as my special counselor and guide from her new position and other-worldly competence.

This incident confirmed my growing awareness of how God was blessing me again in a very special way. My grief was fast receding because of it, and it came to me that real faith includes an unconditional trust. It is a trust that, when authentic, relies on complete surrender to a Divine love, a love that is always there. It is a surrender that entails a confidence that this love is always leading to your ultimate good, and is marked by the complete absence of fear. God had now given me a new life—and now it would seem a new wife.

It was in May of 2006 that Linda and I were married in a beautiful wedding ceremony celebrated at Marygrove College in Detroit. All of our two families attended along with a few of our friends. Children, grandchildren, and even great grandchildren were there. The music, the liturgy, the dancing, the food, the delightful conversation, the beautiful ambience of Marygrove College—all combined to make it a picturesque affair that I recall often and will always treasure. It was an experience that, with some minor guilt feelings, I recalled as far more fun than my first marriage celebration in 1955. This perception, I told myself, had nothing to do with lack of loyalty to, or affection for Trish. It was simply that at this late stage in life, marriage holds little or no fears for the unknown, as you know more about what to expect. Any mystery is more one of anticipation and less trepidation of the unknown. Such an attitude allows for much more enjoyment of the festivities and celebration, especially when your already matured family is surrounding you. My anticipation has certainly proven to be correct.

When I reflect upon the past five years of life as Linda's husband, I am overcome by the magnitude of the blessings that God has continued to shower on me; once again, a happy path has been opened to me. It is a path that clearly continues to lead inexorably to love. I am constantly amazed at the love that Linda shares, not only with me but also to all around her. Our relationship has been so absolutely devoid of any conflict, that it is a source of wonderment for us both. Truly, I am a very lucky man. I have concluded that the Almighty often blesses us in ways that are sometimes very dramatic, sometimes subtle or common, but either way, the path clearly leads toward loving. I am being constantly taught to love. Linda is my new teacher. Love unrelentingly is becoming the essence of my faith.

Chapter 11

The Harvest

"'You of little faith,' He said, 'why did you doubt?'"
—Matthew 14:31

The prospect of marrying again, and so soon after Trish's death, had confronted me with some suppressed guilt feelings—over ever marrying again. Was this a mark of infidelity to Trish's memory? Yet, I also felt sure it was where Trish had led me. I was convinced that I was very much in love with Linda, and that my feelings were focused on her, not on some personal relief from loneliness. She was an amazing person who, inexplicably, was evidently profoundly in love with me also. I considered myself a very lucky guy to find love again, and so soon. It was no surprise that my children were supportive of my decision to marry, as they always accepted me unconditionally. When Linda and I began dating, she had been widowed for more than fifteen years, so I knew that her long period of widowhood was different from mine. I knew she was dating someone at the time, but I'd hoped that it was not one to whom she was committed. When I found out, to my relief, that she was not attached to anyone and resolved to fill that void, I began to confront my guilt feelings. During our whirlwind courtship that culminated in the wedding at Marygrove more than two years after Trish's death, I thought about those guilt feelings considerably. I asked the Holy Spirit if this was really the right thing for me to do. The answer came quite clearly to me, as all doubts simply vanished, and I gave thanks for this new blessing. As I've already described, the wedding was a most happy event for both of us, and I chose the wedding toast that I gave at our dinner to acknowledge publicly the Holy Spirit's answer. It melded our mutual journeys of faith and publically declared our conviction that the ultimate goal of life is love. I noted the seeming novelty of both Linda and I loving two people at the same time, she her late husband, Joe, and me Trish. Was this not a conundrum of sorts? I lifted my glass to Linda, our family, and friends, and in a long-winded acknowledgement to our former spouses, and said:

Here's a wedding toast to Trish and Joe:

Fifty years. Trish. We were married almost fifty years. She was with me when I was better, and she was with me when I was worse. She brought to our marriage a special richness that never left me a poor man. We saw sickness and we saw health. Best of all she gave me six wonderful children. Ah, yes...our children. She taught them well. They in turn have shared their unique and priceless talents. It is her greatest legacy. And these children, here today, they teach me still, each in their own special ways. When death parted us, I grieved more than I could ever tell you. It was a life-destroying loss that cast me into the darkest pit and I was certain that happiness had departed my life forever along with her. But she was not finished giving. The loving God who gave us to each other those fifty years before, allowed her to come back to give to me one more time. "Listen," she commanded, and I did. Then she said: "Go back to PFLAG. It's more important than I thought." And

I did go back. The rest is now history. It's a new history—a new phase of my life—a new happiness which I share with you today. Not long ago, I attended the annual Karle family gathering to celebrate the life of Joe Karle, Linda's late husband. I was graciously allowed to participate in that event and I decided to write Joe a letter to tell him who I was and to tell him how much I had learned about him through his family. I wanted to thank him for his part in bringing Linda and I together. I ended it with a thought which I would like to share with you now:

"Joe, soon now, Linda and I will marry. Not long ago, that would have seemed very strange to me. My beloved Trish was taken from me and the thought of loving anyone again seemed impossible, let alone desirable—a most unlikely event. No one who has not experienced it, I think, can ever understand how a person can love so deeply, two people at the same time. Yet, that's what has happened to me. I have learned from it. I love Linda so very deeply, beyond any words I can find. It's easy, Joe. You can understand that—more than anyone else can. You are the only other person who knows how lovable she is. Still, I too have a special place in my heart for my beloved Trish. I love her too. I always will. It would seem to be a dichotomy, this loving two people at the same time. But I think it's a revelation. It occurs to me that God loves all of us, all at the same time, much as Linda and I experience. Apparently, God has no dichotomies or constraints in loving."

So please join me: Here's to Trish and Joe. We love you both!

That happy time was a prelude to many more to come. It was also a preface to a new activism for both Linda and me as we continued our dedication to the gay community. Soon we were elected co-presidents of PFLAG Detroit. We participated in all the activities—the marches, the meetings, the lobbying of our state government, and letter writing. It was a busy time and a happy one. It continues to be.

Tom and Linda 2011

Once, when we were lobbying our state representatives to pass an anti-bullying bill for state schools, which was opposed by the Republicans because it specifically included LGBT people, we approached the office of a Republican legislator. We were told that the lawmaker was very busy and at most, he could give us only five minutes to speak with him. We waited for more than forty-five minutes and were finally ushered into the inner chamber for our five minutes of face-to-face. Nearly an hour later, after hearing our stories, the representative said to us, "You two are very powerful lobbyists." Later on that day, when the final vote came up, that Republican legislator was the only one of his party to vote in favor of the bill. He later sent me an e-mail thanking us for enlightening him and saying that our actions represented the best of our democratic form of government. "Government is best when the people participate," he wrote.

Another action we developed a passion for was AOC. AOC is an acronym for Always Our Children, which is taken from a letter by that name that the U.S. Catholic Bishops issued in September 1997. The preface to that letter says:

> The purpose of this pastoral message is to reach out to parents trying to cope with the discovery of homosexuality in their adolescent or adult child. It urges families to draw upon the reservoirs of faith, hope, and love as they face uncharted futures. It asks them to recognize that the Church offers enormous spiritual resources to strengthen and support them at this moment in their family's life and in the days to come. [12]

AOC initially began as a program called Putting a Human Face on Homosexuality, PAHFOH. It was conceived and organized through the joint efforts of Linda and Mary Black. They later renamed it after the bishop's letter because of the Catholic focus of the program. Another reason for the name change was that the word *homosexuality* was felt to frighten people away. The program

---

12 The letter *Always Our Children* was initially issued in September 1997 by the USCCB, and then modified via a follow-up letter from the bishops in June 1998 to mollify conservative critics. Nevertheless, it remained a pastoral document.

is a panel presentation by four people—a father and a mother of gay children, a gay man, and a lesbian woman. The presentation consists of the panel members simply telling their stories of reconciling conflicts between a God-given sexuality and their spiritual convictions from their own unique perspectives. The presentation is typically made at a Catholic parish, and is followed by a question and answer period. The program has been very successful and has been copied around the country. It never fails to evoke quite a bit of emotion, as the storytellers have some very moving tales, which often relate to the experiences of many in the audience. We have learned to provide an ample supply of free facial tissues for the audience.

The stories of gay people and their families are the cusp of the effort to educate the homophobic. It is impossible for one to hear the stories of real people describing the pain, anguish, hate, bigotry, and often-physical violence endured by these families and not be seriously moved. Often it involves parent against child, and conflict with strongly held religious beliefs. Too often, the tragedy of suicide is part of the story. It seems every imaginable trauma is part of the reality of being gay in our current culture. I remember one story, which I will never forget, that I heard one Sunday at our PFLAG meeting.

This young man had come to our meeting. It was his first visit. The moment I first saw him, his demeanor alerted me. I knew instantly this was a young man in trouble. I had never seen a person look so obviously sad. He walked slowly with more of a shuffle than deliberate steps. His head was bowed down as if in deep thought. As I walked toward him to greet him, he looked up slightly and I saw a confirming look of terrible sadness on his face. As I introduced myself and stretched out my hand toward him, he grasped it and mumbled his name, apologetically. I put my other arm around him and embraced him as I said, "Welcome to PFLAG Detroit. It was good of you to come." I then led him into the gathering, introduced him to some others, and then moved off to greet other new people.

Part of our PFLAG meeting consists in breaking out into small groups of six or seven people, and spending an hour and a half exchanging our stories. Usually there are three or four groups. As chance dictated, the sad man ended up in my group. His story was unforgettable. He was a young man of about twenty-five when he came to us. He told us that he had recently decided to come out to his parents. He had called his mother on the phone rather than confront her face–to-face. It had been something he had been dreading, since his parents were strict Catholics and he knew his disclosure would be hard for them. When his mother answered the phone, he simply said "Mom, I have something I need to tell you. I'm gay," he blurted out. He said there was a prolonged silence. "What did you say?" His mother asked. He responded. "Mom, I'm a gay man. I'm a homosexual." He said there was a long pause. "Are you sure?" "Yes," came the reply. "I've known for a long time." There was another long pause. Then his mother said to him, "Well, I never want to see you again. Your things will be out on the front lawn when you get home. Find some other place to live."

Then the sad man said to us, "My mother then went into the next room and shot herself. My father now blames me for my mother's death, and I think he now wants to kill me." He went on to describe how his father has threatened his life. He began weeping uncontrollably.

I have heard too many such tales of terrible family trauma, suicide tragedies, violence, school bullying, job losses, housing discrimination, and parental rejection—most of it emanating from sincere, often fanatically religious people who somehow manage to put their misguided faith before family or parental love. It is an infantile faith that has never matured and it is nurtured by unwitting Church-sponsored idolatry of an anti-Jesus dogma devoid of love. While Catholics are in significant ways at the fore of this tragedy, some fundamentalist denominations unabashedly promote violence toward gay people. Indeed, some of them have supported legislation in African countries to establish the death penalty for homosexuality.

Yet God's persistent pursuit, even in the most tragic circumstances of our lives, leads ultimately to happiness. More and more with each passing day, I witness the joyous ways of the Holy Spirit. When I reflect back on the recent tragedy in my own journey, I see clearly the lessons I've been taught. I am glad that those months after Trish's death did not fast-forward as I had wished. Each of those days has turned out to be precious. I realized, too, that Linda and I are a new team. Together we have experienced the immense satisfaction in bringing new understanding and joy to many families. We are two activists with an enthusiastic passion for justice for our gay children. That activism had germinated somewhere in the past in both of us. Now it was blossoming into a growing harvest.

Chapter 12

The Spirit

"But the fruit of the Spirit is love, joy, peace, patience, kindness, goodness, faithfulness, gentleness, self-control; against such things there is no law"
—GALATIANS 5:22–23

It was an early Saturday morning in 1950, shortly after I had enlisted in the U.S. Naval Air Reserve. I was on a weekend period of duty at the Grosse Isle Naval Air Station, which is located on the mouth of the Detroit River, where it empties into Lake Erie. I was filled with excitement anticipating the day's duty as the flight engineer on a Navy PB4Y flying boat, a large twin-engine amphibious aircraft. A training exercise was scheduled for practice touch-and-go water landings. This involved a gentle landing in the river and immediately resuming full power to take off again to return and repeat the whole process. Flight assignment was a coveted duty that we all vied for, and it only came along every three months or so. It also included the added attraction of a flight-pay bonus. But this occasion was unique because water landings held special attraction. They were rare occurrences and it was an experience that added special thrills to the flying adventure. It was a duty no one turned down.

This particular weekend, at morning muster, our executive officer declared that a work crew was needed to prepare for a forthcoming admiral's inspection. Who would be willing to volunteer? Receiving the anticipated no-response, the officer promptly walked up to our formation and selectively pointing, stated, "OK, I'll take you, you, and you." The final "you" was me. I immediately protested, "But sir, I'm scheduled to fly this morning sir!" "Report to Chief Brown, mister," was his stern reply. He wasn't buying any change. I went up to him after muster and pleaded my cause again. I had even gotten a friend to volunteer to take my place on the work detail, and I was certain this officer would relent to my very plausible and convincing arguments, particularly now that I had a substitute. But I was wrong. My persistence was futile. No substitutes; I was his choice, period. It became clear that the man was stubbornly adamant and he was not going to change his mind. I had pursued it as far as I dared. I was assigned to the work crew and felt pretty down about being treated so unfairly.

Some hours, later while performing my assigned cleanup duties, all activity was abruptly interrupted by the startling blare of the airbase emergency sirens announcing some unknown tragedy. I soon discovered that the aircraft I had been assigned to fly on had crashed during a landing on the Detroit River. It was later determined that during water touchdown, one of the wing floats had struck a log floating in the river. This caused the wing to twist severely, rupturing the fuselage, and resulted in rapid submersion of the aircraft.

The sailor who had replaced me as the flight engineer was a close friend. He had been pinned in the small flight engineer's compartment located immediately under the main wing, unable to escape. He was one of two people killed in the incident. His body was later retrieved only after being cut from the wreckage. It was obvious that he never had a chance at survival.

I had clearly escaped from an obvious encounter with certain death. It made a deep impression on me. How could I have been so fortunate? Why was my friend chosen to die, and not me? Was it just fate? Why had our executive officer been so absolutely adamant? They are questions I still ponder. I remember going back to thank the officer who had been so insistent in assigning me to the work crew that day. He shook his head and simply said, "You were lucky, Nelson."

Lucky, maybe. Some would say that my Guardian Angel was on the job. However, if it was my Guardian Angel, I know the Spirit was guiding him, and the executive officer was an unwitting accomplice. I still don't know why my friend died and not me. For some reason, the Spirit had chosen me to live. There are those of us who would proclaim that such incidents are coincidences of fate. There was a time when I would have agreed with that assessment. Now I choose to believe and understand it differently. It's obvious the Holy Spirit was at work. While I still don't know the "why," I definitely recognize the "Who." Perhaps the "why" is that maybe I was considered a person who might be more viable for future enterprises of the Spirit. That's a hope. On the other hand, maybe I was simply the one who was judged as more in need of further improvement. That's probably closer to the reality.

The Holy Trinity, who can explain it? Perhaps some industrious theologians or some of the magisterial experts will confidently proclaim it as a revealed doctrine and try carefully to define it. Yet how does one explain what is essentially beyond understanding—the indefinable? "Three persons in one God" is what the catechism says: Father, Son, and Holy Spirit. My own understanding and acceptance of this concept is that the Holy Trinity doctrine is an admitted mystery; it is a paradigm of God's revelation of Being at a level that accommodates our limited human intellectual capacity. God is incomprehensible, but the doctrine of the Trinity enables us to understand God in a practical way that accommodates the limitations of our humanity.

I have had many confirming experiences of the Holy Trinity in my life. At least I have understood and interpreted them as confirming. The Father and the Son are perhaps more easily comprehended. I can recall many times in my life when I have recognized Jesus, the Son, being very much present and active on my behalf. Most often, it has been His encouragement, or rescuing me from some of my own failures. Certainly, like many, I pray to the Father—at least every time I recite the Lord's Prayer. But what about the Holy Spirit? Recalling my own confirmation as a child, I've concluded that like the disciples of Jesus at Pentecost, the lockable entryway to my soul was opened to the Holy Spirit at that time. Years later, I managed to replace that self-protected, keyed entryway with swinging doors. Still later, I decided to put out a welcome sign. I began to turn my attention toward the Holy Spirit. I began to listen. I encountered a plethora of new graces and they have ushered into my life increasingly wonderful results, and a new awareness. I have also experienced some amazing occurrences. The Spirit tends to be hidden, but sometimes its presence is glaring, and we are given an unexpected and mostly rare clarity.

Looking back, there were many incidents that reflect the Spirit's presence in my life. The Grosse Isle incident was one of the more dramatic ones. I might not have recognized them at the time, but they now seem quite clear. My experience has confirmed that life definitely has many teachable moments that stem from the Holy Spirit. Often we're in a life-teaching class and don't even realize it until the particular incident is long past. We look back and realize that sometimes we achieved honors; other times we flunked. Lately, I've been hoping that I might l be able to make it to graduate school. Whatever the future holds, I often find it educational simply to review old lessons.

There have been other experiences of the more dramatic. Sometimes I think the Spirit revels in drama.

Linda and I had traveled to Chicago for a spiritual retreat at Loyola University. The program entailed two courses in pastoral studies of our choice. It was the second time we had done this, as we had found it to be an inspirational and rewarding experience. At the outset of this particular summer session, I was suffering from a severe bout of osteoarthritis. It had been a progressive ailment that seemed to have settled in my right hand. I was convinced that I had inherited my mother's adverse DNA, as she had endured the affliction in both of her hands late in her life, and would often resort to large and frequent doses of aspirin in her search for relief. My own pain had become severe and it was unrelenting. I had already experienced some unwelcome encounters with this misery and it portended a most unpleasant future. It had started during the stress of Trish's illness, but it had largely disappeared in recent months. Now it was back with a vengeance in my hand, and I dreaded the prospect of a future filled with pain. This week in Chicago I was certain I was getting a preview, but I was in for a surprise.

At the beginning of each class, our professors required the students to stand and introduce ourselves, telling who we were and why we were there. In one of these, a class designed to further our search for greater spirituality through the study of Enneagrams, there were about eighteen adult students present. At the start of the first session, as we each introduced ourselves, one young woman, a nun from Texas [13] told us that she had been given the gift of healing touch. She said it was a strange gift that didn't seem to be associated with prayer or spiritual achievement. She said, "It's just a gift." I made an immediate mental note to speak to this woman at the class break. When the time came, I approached her, held out my afflicted right hand, and pleaded, "Help me. Heal my hand. I have terrible arthritis in it."

My decision to approach her was mostly a bit of a lark. I really had little expectation that anything special might happen, but if she truly possessed a gift of healing touch, I wanted it demonstrated on my afflicted hand. The young nun smiled and gently took my right hand in her left hand and then stroked it softly two or three times. She appeared to say no prayers, but appeared to be in deep thought. She murmured, "It doesn't always work." However, it did for me! Instantly the pain was gone. It was as if she had flipped a switch. I was absolutely amazed and told her all the pain was gone. I clenched my fist again and again; I couldn't believe it. I exclaimed, "It's gone! It's gone! The pain is gone! Amazing!" She smiled and said simply, "I'm glad for you."

During this time, several of the students were looking on and they were all very impressed, along with my wife, Linda. I later told the professor, who had not witnessed my healing experience and he immediately said, "Wow. I'll have to get her to heal my sore

---

13 I have forgotten her name.

neck. It's been a real pain for some time now." I spoke with him later and he said the nun had attempted to heal him also, but it didn't work for him. It has been several years since this bizarre blessing. The pain has never come back. My hands are still free of all arthritis, and I am again puzzling: Why me? Why this special grace received? I don't know. I am blessed. I count it as the fourth special extraordinary spiritual experience, and I am grateful.

Then it happened again, late one night in early November. We were at Paradise Bluff, our lake house overlooking Lake Michigan in the beautiful North Country of Michigan. The trees of the Manistee National Forest had finished their weeping at the death of the summer just past, their tears forming puddles in the sheltered nooks of the windswept bluff, and flooding the forest floor beyond with their colorful display; their anxious swishing in the wind off the lake was harmonized by the din of the water's drama below. It was fall, and when we retired in the evening, we had opened the window slightly that night to hear nature's sleep machine. It was one of the benefits of being so close to the water. Insomnia was rare with the constant symphonic song of the wind and the surf's rhythmic crescendos. This night was no exception. I had long since fallen into intense sleep. What happened later that night to awaken me from such deep and pleasant sleep was something that defies mere words. Like the Trinity, what words can define the indefinable? The experience is now sufficiently past that I am less uncomfortable recalling it. Religious encounters are often best left undisturbed in one's memory for a protracted time in order to permit the firm return of reality. Yet now, it's time. I think I understand it better.

If there are five senses, only one of the common ones was involved that night. It was visual, a brilliance that was everywhere, but there was no form, no figure, only the very intense light. I was once again experiencing a numinous brilliance with an intensity that would have hurt in any wakeful reality. In addition, instantly there was the other, beyond any of the normal senses. It was a new other world dimension—extreme and shocking—something well beyond the merely visual, beyond any of the senses. It was an overwhelming joy, an indescribable rapture, one that I had never before experienced or could have even imagined. Words do not exist that could adequately describe the utterly surreal ecstasy of joy I experienced that night. The closest I can come to describing it is a supernatural joy—a joy that completely enveloped my total being and awareness. The intensity was definitely paranormal—amazing—one that consumed every other sensibility. No human function could possibly create the sensation of joy that I experienced. It was beyond anyone's imagining. I now believe that such surrealism could have come only from the Divine.

"Joy is the most infallible sign of the presence of God"
—Teilhard de Chardin [14]

This event was brief, I think. Who can tell time in a dream? The intensity shattered my sleep, and at some point I abruptly sat up, fully awake, as Linda continued her slumber next to me. I was stunned. I knew immediately that it had been no ordinary dream, and I remember it still, as if it were only a moment ago. It has left an indelible impression that seems never to fade. It has definitely reinforced every aspect of my faith. Skeptics with scientific bent would say I probably had a rush of cranial serotonin for some obscure reason. If that were so, then my brain was drowning in it. Now I think I know what happened. It wasn't serotonin.

Ever since that inspired moment following Trish's death when I earnestly prayed a commitment of my remaining life into the hands of the Holy Spirit, I have not only experienced frequent incidents that I call cajoling reminders, but I have also had rather consistent gifts that sometimes seem to be more entertainment than anything else. Yet they have been a source of renewed faith and inspiration. They are always plain and obvious when they happen, but even more so in retrospect.

---

14   Pierre Teilhard de Chardin SJ, 1881–1955, was a controversial French philosopher and Jesuit priest who trained as a paleontologist and geologist. His ideas were condemned by the Church mainly for a stance that was deemed contrary to the doctrine of Original Sin.

The Spirit seems like an old friend now who is always there—my own private cheerleader and comforter; a coach, easy to recognize, sometimes teasing, but always fun to talk with. That night at Paradise Bluff was perhaps the most paranormal of all the Spirit's gifts. It was a humbling but inspiring thing. I have since interpreted that, for a brief moment, I was treated to a small taste of the sensitivities of the human soul, unencumbered by the human body. Recalling Saint Paul's declaration that, "Eye has not seen, ear has not heard, what God has ready for those who love him," I conclude I that I have been given the smallest glimpse of what he spoke. It was a special gift to me from the Holy Spirit, I have no doubt. It was the fifth and most recent extraordinary spiritual experience of my life.

The Spirit isn't always so dramatic. The very morning of the day I wrote this chapter, I received a little more mundane gift that lifted me up from a bit of a funk and left me smiling—once again giving thanks for the sometimes entertaining grace of God. It was the morning after celebrating with my brother, his wife, and family on the occasion of their sixtieth wedding anniversary. It was a natural inclination at that event to indulge in an extensive amount of nostalgia. Old memories, photos, and stories were the highlight of the evening. Thus, the next morning, I awoke and immediately, upon recalling the prior evening celebration, began again to drift into a nostalgic state. This quickly became a self-focused vision of my onrushing mortality. The reality of old age sent me into a pensive, somewhat depressing, and contemplative mood—a bit of a funk. It would soon be New Year's Eve, not a time for moping. I think the Spirit had a little more merriment in mind. Sitting down to breakfast in this somber mood, I began browsing through the morning *New York Times*. The first article upon which my eyes came to rest was on the Op-Ed page and an article entitled "*Real Life among the Old Old*" by Susan Jacoby. In an eerie fashion, it fit right in with my momentary melancholy. Jacoby concluded her uplifting article by stating that she will consider her life a success if at the end, she will be able to say like her grandmother, "It's good to know that the beauty of the world will go on without me." I nodded in agreement, and smiled when I recalled my oft-repeated resolution to grow old gracefully. Then, too, I was cheered when I read that at my age, I'm not yet officially one of the "old old." At this point, Linda walked into the room. I jumped up and gave her a hug. She was a bit startled and asked, "What's going on?" I replied, "Oh, nothing. The Holy Spirit is just nudging me again."

Some would argue that my relationship with the Holy Spirit amounts to nothing other than serendipitous coincidence. I would disagree. My engineering mind says that the statistical odds of such continuing coincidences and their timing being attributable to mere chance are virtually zero. I would also add that, finally, after eight decades of life, I have learned a bit how to *listen*.

Does listening extend to others in this world? Does it extend to our "Christian USA"? Are we really a Christian nation? I've thought about that and wondered if the Spirit has communication problems in our country. My perspective would suggest that there is a major problem. Surely it's plain to see that the current political environment is producing the usual inane distortions, lies, and half-truths. The lack of intellectual engagement and civility seems mutually endemic to both of our political parties. Most often, critical thinking seems a rarity. American politics has evolved into a kind of unending football game. It's "my team versus your team, win at any cost" mentality, and the country's welfare takes the hindmost. We cheer at our opponent's gaffs and ridicule any perceived weakness. Character assassination is applauded as legitimate. Gentleness, civility, and courtesy are seen as weakness. It seems we have descended into a despicably demeaning state more than at any time in our past. One would wonder how in the world we could expect any decent normal person ever to be attracted to high office in this land. It is a tribal mentality that portends sad consequences.

It is easy to hear impassioned discourse about how America is a Christian nation. To be sure, there are some who indignantly protest that proclamation, insisting that our Constitution protects us from any version of theocracy. It is baffling however, as to just what a "Christian" nation apparently looks like to those who rant such belief. I look at my country and its performance on the world stage in the recent past, and I see anything but Christian behavior. Christian? It would seem that most of us don't even know what the word really implies. I'm no theologian and I'm not a biblical scholar, but I've been around long enough to recognize a Christian when I see one. I've come to the conclusion that a real Christian is a pretty rare thing—nation or individual. It surely isn't somebody who just says he is one, or one who holds to certain dogmas. You can't use church attendance as a measure. A nation doesn't qualify because it simply proclaims that mantle. Many of us are pretty good at being pseudo-Christians—we're good at the masquerading. We go to church every Sunday, pay our dues, and maybe wave the flag a little. We feel pretty good about ourselves. Smug may be overstating it, but to me, calling oneself or one's nation "Christian" demands a much higher standard than we have set. It's a standard that seems beyond even our awareness.

Let's try an example. September 11, 2001. America is attacked. Thousands of innocent people die. The scene inspires revulsion at the perpetrators, and a huge tide of patriotic anger. "This will not stand." We are all in agreement that someone will pay. Retribution can neither come too quickly nor be too severe. Our enemies beware. We will destroy you! But wait a minute. Aren't we Christian? What's the Christian response? "Turn the other cheek!" Is that what our "Christian nation" did? Have we ever done it? Indeed, has any nation ever done it? When? What would it look like if we did?

Supposing we had actually tried something like that. Supposing we woke up on September 12, 2001, and heard our leader asking the world: "What have we done to offend you so? Why do you feel compelled to commit such a horrible atrocity against us? What can we do to allay the terrible hurt that you must feel we have inflicted on you, a hurt so grievous that you would justify such murderous recompense? Will you take our hand if we offer it? Can we talk rather than kill? Let us now sit down and work out our problems in peace."

What would have followed such an announcement? Impeachment? Assassination? Would our president have been interred in an asylum for the insane? Something like that, I suspect. No elected official was "turning the other cheek." Nobody was.

We "Christians" are seldom really Christian. We leave out the hard parts of the concept Jesus gave us. Occasionally an exception comes along, like Mother Theresa. Some of us are better than others, but most of us cannot really claim to be fully practicing Christians yet. We may be working at it, but we have a long way to go and it's a difficult path. Jesus warned it would be. I'm convinced that to be a Christian requires us to honestly see and admit where and what that path really is, and how far off from it we are traveling. We could start by treating our political contests with a kinder, gentler dialogue and less like the weekend football game. We could start by figuring out what it means to "turn the other cheek." We could start by learning to listen a little better. The Holy Spirit has much to say to us, but it requires someone on the receiving end. Can we listen?

A central question surrounding issues of faith in this regard is this: Can the Church listen? More specifically, can the hierarchy listen? Of course, I can't answer that, but I can observe that it would seem that many of our Church leaders sincerely seem to believe that the Holy Spirit stopped talking to us quite a few centuries ago, and if any new Spirit messages are sent, it's rare and they go only to the hierarchy. "We know it all" is the mantra at the top. "All revelation is past, and there is nothing new to learn. It is written in our tradition. If you have any questions, just ask us. We are the keepers of the absolute truth, and it is unchanging" If perchance we do submit a stumping question to them, the attitude is the equivalent of, "We'll check with God and get back to you." It is an arrogant attitude that effectively turns off any listening capability. Their hearing is muffled; in some areas, they are deaf.

This is nothing new. Human history is a continuing tale of repetitive error. It is the proverbial "two steps forward, one step back." Thankfully, we somehow seem to gradually progress. Many of the things that we lament today are not that much different from our frustrations of yesterday. Yet one can look back and see progress. In this country, slavery is gone. Segregation is dead or dying. Women are treated more equally. In the Church, the inquisition and the Crusades are history. There are many things we humans have accomplished. I remember author and teacher Diarmuid O'Murchu speaking at Loyola University, Chicago, saying, "Most of the time, we humans get it right." He was addressing aspects of the doctrine of Original Sin at the time. It was a good and encouraging thought. Somehow, the Spirit gets through to us despite our hearing impairment.

Perhaps our impairment could be helped by a better perspective than the most common notion of the Holy Spirit. Dr. Elizabeth Stuart, [15] in *Daring to Speak Love's Name*, gives us a different view. She writes:

> In the Celtic tradition of Christianity, the Holy Spirit is not represented as a white dove, tame and pure, but as a wild goose. Geese are not controllable, they make a lot of noise and have a habit of biting those who try and contain them. Gay and lesbian Christians (and their parents) know that God's Spirit is not a tame dove but a wild goose, free of ecclesiastical attempts to control and confine it, that makes its home in the most unlikely places. The Spirit comes not in quiet conformity but demanding to be heard. And its song is not sweet to many. This Spirit drives people together, demanding that they support and travel with each other. And it often forces those on whom it rests to become noisy, passionate, and courageous guardians of the gospel.

I love that description. It seems more in tune with the New Testament's depiction of the Spirit as tongues of flame. It also suggests to me that the Spirit creates activists. And yes, I have repeated it often because I have so consistently found it to be true—the Spirit leading where we do not want to go. Often I am nudged when confronting some annoying obligation that I would prefer to avoid, and that little unrelenting mental message comes: "You said you would go anywhere, do anything, no caveats." I immediately recognize the Holy Spirit, the Gentle Reminder.

---

15   Dr. Elizabeth Stuart, professor of Christian theology at the University of Winchester, Hampshire, England, and founding chair of the Centre for the Study of Christianity and Sexuality.

Sign of the Spirit

I have a card that I always carry with me that has on it a prayer to the Holy Spirit. I don't know the source, but it is my favorite. It reads:

Spirit of God
I know that I need to be
Prodded and challenged,
Awakened and consoled,
Inspired and chastened.
But most often, I need to be sustained.
In all the ongoing burdens
Of my responsibilities, in the use
Of every gift you give me,
In every thankful moment of my life,
I need your grace.
Be with me in ordinary times,
In every time.
Be with me forever. Amen

On the back of this card, it says:

We attribute the beginning of our lives to God as Creator. We associate the end of our life with Jesus who will return in glory and welcome us into God's kingdom. But the middle of our life is the domain of the Spirit. The Spirit is the ordinary breath of God which sustains us through all the ordinary moments.

Chapter 13

A New Brood?

"They tie up heavy burdens and put them on other people's shoulders, but they themselves are not willing to lift a finger to move them. Everything they do is done for people to see: They make their phylacteries wide and the tassels on their garments long; they love the place of honor at banquets and the most important seats in the synagogues; they love to be greeted with respect in the marketplaces and to be called 'Rabbi' by others"
—MATTHEW 23:4–7

What can be said about religious institutions that have cast aside the most fundamental teaching of Jesus? Love of God and love of neighbor are supplanted by man-devised rules that emphasize exclusion: exclusion of those who hear God differently; exclusion of those who don't conform to their doctrine; exclusion of many who simply don't fit the image that they have established and then claim that the image comes from God. They have created a golden calf by substituting their own views for those of Jesus, and then they claim themselves to be the sole source of Divine wisdom. God's speaks only to them. They claim it to be *revelation*, one that God reveals exclusively to them. Many of our mainline religious institutions have fallen into this pit of arrogance and the ordinary among us suffer the consequences. They are the new brood.

I focus on the Catholic Church because that has been the place where my journey of faith began and where it continues. Other denominations have similar failings, but the Catholic Church in many ways perhaps, fails more visibly. My own perception of this is that somewhere along the way, my Church has lost humility. Church leaders have constructed an exclusive men's club and set themselves above everyone else, proclaiming themselves our spiritual rulers, that they alone speak for God; that they alone hear God. Unmistakably, our Church leaders rule, not serve. Yet, Jesus clearly asked that they *serve*. Over the centuries, the overriding focus became secular power disguised as spiritual authority. The contest for power began very early in Church history. It was marked by constant maneuvering for higher ranking; at times, the pontiff was indisputably the most powerful person in the known world. There seems to have been zero recognition of Christ's admonition to serve. Humility has been and continues to be the antithesis of Roman behavior. The very title "Supreme Pontiff" accorded the pope suggests emperor-like status, a self-ennobling stance antithetical to humility. God speaks only through him. The pontiff speaks infallibly with Divine authority. How does this differ from the ancient Roman emperors who pompously proclaimed their divinity?

The hierarchy seems to have it backwards. When, on occasion in the past, I have attended the ordination of candidates to the priesthood, I witnessed how, at one point in the ceremony. the priests-to-be lie prostrate on the floor, and declare a solemn vow of obedience to the bishop. The bishops in turn vow obedience to the pope in similar fashion, the pope being supreme "end-of-the-line" in the structure. How does this correlate with Jesus admonition to serve? Who does the pope serve? Of course he would answer: Christ. I think that's baloney. Everyone serves the pope. It's why he's called "supreme." It seems to me that logically, what Jesus had in mind is the reverse. The pope should be serving the bishops, the bishops serving the lowly priests, and the priests serving the laity—which most of them already do. The hierarchy's focus on their "holy" state demonstrates only an arrogant vanity. They have appointed themselves as a special class above all others, the opposite of what Jesus advised. They only have the truth.

Opposing religious views and clergy from any other denomination are heretical at best in the official curial view. Indeed, many of our Catholic leaders would even today decry any form of ecumenism, and there is an ongoing, thinly disguised effort to maximize Church secular power and influence as well.

Catholic Church bishops consistently attempt to thrust Catholic doctrine on the nation under the pretense of "religious freedom." It's easy to see that the true objective is to "do it our way," and it has nothing to do with religious freedom. Our bishops believe that they are obliged to impose Catholic concepts of morality on all non-Catholics in our country in a Taliban-like plan of Roman doctrine for all. It is a poorly disguised effort for a theocracy.

It is not an exclusively Catholic idea. Other fanatical religious denominations have raised the Bible to idol status and teach literal interpretations with the presumption that God definitely stopped speaking to us some two thousand years ago, and that the world and human culture is unchanging. They, too, insist on the imposition of their brand of morality on the rest of us. All of these approaches suffer from the same malady: lack of humility. Even Saint Augustine admitted, "God is not what you imagine or what you think you understand. If you understand you have failed."

Certainly, God must still be revealing God. I know from my own experience that God speaks to all. I have heard God speaking through many people. On a recent Saturday, I listened to God speaking through a black woman minister who spoke a homily with exceptional eloquence and clarity. Only a deaf person could not have heard God speaking. Deafness to God's speaking can come from a lack of humility. Jesus called those so afflicted "vipers."

The host of heart-wrenching stories that I have heard over many years of listening to families of gay or lesbian children has painted a picture that condemns most religions for a glaring lack of compassion and love. A self-righteous dogmatic judgment is leveled on these outcasts. It is in direct opposition to the magnificent love of Jesus for all of us. It is an injustice that cries out for correction—a far cry from real Christianity, and it is particularly true of my own Catholic Church. Doctrinal intransigence inflicts heavy burdens and ignores approaches that are more compassionate. It also ignores the experience of the ordinary people. Rigid Vatican teaching on many issues seems an obvious contradiction to Christianity, especially in the area of human sexuality. While many Protestant denominations have adjusted their thinking more in tune with modern scientific discovery and comprehension of human sexuality, the Catholic Church is not among them. It remains entrenched in fossilized convictions, espousing a doctrine that is embedded with contradiction and devoid of any consideration of new understandings in human sexual psychology. Regarding homosexuality, the Church's words are anachronistic and mostly harsh. On the one hand, it states, in a manner that suggests it has indeed considered new understandings:

> According to contemporary scientific research, the human person is so profoundly affected by sexuality that it must be considered as one of the factors which give to each individual's life the principal traits that distinguish it. In fact, it is from sex that the human person receives the characteristics which, on the biological, psychological and spiritual levels, make that person a man or a woman, and thereby largely condition his or her progress towards maturity and insertion into society. (CDF, Persona Humana, 1975) [16]

Thus, sexuality is at the core of the human person. Yet, in the same document, the Church contradicts this more contemporary understanding of sexuality, and declares with feeble rationale that these innate characteristics must never be accepted by acting upon them. Homosexual persons must never engage in intimate human

---

16   Cardinal Franjo Seper, *Declaration On Certain Questions Concerning Sexual Ethics, Persona Humana,*
December 29, 1975, http://www.vatican.va/roman_curia/congregations/cfaith/documents/rc_con_cfaith_doc_19751229 _persona-humana_en.html.

love: Intimate love for them is sinful. Their nature is somehow unnatural and precludes loving intimate relationships:

> Homosexual acts are intrinsically disordered and can in no case be approved of.

This edict clearly implies that God created some of us to never experience an intimate human relationship. How does such a concept equate to the primacy of love? The reaction to this mostly negative document has demonstrated that the homophobic found in it sufficient justification for frequent demeaning discrimination and criminal abuse. Charity was obviously missing from this teaching, with little concern for the effect of these words. From such demeaning rhetoric flows the cries *God hates fags,* and the like. At the very least, injustice is unmistakably demonstrated by the result.

Thus, more than ten years later, perhaps recognizing the negative results of this teaching, in a new document, Church leaders attempt to ameliorate their demeaning dogma. Despite their disordered nature, discriminatory behavior toward homosexuals is wrong:

> It is deplorable that homosexual persons have been and are the object of violent malice in speech or in action. Such treatment deserves condemnation from the Church's pastors wherever it occurs. It reveals a kind of disregard for others which endangers the most fundamental principles of a healthy society. The intrinsic dignity of each person must always be respected in word, in action and in law. (CDF, Letter To The Bishops Of The Catholic Church On The Pastoral Care Of Homosexual Persons, 1986) [17]

The struggle to make sense of the convoluted reasoning of the Vatican would be humorous were the consequences not sot so

---

17 Cardinal Joseph Ratzinger, Letter to *The Bishops of the Catholic Church on the Pastoral Care of Homosexual Persons,* October 1, 1986, http://www.vatican.va/roman_curia/congregations/cfaith/documents/rc_con_cfaith_doc_19861001_homosexual-persons_en.html.

hurtful to so many. Juggling charity, the modern understanding of sexuality as one of the *principal traits* of an individual's life, and an archaic dogma on sexual mores is an impossible jumble of contradiction. Wary of possible inconsistencies conflicting with their image as sole holders of the absolute truth, and leery of being seen as allowing licentiousness, Church leaders are driven to defend the indefensible. The Vatican decides to ignore rationality and simply reiterate: violent malice in speech or action may be deplorable, but the overriding issue is, these folks are "disordered."

> Although the particular inclination of the homosexual person is not a sin, it is a more or less strong tendency ordered toward an intrinsic moral evil; and thus the inclination itself must be seen as an objective disorder. (Ibid)

God made them *disordered,* not *good,* and therefore, being disordered, they must be denied certain human rights that may conflict with our past absolute, revealed truth. A homosexual person loving another human being is simply not a recognizable right. It is forbidden because their love would be an "intrinsic evil." It's evil because we say it is—it's 'natural law'. In addition (despite any violent malice resulting) it's decreed that gay people's difference, just being who they are, demands special exclusions: They can't teach in schools, coach athletics, be foster parents, and so on. They can't live or work where heterosexuals don't want them. (They're an abomination, but we don't like that offensive designation. We prefer the more nuanced term, *disordered.*) Moreover, since the Holy Spirit speaks only to the magisterium, and they've declared themselves infallible, no one may challenge their *truth*—again, homosexuals, who were created with the "principal traits that distinguish" them, are not *good,* but *disordered.* The Creator obviously erred.

Persisting in this convoluted argumentation, and responding to the bewildering dichotomies they've created, they try to explain further:

> Sexual orientation does not constitute a quality comparable to race, ethnic background, etc. in respect to

non-discrimination. Unlike these, homosexual orientation is an objective disorder and evokes moral concern. (Some Considerations Concerning the Response to Legislative Proposals on the Non-Discrimination of Homosexual CDF Letter, 1992) [18]

Yes, it's that objective disorder thing. Forget that we said earlier, that "The human person is so profoundly affected by sexuality that it must be considered as one of the factors which give to each individual's life the principal traits that distinguish it." Just ignore that, dear Christians, it's really OK to discriminate:

There are areas in which it is not unjust discrimination to take sexual orientation into account, for example, in the placement of children for adoption or foster care, in employment of teachers or athletic coaches, and in military recruitment. (Ibid)

The author of this document obviously equates gay people as being the equivalent of sex-crazed monsters who will always be lurking to corrupt the innocent heterosexual. *Keep them away from children!* is the sick perspective. In further demonstration of moral dementia, it is arrogantly stated, if people get hurt, it's to be expected:

When civil legislation is introduced to protect behavior to which no one has any conceivable right, neither the Church nor society at large should be surprised when other distorted notions and practices gain ground, and irrational and violent reactions increase. (Ibid)

This is a loving, Christian concept? Read that again. The Church in effect is saying we *must* discriminate against gay people.

---

18 Congregation for the Doctrine of the Faith, *Some Considerations Concerning the Response to Legislative Proposals on the Non-discrimination of Homosexual Persons*, 1992, http://www.vatican.va/roman_curia/congregations/cfaith/documents/ rc_con_cfaith_doc_19920724_homosexual-persons_en.html.

It's OK to fire them, deny them housing, marriage, family, and a host of other civil rights. They don't deserve these rights, and "violence will ensue if we if we try to legislate equality." This dogma clearly holds homosexuality to be the seeds of pedophilia.

We can expect violence if we *don't* discriminate! We must therefore deny gay people civil rights. Because they are *objectively disordered*, they are not worthy of equality. Discrimination is justified, because their difference is unacceptable in the Church's view. Gay people have *no conceivable right* to love another human being. They can't have the rights the rest of us take for granted.

Absurd! This new standard of justice is a standard of injustice. It is blatant homophobic bigotry born in hypocrisy and nurtured in hatred and arrogance This from "a supreme pontiff?" Ludicrous! It is from a sick Church, a new brood. If I'm a gay person, what I hear is that any attempt to attain equal civil rights will justify violence against me. I may never love another human being intimately; *it's intrinsically evil.* No matter how they phrase it, the Catholic magisterium truly believes God created me an abomination. They assert that God created gay people, *disordered*, and denied them intimate love for a lifetime. Why would any gay person ever want to be Catholic?

I ask my Church leaders: "Is this is a concept of Divine love?" No, it is a pejorative teaching that is more a blasphemy. It is a mockery of God's unconditional love. It is the product of deafness, blindness, and arrogance born of the common human sin of pride. It is the product of "an old boys' club." It is the voice of vipers.

The viper's voice is blaring today. Recently, the prince of the Chicago archdiocese announced his conviction that the gay community is tantamount to a modern-day version of the Ku Klux Klan. What an idiotic and ignorant statement. Such rhetoric seems born of emotional frustration over the obvious logical correctness of the gay community's drive for civil rights. Cardinal George is lucky his vocal diatribes are baloney. If they weren't, we'd definitely have seen some lynching of bishops by the gay community. (He has since apologized for his remarks)

Then there's the nonsense emanating from the duke of New York, Archbishop Timothy Dolan. This jovial "leader" contrived the ridiculous idea that same-sex marriage is a threat to religious freedom. Apparently, his idea of religious freedom entails the enforcement of Catholic dogma on the rest of society. If we don't do that, we're usurping his religious freedom. Like the rest of his colleagues, he ignores the reality of the 50 percent divorce rate accomplished by heterosexual couples. Divorce is the greatest threat to marriage, your eminence.

It's all reminiscent of the twisted logic that justified slavery, seg-regation, and anti-Semitism and many other errors. It's reminis-cent of the inquisition and burning people at the stake. (Anyone who disagrees with us will be executed!) Just as homosexuals have no conceivable right to the civil rights that the rest of society enjoys, slaves had no conceivable rights either. Neither did the Jews who were consigned to ghettoes by the papacy. When violence results, "We should not be surprised." (I don't suppose the slaves or Jews were surprised either, when they attempted to flee their abuse and encountered a violent recompense.) Is this not a rationalized justification for violence? How can this *not* be an evil stance the Church espouses? I say to the magisterium: Such rationale nicely matches the one that gave us the Holocaust. Where is love in this philosophy? Is this what Jesus would do? How can anyone justify silence in the face of such bigotry? It is a disgrace to the Church.

These excerpts are a mere snippet of the official teachings of the Church in recent years on the issue of homosexuality. It clearly defies rational Christian thought, because it is blatantly opposed to human love and justice. The Church wants to ignore the conse-quences of its condemning and demeaning rhetoric. The denial of any responsibility for the consequences of the anti-Semitic Roman Catholic history that preceded the Holocaust is sadly similar. It is prototypical to couch doctrine in high-sounding academic rheto-ric and cloak it in an aura of infallibility. Unfortunately, while it may sell, words matter. The reality of violence matters. The reality of bigotry and prejudice matters. It reveals only an ill-concealed attempt to ignore real-world experience, and exposes an institu-tion drenched in hypocrisy and deceit. The last quote from the CDF (Congregation for the Doctrine of the Faith) above surely hints at some recognition of the inherent contradiction and tragic consequences of such doctrine when it says we *should be surprised when other distorted notions and practices gain ground, and irrational and violent reactions increase.* The Church cannot claim innocence from the universal violence against gay people any more than it can claim innocence of the injustices of slavery and anti-Semitism. Words do matter.

My experience over the last thirty-five years of studying homosexuality and ministering to the gay community clearly demonstrates how terribly wrong the Church's teaching on this issue is, and the terrible misery inflicted on innocent families. Today, there are places in the world where gay people can be executed by the state for their orientation. Yet the Catholic Church is silent over such heinous injustice. Beyond the silence, Church rhetoric actually supports such state-sponsored violence. It's a familiar silence—a silence that history now condemns. I conclude that our Church leaders are afflicted with a Pharisee-like mentality that is spawned by arrogance. When one considers the horror of the sexual abuse of children, the continuing cover-up, and the ongoing lack of chaste living among many of our clergy, one sees a pattern—a continuing culture of a malignant mendacity sorely in need of reform.

The problem with the self-righteous who claim to represent God and castigate gay people, is they believe their own negative stereotypes. My own stereotypes of gay people comes from personal witness. I know many, many gay people—far better than any Church "experts." What our Church princes don't see is something I see consistently. I see the unheralded and most amazing charity by so many in the gay community. For me it has become a stereotype; it is a prevalent and most unique thing. I see gay couples doing heroic acts of charity; adopting society's cast-offs—cast-offs of all ages, and then raising them in the most loving environments. They do it often at great sacrifice, a sacrifice that is exacerbated by a society that legislates, among other things, denial of mutual medical coverage for gay partners *and their children.* I see gay people often assisting the elderly, the disabled, the helpless. I see them taking the homeless into their homes, demonstrating a profound Christian love; a giving service to desperate people, ending only when these homeless are able to resume an independent life. I see their charity as such a common characteristic, that I cannot fail to be impressed. It is above and beyond.

In one case, I observed a gay man assume the death watch of a severely disabled neighbor. He daily took responsibility for the mundane needs of a dying women in her final days. In the end, he followed up by arranging and paying all burial expenses, as well as her final medical costs, because there was no surviving family member to do so. It was an amazing display of love of neighbor. It was a gay man taking on a charitable responsibility for an elderly disabled women, because he saw that no one else would.

My gay brothers and sisters do these things absent any support from most religious communities, who seem bent only on decrying their "evil." Heroic charity by the gay community seems far more common than in our "straight" enclave. If I want to find a "Good Samaritan" at anytime, I know where to go.

Not too long ago, when my wife of fifty years was dying of cancer, two gay men showed up at my door one Saturday with a hospital bed for our use. It was a very welcome and unsolicited gift which made our difficult journey a little more bearable. After my wife died, they returned with their rented truck to retrieve their bed (to gift to some other suffering soul.)

The Church sees only sex. The broad obsession with sexual activity reveals a fundamental cancer at the very core of Catholic Church doctrine. Over the centuries, it has wittingly or otherwise been used as an instrument of power and control, keeping the laity in line by laying on impossible burdens, all the while presenting the deceitful image of celibate chastity. It is striking that the Catholic perspective on the nature of human sexuality, while having roots in ancient Greek, Roman, and Stoic philosophies, essentially was initiated by Saint Augustine. His supposed expertise includes a background of having fathered an illegitimate child and then abandoning both the child and the mother to their own devices while moved off to "a celibate life dedicated to God"—all with an effective disregard for the terrible injustice he inflicted on his mistress and progeny. While many aspects of Saint Augustine might be worthy of praise and emulation, and no man is without faults, his qualifications as an authority on human sexuality certainly seem suspect at best.

Saint Augustine is a much-admired religious figure and, while I hope sometime in the future I might get to meet him, I confess that I am not a student of his life. What little I know of him is constrained by the distance of his life from mine and the mundane demands of my life that seem to preclude sufficient intellectual pursuit or study of the Augustinian legacy. That he's been proclaimed a saint says more of his eminence than I can. His singular struggles with sexuality certainly give him modern appeal, but I'm quite sure his conclusions on human sexuality would not agree with my own, and they certainly don't reflect contemporary human knowledge in the field. I suspect his views stem from the throes of a deep-felt personal guilt. Then I know I'm not going to be proclaimed anyone's saint.

He was bishop of Hippo, but that doesn't help me either, as I regard more than a few bishops (and cardinals—and popes) as naive individuals who are trying to tell us they speak for God and only they know God's plan. They freely ignore the reality of a limiting humanity common to us all and the undeniable value of human experience that contradicts their teachings.

Recently it has become common practice for our Catholic bishops to castigate theologians who might hypothesize some new insights. Our bishops have such an arrogant view of their sacrosanct position that they don't even extend the courtesy of discussion with the offending theologian before they read them out of the party. In mid-2011, the bishops publically condemned theologian Elizabeth Johnson's[19] new book, *Quest for the Living God,* without ever engaging their own review process, arrogantly implying, "Don't ever publish until you check with us first. You must not challenge our version of truth." Ms. Johnson replied: "The task of theology, classically defined is faith seeking understanding; it calls for theologians to wrestle with mystery. The issues are always complex."

The aristocrats are mighty protective of their positions of power, and they prefer that no one else engage in any independent

---

19   Elizabeth A. Johnson, professor of theology, Fordham University, is a teacher, author, editor, and public lecturer in theology.

thinking. They have very effectively entrenched their system of rigid conformity by incorporating strict obedience into the clerical culture. Their solemn vow of obedience to the next in the power line is most definitely an *intrinsic evil,* as it makes it impossible for a cleric to follow his conscience freely, if it conflicts with the party line.

Not every bishop accepts all of that party line, however, and there are definitely many lower-level clergy who, being closer to the ordinary people, have admirable humility and spiritual insight. Their exceptional presence is a refreshing contrast. Yet unfortunately, like Jonah, many of our bishops would definitely benefit from some time in the belly of a whale, so as to comprehend their limitations. They should undoubtedly be accompanied by a few cardinals and popes as well.

Yes, Saint Augustine was bishop of Hippo. As such, he certainly must have been afflicted with the adulation that rank always engenders. It probably, like many of his current successor bishops, enabled him to tout many convictions with an unlikely certitude. This is despite his own proclaimed stance that "we can't understand God."

As I hear him, he also seemed to think that few would be saved; most will be damned for eternity. This strikes me as someone with pretty pathetic fears that seem antithetical to unconditional love. I sure wouldn't treat my children as severely as Augustine posits that God treats His. It seems more like a reflection of guilt over one's past failures—an understandable human reaction. It is certainly not a concept of Divine love. Fear is historically a magisterial tool used for spiritual torture and one that seems ingrained in our nature. Fear is certainly not the earmark of the Jesus I have come to know and experience in my life. Fear is a depressing perspective that I don't share. When fear attacks, it is often a mark of a temptation of faith. Ironically, the most common phrase in the scriptures admonishes us to "fear not!"

Sadly, my Church has a long history of ignoring this plea. Instead, it essentially denies the reality of God's innate love and opts for promoting fear. Perhaps it stems from the fact that God's love is so completely incomprehensible as to be unbelievable— and maybe particularly so for the celibate mind.

Unfortunately the Saint Augustine syndrome of indigenous sexual misconduct—all sexual pleasure is suspect—is alive and well in the Church today. Thus, celibacy has been elevated to idol status and strictures on sexual activity have become an obsession. Ironically, based on several recent studies that indicate many priests, bishops, and even cardinals are sexually active, celibacy is quite obviously a myth[20] in practice. It is more evidence of a facade that condemns the ranks of the hierarchy by their own behavior, and reveals a deception and hypocrisy that Jesus so threateningly condemned. While they preach an Augustinian-based doctrine on sexuality at which they themselves fail, they also violate an even greater proscription of Augustine's regarding deceit. The sexual abuse cover-up scandal is stunning evidence of it. It not only continues, but the negative implications for the entire Church multiply. The probability is, that the ultimate resolution of this disgrace will come only through civil intervention. The institutional Church is so steeped in a culture of deceit and arrogance as to make any self-correction exceedingly unlikely.

When the Church is viewed from an historical perspective, it is easy to recognize the many past evils and sins committed by those in high places. The accuracy of Lord Acton's[21] dictum is obvious: "All power corrupts, and absolute power corrupts absolutely. Great men are almost always bad men."

It's ironic that Lord Acton wrote this wisdom to Bishop Mandell Creighton while expressing his opposition to the First Vatican Council's declaration of papal infallibility. Clearly, the Catholic hierarchy exercises absolute power in the Church. There is no appeal from its aristocratic dictates. Then one wonders: Have our Church leaders corrupted themselves and forgotten Jesus's stern warning to the Church leaders of His day? On one occasion, in decrying their hypocrisy, He said to them: "You brood of vipers, how can you say anything good? For out of the overflow of the

---

20   This is a common theme expressed by Richard Sipe, a sociologist and author who spent eighteen years serving the Church as a Benedictine monk and Catholic priest; http://www.richardsipe.com/.

21   John Emerich Edward Dalberg-Acton, First Baron Acton (1834–1902) was an English Catholic, historian, politician, and writer.

heart, the mouth speaks" (Matt. 12:34). On another occasion, He said to them: "You snakes! You brood of vipers! How will you escape being condemned to hell" (Matt. 23:33)?

Have we now, in this time, allowed the creation of a new brood of vipers? Has anyone the authority to answer or even make such an accusation? Perhaps only Jesus can do that. However, His harsh rhetoric would worry me if I were a Church leader. One cannot judge, but blatant deceit and corruption is easy to see and hard to ignore. It is readily apparent in the hypocrisy of the abuse scandal and cover-up.

It is also apparent in the broad power and corrupting influence of money and the attendant secrecy and fraud that is all too prevalent throughout the Church. Speaking to financial fraud, Jason Berry in his recent book, *Render Unto Rome*, stated:

> Amid mounting bankruptcies, bishops have been selling off whole pieces of the infrastructure—churches, schools, commercial properties—while the nephew of one of the Vatican's most powerful cardinals engaged in a lucrative scheme to profiteer off the enormous downsizing of American church wealth. [22]

Clear and accepted accounting of the Church's financial status is a rarity throughout the world. Secrecy is an all-pervading practice in matters material as well as spiritual. Like the rest of humanity, the Church struggles with the sin of avarice.

Humility is always obvious and pleasant when it's encountered. Recognizing humble, loving people when they appear on the scene is truly a refreshing event. There are many humble and loving people in Christ's Church. I witness them most often in the lower ranks of the clergy—those who are closer to the ordinary people. Yet, Pope John XXIII certainly seemed to meet the characteristics of loving Christianity, and to display a level of humility that was uncommon for his exalted office; he was definitely a pastoral leader. Unfortunately, his attempts at Church reform via the Second Vatican Council are being met in this time with

---

22   Berry, Jason. *Render Unto Rome*. New York: Crown Publishing, 2011,

continuing efforts of nullification and retrogression. Too often today, one sees and hears only demeaning words of judgment and actions that defy a loving, pastoral approach. Instead of love, there is often arrogant bullying. It is a condition that seems to ebb and flow, and we are in a flood tide.

Some fellow Catholics would object to what I have written here. I may perhaps be rightly accused of stridency, but is not the Church strident when it condemns my gay son as disordered? I can never accept that an all loving God means to deny all gay people the virtue of loving. When I survey all the lessons I have learned in this life, I conclude that the greatest of these is learning to love. I observe that loving has given me joy beyond anything else. More than being the greatest of the virtues, it is the virtual essence of life. Claiming that the Creator intends that my son and those like him should be denied this gift, is a blasphemy. Can anyone claim that we must not love? Blind brood!

I have tried to state the things I have witnessed with accuracy, not malice. One cannot judge the culpability of those in the Church seen as having strayed from the message of Jesus. Actually, it is probably more accurate to assess the hierarchy as victims rather than perpetrators. We laity have contributed to a cult of adulation by allowing and supporting a system that methodically militates against the virtue of humility and cultivates corruption. We do it by our silence. We do it by according a virtual divinity to the papacy. We do it by our "pay, pray, and obey" mentality and our penchant for silence when protest is called for. We do it by our complacency and refusal to utilize our intellect.

I am not optimistic that meaningful change will come to our institutional Church. People get what people allow. Most Catholics are complacent and apathetic. By being complacent, we are guilty of complicity. Our silence is not unlike those who witness child abuse but fail to report it to the civil authorities. It reminds me of the old saying, "If you keep doing what you're doing, you'll keep getting what you're getting." I fear the forecast: We'll keep getting what we've been getting.

I would not presume that differing views have no merit, yet one can rightly be judgmental of words and actions of injustice.

We are truly living in the midst of a new type of holocaust. To be silent in the midst of it is to be complicit. Today's holocaust may be less hideous and of less magnitude than the infamous tragedy of Auschwitz-Birkenau, but the process is analogous. It may be more hidden as there are no gas chambers, but an indefensible and terrible persecution nonetheless exists. Too many of us are oblivious. The occasion to witness it surrounds us. It's there to see—if one has the eyes and the willingness to see. I have seen it—too often.

The Church is obviously divided into two opposing camps. The conservative camp is currently the ruling camp and has been since Vatican II. This division is tragic because rather than complementing one another, there is only conflict. That's regrettable as both views have much to contribute. It would be better to learn from each other. Yet, human failing in the Church is historic. It existed in Saint Paul's time; it existed throughout Church history; it exists in our own time. This conflict has consequences—disastrous consequences if you happen to be gay. Despite their obscurity, many ordinary laypersons are the victims. They cry out for relief. The modern Church is breeding much human suffering when it should be leading the struggle against it. The evidence is saddening and a direct affront to rational thought. Divisiveness is a worldwide problem, not just a Catholic one, and it seems to be growing in intensity. It is a phenomenon I don't understand. The hideous genocidal crimes of history that persist even today stagger any understanding.

How can I reconcile this conflict of faith and Church? While I conclude that my views are the product of my personal experiences, and that we all travel different journeys while aiming for the same destination, it seems to be part of God's plan that we travel these different paths. Our created differences suggest that differing views should be expected. If one looks carefully at God's creation, an immense, unfathomable variety is clearly evident. One almost senses that uniformity and regimentation is anathema for the Creator. Who knows? One can only surmise. Yet, surely, we are meant to complement one another, much like the amazing balance we witness in the universe around us. There, the pattern is one of endless variety, which has somehow come together in coherence, like some gigantic puzzle—each piece different from all others, yet all fitting neatly together. Similarly, while our personal views and beliefs may differ, they have special places and are a necessary part of the whole. The personal experiences and the lessons that we each learn in the course of living are perhaps meant to meld into a unity of understanding as we together try to comprehend the Creator. Such melding can only come about through love. Ideology is not an answer.

The terrible injustices of the institutional Church, which is supposed to be the voice of Jesus, are evidence of the *new brood*. The pastoral ones who are the exceptions are the very ones in the Church who are being removed or punished by the leadership.

I also see another dichotomy in the Church's stance that is bewildering. The Church's historical teaching on social justice is one I can enthusiastically applaud. It is a view that is probably more progressive than my own. For me, this championing of justice for the poor and downtrodden among us does not seem to correlate with the simultaneous denigration of women and gays. I can only look to the Spirit for the enlightenment to understand this paradox. I ask myself: What am I to learn from this? Is the Spirit speaking to the Church? Is the Church listening?

When I consider the many outstanding clergy who truly do follow Jesus and the Church's love-centered teachings on social justice, I realize that one cannot so easily critique such a complex institution. There is risk of oversimplification. I can only pray and trust that my own convictions of the need for reform stem from where the Spirit has led me. I try to listen. I try to learn from my experiences. While the Spirit seems to have led me toward a diminished regard for the commands of the magisterium, I know that perhaps, they too contribute to God's plan. They too have their measure of sincerity, however arcane and fallible their teachings. Their contribution is sometimes veiled from me, but I think our disagreements present a challenge to blend our views in a spirit of love. It is difficult for me, particularly the prejudice against gay people like my son. I pray about it.

We all are at risk of the brood syndrome. Human failure is universal. We all fail. Yet, our lives are assessed not by our incidents of failure, but by the totality of our journey. I believe that any final assessment will focus on our progress toward loving. The Holy Spirit persistently leads us toward this goal. Our mutual challenge will constantly be to attain the requisite humility that will allow the Holy Spirit to guide us to this end. I hope and pray that we can achieve such humility and that the hierarchy will partake in that achievement. If so, it will probably evolve slowly. It will take a long time, and a heavy dose of Divine grace. We can't do it by ourselves.

Clearly, my focus throughout this book is on the Catholic Church and her shortcomings. As I've already stated, this is natural since it is the source and sustenance of my faith. However, much of what I criticize is applicable to other Christian denominations. This seems particularly true of the evangelical Christian fundamentalists. Many of these, who claim the mantle of Jesus, grossly distort His most basic teaching, not unlike my Church. Unfortunately, all of us find the task of loving one another to be daunting. The search for an authentic Jesus-centered faith is constant for all of us, but some seem closer to it than others. Despite my focused critique of Catholicism, I believe we are all deficient and always in dire need of listening to the quiet voice of the Spirit.

Chapter 14

Always Sinful

"But, since even the lawful intercourse of the wedded cannot take place without pleasure of the flesh, entrance into a sacred place should be abstained from, because the pleasure itself can by no means be without sin"
—Epistles of Saint Gregory the Great, circa 600 CE

The above quote reflects the historical nature of the Church's medieval comprehension of human sexuality. There seems to be an all-pervading fear of anything pleasurable in our Catholic history. Life must be a vale of tears to be acceptable to the Almighty. As a parent, this is the exact opposite of what I would want for my children. Does God really want us to exist in misery? The Church=s fear-based teaching on sexuality reveals a distorted understanding, and the virtual pathological focus on the sex act. The emphasis of genital behavior borders on obsession. Could it be partly the product of a celibate mindset?

Human sexual activity is actually a very minor aspect of human love and marriage, notwithstanding our current culture's distortional overemphasis on, and abuse of sex. The moral focus in human sexuality, in my view, should more rightly be on the relational aspect, not on physical pleasure or the act of copulation. The pleasure is fleeting and is designed to move us toward love. A celibate perspective to understand this will be handicapped because by definition, celibacy denies one the experience of engaging in intimate loving relationships. This reality is the core of celibacy's fundamental flaw. In my view, the love relationship with another human being, not the sex act, is the primary essence of marriage. Sex, though a powerful drive, is only a very small factor in intimate loving. Love is not sex any more than sex is love, nor is marriage about sex. Marriage is about loving. Love is about giving. Love is about serving. Love is about relationship and family. Sex is like a fuse that ignites our ability to love. After more than eighty years of living and nearly sixty years of marriage, I can unequivocally state that sex is a very minor part of marriage as I have experienced it. The primary purpose of sex in my view is to attract, promote, and enhance a loving relationship. Sex is the *flower* that attracts us to the honey of loving. A true loving relationship aims at an ultimate bonding that is ontological. No other human experience can match it. It is virtually an indescribable and incomprehensible plane of existence that is probably the closest we can get to the divine in this life.

If a doctrine of sexual morality placed loving relationships as the principal objective, rather than the focused fury on the correctness surrounding the physical act of sex, we would have a much different perspective. If the emphasis were on self-giving and how to achieve it, I suspect there would be much less divorce and better families as a result. This is not the Church's present posture. The obsession with sex is distortional. Obviously, this is not an exclusively Catholic position. Other denominations mimic the Catholic confusion. The myopic focus on sex misses the object of it all. The idea that procreation is the primary end is wrong also. The constant focus on pleasure, and whether it's legal or illegal, moral or immoral, represents a distorted obsessive-compulsive mindset. This ancient academic concept was born in an ambience devoid of a true understanding of real human love and sexuality. Our Augustinian based understanding is an anemic concept. It is probably one reason that real human love is too rare in our culture. Our celibate moral leaders are mostly ignorant

Some of us learn to truly love only after a lifetime of learning. It is easy to witness a real human love in a great many elderly married couples. The experience of a long marriage can teach uniquely. It is why some marriages last into the sixth decade and beyond. I have been fortunate to experience it myself. People who have been married for many years and have managed to attain the mystical bonding of true love, could in turn teach the rest of us with much greater authority than what our Church leaders can offer.

Catholic doctrine on human sexuality has been very slow to develop and is constrained by ancient fallacies with little recognition that anything new has been discovered over the past two millennium. It is a position that is many centuries behind current psychosexual discovery and understanding—one that persists in a continuing emphasis on sex and pleasure, not love. The anemic arguments that tout natural law come from an institution that has historically opposed any new understanding of it. It reflects a virtual flat-earth mentality that promises only future apologies. We don't have to go back to the sixth century to find the origins of this doctrine.

The Church's teaching on sexuality is a continuing challenge to juggle easily transparent dichotomies. The doctrines relating to sexuality seem to infer, among other things, that in essence, any pleasure in marital intercourse is essentially a necessary evil. Any sexual pleasure outside of marriage is grounds for damnation. Don't even think about it! Despite an obvious struggle by the Church to bring a common sense "mutual satisfaction" element into its teaching on marriage, procreation keeps surfacing as the only legitimate object of sex, and it must be between a man and a woman. Vatican II's statement that, "The love and mutual satisfaction of the spouses is coequal to the procreation ends of marital intercourse"[23] remains a contentious view in the traditional perspective. The procreation imperative is the basis for the unequiv-

---

23 This quote is a common synopsis of Vatican II's *Gaudium et Spes* statements on the nature and purpose of marriage. It is a general consensus that the statements in Chapter 1, *Fostering the Nobility of Marriage and the Family*, are reflected in the quote noted here.

ocal condemnation of homosexual sex. All sex must be open to procreation and must never be thwarted—thus the prohibition of artificial contraception. However, turn the page, and we hear that the rhythm method is OK. No one would deny that the object or intent of rhythm practitioners is to thwart conception. It is a clear portrayal of a physicality-centered theology that seems quite irrational and little related to our "nature," despite the touted thesis of "natural law."

How does one square rhythm's approval with what I was always taught at an early age by my Jesuit teachers: intentionality—that the morality of an act is dependent, among other things, on the *intent* of the individual? There is a poorly concealed contradiction here. It is similar to the Church's less-than-sly acceptance of the dissolution the marriage bond. It's called annulment rather than divorce, an obvious hypocrisy. Yet the colloquial understanding of this process is "Catholic divorce." Few people are fooled; most understand the dissimulation.

So what differentiates intent in the case of contraception? What's the answer to this contradiction of rhythm versus artificial contraception? Easy, some would say. What does the pope say? Rational thought by the laity or scientific understanding is irrelevant and invalid. The magisterium's message is, "Get back in your pew, be quiet and sit down, you ordinary person."

Occasionally, some hints of understanding and struggle to change creep into view. In 1930, Pope Pius XI, in his encyclical "Casti Connubii," [24] despite an emphasis on a traditional Augustinian-based concept of human sexuality, stated that the *mutual love* of husband and wife "can, in a very real sense, as the Roman Catechism teaches, be said to be the chief reason and purpose of marriage..." Now I don't know what "Roman Catechism" he's talking about; it's sure not the one I remember. Ensuing theologians who picked up on this concept of the primacy of "mutual love" were quickly silenced. One cannot change the "absolute truth" that procreation is supreme. It is my own contention that

---

24 Pope Pius XI, *Encyclical Letter of Pope Pius XI, On Christian Marriage,* December 31, 1930, http://www.vatican.va/holy_father/pius_xi/encyclicals/documents/hf_p-xi_enc_31121930_casti-connubii_en.html.

mutual love, if it is defined as the giving of self, is definitely the prime function of marriage, not procreation.

As an engineer by training, I like to look at the data. Thinking about the relative importance of sex in marriage, I decided to do just that. What does the data say? If sex is so important, just how much sex does marriage entail? Looking at my own experience as an ordinary married person, I have concluded I probably am just that—*ordinary*. That is, I have been neither consumed by concupiscence nor devoid of passion. Note that I have fathered six children, which speaks for itself. (Sex was a part of that.) So, looking back, I have calculated the estimated time I have spent in marital sexual activity and compared it to the total time I have been in the married state. The resulting comparison should be some indication of the relative importance of sex in marriage, at least from an empirical standpoint. In the case of this ordinary man, in nearly sixty years of marriage, sex has occupied the full attention of my wife and me less than one-tenth of one percent of my total time in the married state. Put another way, 99.975 percent of the time, my spouse and I were engaged in some nonsexual activity. I suggest that such a perspective makes the Church's doctrine on sex and marriage seem at least a little humorous. As an afterthought, I would add that in my current state as an eighty-two-year-old married gent, the 99.975 percent now has a lot more nines after that decimal point. Significantly, my marital joy is higher than it has ever been. I think that's because, at my age, I've learned quite a bit about the joy of loving. The result is a truly blissful experience.

Contrary to the Catholic doctrinal understanding, procreation is a secondary purpose in marriage as married people actually experience it. The Catholic position prohibiting contraception is a result of a fundamental misunderstanding of human sexuality in my view. Rome has historically associated marriage as a solution to the struggle against concupiscence. While this Augustinian-based idea is perhaps a prevarication of some very positive insights on marriage posited by that great saint, it nonetheless forms the distorted foundation for Church understanding of sexual mores.

I would expect that most Catholic couples successfully married for a sufficient period, would applaud support for my understanding of married sexuality. Yet Vatican dogmatists won't even consider such a concept. Beyond their rejection of change, they cannot comprehend it because have shut themselves off from experiencing a very essential part of life, constructed an abstract "we can't be wrong" syndrome and devised an academic dictum of a superior masochistic-celibate state that they themselves cannot follow. It seems absurd. It is sad. They have raised celibacy to the level of idolatry and through their self-imposed rigidity have laid on burdens that *threaten* marriage, not enhance it. (I know about that.). Worse than that, the consequences of this terse stoicism have inflicted much pain and suffering on millions of people, now and in the past, both heterosexual and homosexual. One could argue that the Church has long been afflicted with a cult form of sadomasochism—and in more than matters sexual. The recollection of the medieval promotion of self-flagellation as an act of piety comes to mind.

The historical nature of the Catholic Church's absurdities when it comes to human sexuality has many humorous anecdotal proclamations from our "infallible" popes. One such idiocy is the former teaching that the utilization by married couples of anything other than the missionary position was a mortal sin.

Denying themselves the most fundamental aspects for learning about human love and sexuality, Church dogmatists tout themselves to be experts on these matters. This is at best unlikely. They proclaim virginity superior to marriage. How self-congratulatory! This concept is justified by the remote idea that the celibate love God in place of loving another human. Yet how can they know about love? Human love seems a natural precursor to Divine love. Their concept proceeds from a perspective of one who has never engaged in intimate, committed, human love and then proclaims that the experience of human loving is an inferior virtue. (Actually, I'm not sure they would even consider human love a virtue.) Only celibate love fulfills the better goal. In a sense, the conclusion can logically be made that not loving is superior to loving. How can that not be absurd? My own experience of truly loving another human being has taught me far more about a loving God than any biblical or Church exhortations.

A distorted understanding of human sexuality is the fundamental cause for the castigation of homosexual persons. Because of a tunnel vision that sees only illicit pleasure, and an attendant legalism that constructs the plethora of academic-based esoteric rules and regulations, it is decided that a large component of the human race can never even attempt to achieve a loving human relationship. "God made you disordered so love is not for you." I very nearly destroyed my own son with the application of such a love negative philosophy.

It is much less effective to learn, let alone teach about something, from a solely academic perspective than it is by combining experience with study. Academics can be helpful, but experience is vital. One can read about how to swim, but you won't really know what it's all about until you jump into the pool. Church leaders think they know about human sexuality, but they haven't even gotten their feet wet, let alone jump into the pool.

When it comes to human love—the total giving of self—no one is qualified to teach me or anyone else until he has experienced the challenge to intimately love another human being. From a deficient celibate status, in the vernacular, you have no clue. My dear celibate brothers: neither procreation nor sexual mechanics are the issues!

Relating these perhaps judgmental observations, I am moved to remonstrate myself a bit by admitting that mine is a one-sided perspective. I know that any traditionalist who might have gotten this far (unlikely) will be scoffing at best. I will readily concede that my convictions stem from an ordinary intellect, and that there are times when I would do well to listen to the Church magisterium, even in areas in which I tout to have some expertise. Academics can complement experience. I state firmly that I do listen. An example that comes to my mind is Benedict XVI's "Deus Caritas Est." [25] His encyclical on love resonated with my own experience and belief. In describing the maturation of human love, he states that we gradually move from what I would paraphrase as immature love to a mature love. Benedict refers to them as *dodim* and *ahab*, or *agape:*

---

25 Pope Benedict XVI, *Encyclical Letter of Pope Benedict XVI, Deus Caritas Est,* December 25, 2005, http://www.vatican.va/holy_father/benedict_xvi/ encyclicals/documents/hf_ben-xvi_enc_20051225_deus-caritas-est_en.html.

Dodim, a plural form suggesting a love that is still insecure, indeterminate and searching. This comes to be replaced by the word *ahabà*, which the Greek version of the Old Testament translates with the similar-sounding *agape*, which, as we have seen, becomes the typical expression for the biblical notion of love. By contrast with an indeterminate, "searching" love, this word expresses the experience of a love which involves a real discovery of the other, moving beyond the selfish character that prevailed earlier. Love now becomes concern and care for the other. No longer is it self-seeking, a sinking in the intoxication of happiness; instead it seeks the good of the beloved: it becomes renunciation and it is ready, and even willing, for sacrifice.

I found that description, while decidedly academic, a rather precise portrayal of my own experience. The only minor critique I would add is that mature love is more than a *willingness* to sacrifice; it is a *desire* for sacrifice, and that sacrifice results in an *intoxication of happiness*. However esoteric the prose, Benedict's analysis is perceptive, especially for a celibate person, a fact that might moderate my rhetoric. I only wish he could apply such thinking to the Church's understanding and teaching on marriage and human sexuality. But, of course, I would suggest that his inability to envision such a new paradigm flows from his celibate state and a hierarchical mindset devoid of humility. "We said it, therefore it must be so." (We cannot change our infallible pronouncements.) My own conviction on marriage and sexuality is that the greatest need is to shift from a philosophy of self-focus to loving God and one's neighbor. Realizing that loving entails primarily giving, not receiving or selfishness, is not much different from Benedict's encyclical statement.

What Benedict describes is a primary aspect of what I have learned about loving. I learned far more about loving from intimate experience than any academic endeavor. It is a common experience of ordinary laypeople. Marriage and family, a gay child, six children, the loss of a spouse—these more than anything else have taught me about love and the all-loving Creator. The overwhelming blessing of being loved by a woman who was so exceptionally giving, so loving, in turn taught me how to love. It was a joyful lesson. The Church's focus on contraception, complementarity, procreation, and so on, is way off the mark to old married people like me. Maybe our clergy needs to open its club to the girls. I think it would help.

Despite such encyclicals as "Deus Caritas Est," the magisterium seems deficient in truly understanding intimate human love. Their self-acclaimed expertise on human sexuality reveals a broad deficiency when compared to actual human experience and the reality of recent events. Despite protestations to the contrary, the sexual abuse scandal is a clarion call to end celibacy. The institutional Church's handling of this scandal dramatizes that a fundamental deficiency in understanding human love and sexuality must exist. Whether the source is celibacy, hierarchical structure, doctrinal, or some other failing may be immaterial, but I feel certain that if our clergy members had had their own children, the sexual abuse scandal would never have happened. (I will address the issue of celibacy in greater detail in Chapter 16.)

The magisterium's touting of the Bible to support their doctrine is often a misuse of that hallowed document. The Bible is intended for moral enlightenment, but not necessarily immutable moral rules for all time, and certainly not for scientific truth. Change happens. Humanity evolves. Many religious leaders have misused it in the past to their eventual dismay, as new knowledge exposed errors in a way that could not be ignored. The Galileo debacle, slavery, and the subjugation of women come to mind. Some do not seem to realize it, but God has not stopped teaching us! Humanity's learning process never ceases. The Bible is a text more about culture and morality in a specific time in history; it is not about science. Human sexuality is more a matter for scientific study, about which full understanding has yet to be achieved. The Bible is not a timeless and precise manual about how to live in today's culture. The theologians Salzman and Lawler, speaking on sexuality relative to homosexual orientation, incisively wrote on this very issue:

> Neither the Bible nor the Christian tradition rooted in it
> prior to the twentieth century ever considered the homosexual

condition; they took for granted that everyone was heterosexual. To look for any mention in the biblical texts of what today is called "homosexual orientation" is simply anachronism. One might as well search the Bible for advice on buying a car or a computer. The biblical passages most frequently cited as condemning homosexuality actually condemn homosexual behaviors, and they condemn these behaviors specifically as a perversion of the heterosexual condition they assume to be the natural condition of every human person. In its modern meaning, homosexuality is not and cannot be a perversion of the heterosexual condition because homosexuals, by natural orientation, do not share that condition. Homosexuality is, rather, an inversion of the heterosexual condition that psychosexual homosexuals, by no choice of their own, do not naturally share, and they cannot be held morally accountable for something they did not choose: The context in which both the Old and New testaments condemn homosexual acts is a false assumption, shaped by the socio-historical conditions of the times in which they were written, that all human beings naturally share the heterosexual condition and that, therefore, any homosexual behavior is a perversion of "nature" and immoral. Because that biblical assumption is now scientifically shown to be incorrect, the Bible has little to contribute to the discussion of genuine homosexuality and homosexuals as we understand them today. [26]

My own compulsion to battle the injustices I see in the world surrounding a multitude of issues has naturally focused much on the Catholic Church. It has also focused primarily on the issue of homosexuality. The Church supposedly endeavors to be "the Body of Christ" in the world, but it has too often failed at that goal. It has become more like a doctrinal police department seeking to slay any perceived violator of its "infallible" teachings; an exclusive men-only club with a privileged caste headed by a supreme leader; an emperor-king who envisions himself as the very image of Christ Himself. Can a Church structure modeled after a medieval

---

26   *The Sexual Person*, T.A. Salzman and M. G. Lawler, p. 217

aristocracy, with a claim to be the God-appointed sole possessors of the absolute truth, above everyone else, be what Jesus had in mind? Is this what He meant by serving?

This all is further proof of the unwitting new golden calf, a new brood of vipers. And yes, we laity are complicit when we acquiesce to this aberration by our "pay, pray and obey" practice. It is a perversion of Jesus' plea to be the servants of one another. Despite the many good people in the Church, and the many-heralded accomplishments, it is apparent that too many of our leaders have succumbed to that fog of adulation to which they are so constantly subjected. It is easy to see. Witness their baroque robes, darkened limousines, palatial residences, popemobiles, and the distancing of themselves from the common man—the deference of the laity, none of which has any relevance toward understanding sexuality. They will never understand human sexuality, until they embrace intimate human love and experience it for themselves.

Chapter 15

Prince Versus Peasant

"When the game is over, the king and the pawn go into the same box"
—OLD ITALIAN PROVERB

Failure in the Church is ongoing, and as a layperson, I am driven to oppose those failures, to the extent of my ability as an ordinary Catholic to do so. I have remained Catholic, obviously not because I accept all Catholic teaching, but because I believe that the greater body of the Church, the laity and the many good clergy, are the core of Catholicism. The higher echelons of the hierarchy are another matter. Their demeaning statements and actions, their abuse of power, urge me to voice my objections in every way that I can. In attempting this task and trying for dialogue, one of the greatest hurdles to overcome is crossing the vast gulf that separates the hierarchy from the laity. History relates how difficult it was for communication between princes and peasants. As a layperson, it is essentially just as difficult for me to speak with my own bishop. He may be a prince of a fellow, but his princely position is situated behind a moat that is not easy to cross. On the other hand, I have some tools the peasants of old lacked. One is the U.S. mail. Thus, among other things, I have written my own Cardinal Adam Maida to express my frustrations and impatience with the Church's unwelcoming stance and injustice toward gay people.

Initially, I wrote my first letter after the "activist" affair that Sunday morning when I very publically protested the taped message that I found so hurtful. That initial letter began a series of two-way written exchanges between the cardinal and me. My letters eventually numbered thirteen in all and evoked nine responses that stretched over four years. In the end, I concluded that our exchange clearly demonstrated the frustrating futility of attempting meaningful dialogue with these "princes" of the Church. I was unable to achieve any positive action by the archdiocese to welcome people like my son. I received mostly perfunctory replies. In my first letter, I wrote:

Adam Cardinal Maida   October 18, 2004
Archbishop of Detroit
Your Eminence:

I am writing to you to convey my thoughts and reaction to your recent message played at mass in our parish this past Sunday regarding support for the Michigan constitutional amendment banning gay marriage and civil unions. Your message hurt my family and me very deeply. I am certain that other families were hurt as well. I would like to think that the hurt you have caused was unintentional, but from my perspective, it continues a pattern I have witnessed during your tenure as our archbishop. It seems as though you have a personal vendetta for the gay community. I have seen you effectively throw Dignity out of Holy Trinity, decry the Big Three auto companies' granting of benefits to gay couples, and essentially lead the action against Sister Jeanine Gramick and Father Robert Nugent. While I can understand your dogmatic conviction about saving the institution of marriage, I am utterly at a loss to understand your constant siege against anyone who is gay. From my perspective as the father of a gay son, your actions seem doctrinaire and devoid of compassion and Christian love.

I am the father of six children. I am also a life-long Catholic in the twilight of my life. My formal Catholic education includes sixteen years through the University of Notre Dame. I think I pretty much know the rules and know the reasons of our Church's teaching on morality—at least as well as or better than most laypersons. But I have also had the advantage of God giving me a gay son. This has been, perhaps, the greatest single blessing of my life. I feel that through my gay son, God has taught me much.

I nearly lost my son to suicide early in his life. The fundamental cause of his despair was easily traceable to me, his father. During my children's teen years I had unthinkingly mouthed Catholic moral teaching with doctrinaire certitude as my children searched for answers to the often-vexing issues of that time. During dinnertime conversations, when it was our custom to discuss any issue any family member wanted to explore, on some rare occasions, the topic of homosexuality was ever so timidly broached. My ready answers touted dogma that I suspect would have made the Vatican cheer. I enlightened my children about "natural law, sex is for marriage, an abomination, love the sinner, hate the sin, the virtue of chastity, etc." Little did I realize during those moments that I was stifling my son's attempts to communicate on a difficult subject and that my brilliant pontificating was secretly causing him to question his very worth.

As a result, I nearly lost my son when he attempted suicide. He was alone, many miles from home, during his first year of college. Convinced he was an abomination and that it would be better to end his life and spare his family the knowledge of who he really was, he commenced an ordeal that took him to the brink of death. He survived only through the intervention of God in a very special way. In the ensuing years, I have learned much about homosexuality. I have witnessed many times the terrible consequences of a strict and arrogant application of Church doctrine. It's awfully easy to do.

I have spent much time in recent years ministering to the gay community in any way that I could. This experience taught me much and continues to do so. I think one of the most important things that I have learned is how so-called Christian rhetoric is twisted by many to become fodder for violence against gay people. Your message Sunday most assuredly accomplished that unwanted goal. I have seen parents (Catholic) resort to suicide and even attempt murder simply because a gay child revealed their true identity. The root of such actions invariably stems from a distorted fervor for a doctrine that communicates only "disordered, intrinsically evil, an abomination." This climate of condemnation at best drives many young people out of the Church, and at worst leads to self-destruction. Indeed, the suicide rate for young gay people is three times that of the heterosexual and is the leading cause of death for them.

What has the archdiocese done to aid these modern day outcasts? Nothing substantive that I can see. Is there a need to leave the ninety-nine and seek the lost one? I think so. I am not hopeful though. Saving marriage? That is naive at best and hypocrisy at worst. I cannot see by any stretch of the intellect how granting gay people the right to make loving, long-term commitments threatens marriage. I need not enumerate the many assaults upon the institution of marriage imposed by our hedonistic, narcissistic, egocentric culture. I'm sure you are well aware of the crisis and the causes. However, I have seen many gay and lesbian couples making often heroic sacrifices to live loving lives of commitment while raising adopted children, children who were often castoffs of society. The job they are doing as parents seems far above the norm of society today. Their lives and families are vivid testimony of the fallacy that gay marriage is a threat to the family.

The right wing seems bent upon destroying the "homosexual agenda"! Pass a law! Enforce our dogma! God hates queers! Sadly, that was the message that came through to me last Sunday at my Church. Your intent may have been innocent, but your effect was devastating to my family and me. I am not alone. Despite a history in the early Church of support for homosexual couples, the present Church is focused on persecution. This stance has contributed greatly toward driving my son from the arms of my beloved Church. He feels unwelcome. I feel a terrible burden and at a loss of what to do. My son needs spiritual nourishment the same as the rest of us. The assault by organized religion on the gay and lesbian is beyond my comprehension.

In your message, you said that "God created them male and female." It appears that He also created them gay and straight. I don't pretend to understand why He did the latter, but perhaps it was to test our ability to love one another. In any event, it seems to me that our Church in recent times has failed to achieve a coherent understanding of human sexuality. To rely stubbornly on old tenets without recognition of new knowledge seems to me as arrogant. Will we again have to apologize four hundred years hence?

Finally, for the Archdiocese to spend upwards of $500,000 to fund this antigay amendment, some of which came from donations from me and my family, is grossly unjust. I can't imagine any justification for this political diversion of funds from more worthy causes. I resolve to correct my future donations accordingly.

I know your burdens must be many and great. I regret that this letter must add to them. But I pray that the Almighty will guide you and forgive the Church for the terrible injustice it pursues. I pray too for your brothers in the hierarchy that they too focus less on dogma and more on the practice of "loving one another, as He has loved us."

Sincerely,
Tom Nelson

He replied a short time later:

Dear Mr. Nelson: November 29, 2004
    Thank you for your recent letter in which you expressed concerns about the expenditure of money by the

Archdiocese of Detroit in support of Proposal 2. I appreciate your perspective on this issue from your own personal experience within your family. The source of such funding did not come from the weekly collection offerings or the annual Catholic Services Appeal. The archdiocese has funds from a variety of sources, including specially targeted donations set aside for public advocacy for the common good. As you note, there are many challenges to marriage today. As a Church, our experience has shown that efforts to experiment with marriage over the years have eroded this most basic building block of society. After Proposal 2 was placed on the ballot, the Catholic Church became involved in order to promote the basic understanding of marriage as between one man and one woman. We did so because of what we stand for, not whom we stand against. In our discussion of this issue, we were careful not to target any person or any group. The Catholic Church is opposed to any unjust discrimination and will continue to work for justice for all people.

Thank you once again for your heartfelt insights on this matter.

Sincerely yours in the Lord,
Adam Cardinal Maida,[27]
Archbishop of Detroit.

Characteristically, the first expressed concern by this man of God was money, and where it came from. Nowhere do I detect any pastoral awareness for the concerns for justice and the portent of hateful Church rhetoric. He says, "We were careful not to target any person or any group." Excuse me? Proposition 2 was specifically targeted against gay people. That automatically includes my son. Nowhere do I detect any feelings of compassion for my son or our family. His anemic disclaimer that, "The Catholic Church is opposed to any unjust discrimination and will continue to work

---

27   Adam Cardinal Maida is now retired. The current leader of the Detroit Archdiocese is Archbishop Allen H. Vigneron.

for justice for all people" defies logic. It denies that words matter, but it is fully compliant with the party-line policy. Gay people are "disordered," and discrimination against them is "just."

The ensuing responses from the cardinal were similarly perfunctory. His responses routinely avoided addressing the specifics of my letters and were consistently dispassionate and irrelevant to what I had written to him. It was clearly evident that there would be no response from him that could be conceived, even remotely, as deviating from the party line. My own letters to him continued a pattern of my deeply felt passion and emotion.

It would be unfair or inaccurate however, to imply that the cardinal was devoid of any compassion. His letter above was simply his first response to me. Later, his letters became slightly more pastoral as we became better acquainted, and he apparently did not perceive me as some type of fringe fanatic. Because of my desire to present fairly his image, I present here what I consider his warmest reply—one I have selected from all of his responses:

Dear Mr. Nelson: November 18, 2005
    Thank you for your very humble and sensitively worded letter. I appreciate the fact that you seem to have reached a better understanding of my position as Chief Shepherd of this local Church. When dealing with questions such as homosexuality, on one hand, it is important not to condemn or ostracize people who have such an orientation, but on the other hand, I cannot condone homosexual behavior. I am truly sorry about the abuse you say two of your daughters experienced from a Catholic priest[28].

---

28   This young priest became a virtual member of our family, a surrogate sibling to my children. His was not a classical abuse case, in that it involved only inappropriate touching and embracing. It caused my daughters no lasting distress. Nevertheless, it was uninvited and offensive at the time. It illustrates that abuse is a complex problem. The nature of his dismissal from the priesthood is unknown to me, however, I feel certain there was some degree of duress involved. In later years, following his laicization, he attended my fortieth wedding anniversary in 1995, and we have not seen him since. His aberrant behavior with my girls was more than offset by his loving contributions to our family over a period of many years. He is still regarded with affection by all of us. My

I realize you were suggesting some kind of personal meeting to discuss these things, but, given my schedule, I think it might be best if you could meet with your pastor. I am sure Father Chabala at Saint Fabian's could offer you a good listening ear; he is sympathetic and understanding.

Assuring you of my special prayerful remembrance for you and your family, I remain,

Sincerely yours in the Lord,
Adam Cardinal Maida,
Archbishop of Detroit.

The cardinal's "given my schedule" and his ensuing recommendation that I meet with my pastor confirms the "moat." Princes do not ordinarily meet with peasants. Yet I sensed a softening and more pastoral attitude despite his inability to see the contradiction between his desire "not to condemn or ostracize people who have such an orientation" and the relevant Church teaching that definitely does ostracize and condemn. He is obviously constrained from close contact with the peasantry and any dialogue about doctrine. Church structure promotes a climate of remoteness by the hierarchy that few seem able or desire to surmount.

My main goal in writing to the Cardinal was to achieve a bit more pastoral approach of the Church for excluded people. In particular, I tried to persuade him to make some kind of conciliatory outreach, or welcoming gesture to the gay community. My motivation included a hope that the Detroit archdiocese would initiate a welcoming, similar to what Bishop Terry Steib did in his diocese in Memphis, Tennessee.

---

own assessment of his problems is that he is more victim than offender. The details of his youth and his ensuing lack of sexual maturity are not uncommon among some young men and the outcome should not surprise us. It is a logical consequence of mandatory celibacy, at least for a segment of young persons committing their life to the priesthood.

Meeting the Cardinal

I was hoping to persuade the cardinal to at least indicate that gay people were welcome in the Detroit archdiocese. I would not ask him to risk any threats to Church teachings, just a little "welcome." He totally ignored my repeated pleas for such an action, despite the Memphis precedent.

Bishop Steib is cut from a different cloth. An obviously compassionate and pastoral man, he had lowered the drawbridge across his moat. He very publically acknowledged this when he wrote a letter to the people of his diocese, published in the *West Tennessee Catholic,* the Memphis Diocesan newspaper, on May 17, 2005. The letter received wide publicity due to its uniquely pastoral tone. I wanted to include here the letter Bishop Steib wrote in its entirety. It represents such a rare exception coming from a bishop, that I wanted to show that there is some "love at the top." However it was not to be.

When I contacted the Memphis diocese to request permission to include herein the Bishop's letter in its entirety, I was denied such permission. My conversation with the *West Tennessee Catholic* diocesan person issuing the denial and subsequent investigation through a local Memphis Catholic layperson, confirmed what I had expected. Even in this more pastoral place, fear dominates. The denial response and follow-up clearly indicated that the Bishop operates under the handicap that Rome frowns on his loving approach. The message is plainly:"Don't even hint at thwarting our rule." *Fear not?"* No, it's more *"Be careful bishop—we are watching you."* Fear is nurtured in the Roman Catholic Church at all levels. The bishop's staff was clearly saying to me: We cannot risk you rocking our boat."

Bishop Steib's letter described how he came to the realization that the Church is home and a community of faith, but that we are shutting out some of our family members from that home. He undertook an extremely unlikely thing. He personally met with some gay people and their families, and listened to their heart wrenching stories, concluding, that judgmental exclusion was not the way of Jesus. He resolved that he would initiate a ministry in his diocese to correct this offensive distortion, and said:

...We are called to *be* church to one another, to be God's family to one another. In giving us this Church, God has given us a spiritual home here on earth. This spiritual home is to be a precursor of the home we will have for eternity when all walls have come down and we are truly and completely dwelling in union with God and with one another. Our task while we are in this earthly home is to do all we can to help each other grow into the home we will share in heaven.

To be sure that we do not leave anyone behind, to be sure that all are welcome in their own home, and to be sure that we promote genuine gratitude and reverence for the gift that each one of us is to the Church, we have begun to lay the foundations for a diocesan ministry with Catholic gay and lesbian persons.

Bishop Steib concluded his lengthy letter by saying:

...The message of Jesus is clear: "Love one another as I have loved you." In my meetings with gay and lesbian Catholics, I told them that God does not withhold love from any of us. I believe that wholeheartedly. God's love is unconditional and that is the gift God offers us in Christ Jesus: the gift of loving each other with that same Godly and unconditional love.

Please pray for this ministry. Participate in the work of welcoming the entire family into the home which is our Church, where all are embraced by a God's unconditional love. Let us all dare to love as God loves. [29]

Powerful and welcoming words from this duke of the Church. Bishop Steib is an example of compassion and a pastoral attitude that fits my understanding of how our Church leaders should be leading. I fail to see how Rome could consider this man a "threat" or why they would ever want him to fear. On the contrary, his focus on God's love impressed me particularly. Unfortunately, he is a rare exception. While I know and have met a few others in the Church hierarchy who are similarly inclined, that cloud of threat is always on their horizon and their fear of a coming storm is real. It is a sad commentary on the *brood* posture in Rome.

It is my own observation, that these exceptional men often hold a different view from the official Church doctrine because they have come to know some gay people. Others have struggled to learn on their own simply by studying and being open and

---

29   The letter in its entirety can be viewed on the website: http://www.cdom.org/gayandlesbianpersons/news.htm

listening to opposing views. Some of them have gay siblings. I believe that some have changed over a lifetime mainly because of their own humility and a willingness to listen to the laity. It's been my experience that the Holy Spirit most often speaks to me through other people. I suspect that similarly, the Spirit attempts to speak to Church leaders often through the laity. To most of the magisterium, such an idea would be tantamount to heresy, despite the reality of historical precedent that change has most often come from below. Those bishops who do listen have frequently opened their ears to all sources of the Holy Spirit and embraced a desire to learn. They have not relied solely on the "infallible truth" mantra coming from Rome. These bishops are mostly regarded as renegades and do so at considerable risk to their own welfare, as Rome is consistently punitive toward anyone who is seen as straying from the Vatican line. Interesting to me is one unmistakable observation. All of these men who are "listeners" have one common characteristic. They all tend to display an exceptional awareness of the overriding unconditional love of God. Their conservative counterparts spew only a "crime and punishment" doctrine.

It is encouraging, that some of our bishops really do attempt to think independently, even while knowing that the absolute truth may be just beyond reach. Another example of this is contained in a letter written by a U.S. bishop to one of our Fortunate Families board members after meeting at a New Ways Ministry Conference. The two had exchanged letters about the non-pastoral nature of recent statements by the U.S. bishops on marriage. It reflects, I think, a sincere struggle to learn as opposed to rote reciting of magisterial dogma. Here is a bishop who is trying. He wrote in part to my fellow board member:

> Yes, I remember you telling me that I did not know my subject well at the New Ways Ministry Conference. I was more conscious of that than anyone. I had six months to write the talk. I started many times but ran into my basic problem. I then knew relatively little about homosexuality or the gay and lesbian communities.

I still don't, but nonetheless since that time, I have been drafting articles about the subject. However, I still can never satisfy myself. I am still at it, trying to write something that will set a good focus on same-sex couples and how we as Catholics should be open to them. I know a little bit more than two years ago, but still not enough to go into print. Each draft ends before I can get what I feel will convince me of what might be said.

I link that with the experience I had with a high school candidate preparing for confirmation. I asked the question: As a Catholic, how do you react to hearing about homosexuals? "They are human, just as we are" was the reply. "Right on," I said. That is where we must start.

To be candid, I do not agree with what some have said: "We are all God's children, all made by God, we should be considered the same as other couples." Yet I am also convinced that we bishops have not yet gotten to the very heart of the whole issue.

Say a prayer for me. If I do get the draft written, I will send it to you for a critique. I am closer to it but not there yet.

This bishop is struggling to understand. He recognizes at least his own need to do some critical thinking. The exchange between Cardinal Maida and me, on the other hand, reflects the bunker mentality so common in the broader Church. The refusal to take responsibility for the consequences of their stance or even engage in dialogue is arrogant and hypocritical. The very real promotion of violence and discrimination, stemming from a dogmatically proclaimed demeaning doctrine, even when dispensed in sincerity, is a sad distortion of the message of Jesus to "Love one another, as I have loved you." People are being led toward violence, wittingly or otherwise.

In early fall 2005, the Vatican issued a document[30] in which it called for an investigation of Catholic seminaries in the United

---

30   Cardinal Zenon Grocholewski, *Congregation For Catholic Education, Instruction Concerning the Criteria for the Discernment of Vocations with regard to Persons with Homosexual Tendencies in view of their Admission to the Seminary and to Holy Orders,*

States to cull out all who might have homosexual orientation. The clear intent was to place the blame for the ongoing sexual abuse scandal squarely on the backs of gay clergy. The Vatican pronouncement was highlighted in an article in the *Detroit Free Press*. It sparked an emotional letter to the editor from me. I wrote in part:

Our Catholic Church's latest announcement that it intends to purge homosexual persons from the priesthood as a reaction to the sexual abuse crisis is simply an amazing and arrogant display of ignorance regarding human sexuality. The obvious conclusion the Vatican would have us accept is that homosexuality equates to a risk of sexual abuse of minors. The implicit assumption is that since more boys were abused than girls, the problem is basically homosexuality. Such a stance is not supported by current understanding of this problem by relevant professionals and reflects a shallow understanding of the underlying factors in the sexual abuse of minors. This position by the Church is not new. It is longstanding and is reflected by the Vatican's past ill-advised admonitions against any homosexual's employment in an environment involving children. It also seems implicit that either heterosexuals are somehow devoid of such flaws of character, or that abuse of young girls is definitely less serious. One could argue that this logic, which aims to make the priesthood exclusively heterosexual, would result in the abuse only of girls, and that this would be a distinct improvement from current conditions. As the father of five daughters, I find that thought particularly reprehensible. It sometimes seems to me that the Church's entire understanding of human sexuality has not progressed much beyond the fourth century, and it steadfastly insists on maintaining this state of ignorance.

This latest ludicrous launching from the Vatican reinforces the belief that all homosexual persons are potential child abusers. That would necessarily include my son. Such idiotic stances

November 4, 2005, http://www.vatican.va/roman_curia/congregations/ccatheduc/documents/rc_con_ccatheduc_doc_20051104_istruzione_en.html.

are further fuel for those inclined toward violence against gay and lesbian people, and any bland commentary by the Church denying an accessory responsibility for such violence is simple denial and hypocritical in the extreme. This is a blatant philosophy of violence and bigotry.

I am deeply troubled by the Church's actions. My family and many friends feel similarly. Labeling God's creation as "disordered and intrinsically inclined toward evil" is an abuse no less violent than that of the Inquisition. I'm sure that the perpetrators of that terrible ancient injustice were equally sure of their righteousness, just as the Church is today in their teachings on homosexual persons. While much of the Church's past reflects some great and holy accomplishments, my reading of history also recalls many grave errors and terrible injustices that she inflicted on society for which we now wince, wonder, and apologize. Will future generations also wince and wonder about us? It seems the magisterium continues the erroneous conviction that the Holy Spirit speaks only to them. Nevertheless, we parents hear from Him also, and His message is pretty clear and insistent.

The letter evoked no response from the *Free Press*, but it stablished a relationship for a future resource as a Catholic parent of a gay child.

My gay son has not gone without his own protests against injustice toward gay people by the Church. In some ways, he has written off the Catholic Church. He maintains an ongoing Christian life, often engaging in unheralded charity toward his neighbor, yet he will not accommodate a Catholic alliance or any other denomination. Institutional religion has become anathema. Recently, when approached to continue his support of a Catholic charity, he responded in a manner that illustrates well his mindset. It is a reflection of his hurt and the sense of rejection experienced by most gay Catholics, and indeed many of his gay non-Catholic contemporaries. He wrote:

Dear Father Kohler,   November 30, 2005

In years past, it has given me some joy to think that my financial contribution to your annual children's Christmas party has
contributed in some small way to bring happiness to the participating children. It is with some sadness therefore, that I must
decline your request to contribute again this year.

Please consider: After many years of personal spiritual and
emotional turmoil, I found Dignity Detroit's weekly masses at
Most Holy Trinity to be a great source of solace and reconciliation with God. These were truly an experience of God's Spirit
of love. It was very hurtful, therefore, to be effectively kicked
out by the very Church that I would expect to promote such an
experience.

This same Church has now chosen to support and invest
in a political campaign of slander and attack against the loving committed partnership I have with my partner of fourteen
years. These attacks have been promoted in spite of overwhelming scientific evidence showing that a homosexual orientation
is neither chosen nor unnatural in any way. This scientific evidence is coupled with recent exegesis revealing that there is no
biblical basis for a condemnation of such homosexual partner-
ships. In fact, it seems that there are indeed scriptural refer-
ences to some such historical same-sex relationships as being
exemplary of God's Spirit of love.

If the Catholic Church were merely guilty of a willful refusal
to recognize these facts, and of failing to fulfill its role of spiritual leadership by educating the public about them, I would
consider it negligent. But our Church has gone well beyond
negligence by choosing instead to proactively support the politics of hate surrounding the issue. This shameful injustice has
caused me and many like me a great deal of hurt. To commit
such offenses under the guise of restoring morality to our culture adds a great deal of insult to the injury!

I hope you can understand, therefore, why I feel that a
request for financial support from any organization affiliated
with the Catholic Church at this time greatly overestimates my

capacity for forgiveness—although I will continue to pray for the grace to achieve this. I must conclude that if our archdiocese has half a million dollars to fund such vicious attacks, it does not need my small contribution for anything. I have chosen instead to direct what financial support I can offer to The Plan, a secular group dedicated to working to improve the lives of impoverished children and their families around the globe.

In the heartfelt hope that we can one day heal these wounds together I am,

Sincerely,
Mark Nelson

My son speaks well. My girls could speak just as eloquently about their own hurt. When I consider their view, I realize that the affliction I experience with my Church goes beyond its denigration of the gay community. It goes beyond a fallacious understanding of human sexuality. I am constantly challenged to maintain my calm when I consider the Church's stance on women. The Church's discrimination against gay people is matched by its doctrinally biased view of women as a second-class gender. These two issues, the Church's homophobic and misogynistic doctrines, are definitely at the center of my personal radar screen. I think there is a logical reason for such abusive ignorance. The dividing gulf between peasant and prince has resulted from it. It has spawned many failings. That reason is, I believe, simply celibacy.

Chapter 16

Celibacy

"Celibacy, like the fly in the heart of an apple, dwells in perpetual sweetness, but sits alone, and is confined and dies in singularity; but marriage, like the useful bee, builds a house, and gathers sweetness from every flower, and labors and unites"
—*JEREMY TAYLOR, CIRCA 1648*[31]

A m I a Catholic? Some of my friends ask that question and my answer is usually circuitous and probably confusing. Some of my readers at this point might be asking a similar question. My more traditional friends would argue that I have effectively left the Church, or perhaps simply that I am a heretic— a view that I consider personifies the problem with the Church today. My answer can best be described by stating that I am less of a "Roman Catholic" and more of a "Roaming Catholic." While this description fits in with our being members of Holy Trinity Episcopal Church in Manistee, Michigan, it also fits my mindset. I presumptuously go where the Spirit leads.

---

31   Anglican, Writer and Bishop, 1613-1667

Joining the Episcopal congregation at Holy Trinity came about after we withdrew from the Catholic parish near our home in Manistee. The Catholic pastor there bluntly, and with the usual conservative certitude, affronted our sensibilities with a very homophobic homily one Sunday. In essence, he proclaimed that our gay sons were a fundamental evil, of whom all should be wary. When we spoke with him after Mass and related our feelings as the parents of gay children, his response offended us. We heard only reiteration of the usual demeaning Church rhetoric and doctrine, emphasizing that homosexual relationships are evil. He employed no pastoral sensitivity; no empathy. It forced us to conclude that we could find no spiritual sustenance in such a place.

We joined Holy Trinity as a result and quickly experienced a distinctly opposite stance. Not only was Holy Trinity a welcoming community, but as an added bonus, the pastor was a married women and a former Catholic. She had wanted all her life to be a priest, but of course, her Roman Church would not even allow discussion of such a doctrinal affront. (Heavens, she was not only female, but she was also married!) This woman proved to be a marvelous homilist, and an effective leader of a very warm and welcoming congregation. It was certainly a unique experience for us—pleasant in every way.

Mostly, our experience at Holy Trinity differs little from our Roman one. Episcopal liturgy is almost identical to the Catholic version. Indeed, at Holy Trinity we kneel at the altar rail for the Eucharist, which was the traditional Catholic approach prior to Vatican II. Some of the prayers are unique and the music is quite different. The latter is something of the Roman Church that I miss at Holy Trinity, but it probably stems from my lack of familiarity with the music, a factor that I expect will change with time. Liturgical rubrics differ obviously, but other palpable differences are more important. One of these is the overriding ambience of welcoming acceptance and inclusiveness. It highlights the Holy Trinity experience. There is an ambience of love. The nearby Catholic Church lacks such enlightenment.

I recently had the startling experience of hearing a homily at this little church that related the story of a gay man's struggle of coming out to his parents and their ensuing rejection of him. Our pastor homilist was declaring from the pulpit that such homophobic behavior was not a Christian response and certainly not one espoused by the Episcopal Church. Never before, in more than seventy-five years of listening to Sunday sermons, have I ever heard such a relevant voice of justice for the homosexual person. Indeed, it was the first time I've ever heard anything from the pulpit about gay people that was loving or reflective of real-life experience. I think this experience all stems from a married clergy more than any doctrinal stance. Celibacy is not a requirement for the Episcopal priesthood.

The Episcopal Church hierarchy has a cognizance, an intellectual reality that is absent in their Catholic counterparts. Long ago, the Episcopal Church in America accomplished a reform that the Roman Church will not even consider acceptable for dialogue. The Episcopalians allow woman priests, married clergy, openly gay bishops in committed relationships, and a governing structure that embodies lay participation. The Episcopal Church appears much less concerned about conformity of doctrine and the sacrosanct absolute (infallible) truth that characterizes the Catholic position. Definitely the most noteworthy and fundamental difference from my Catholic environment is that the Episcopal Church has opted for a noncelibate clergy.

My personal experience with Episcopal priests reinforces my views that celibacy is an affliction for the Roman Church. The current pastor of Holy Trinity in Manistee, Father Michael Bell, is a good example. He does not hide in some private rectory, alone and sheltered from the surrounding community. On the contrary, this man and his wife both make a serious effort to connect with their neighbors, church members or not. They both obviously consider that reaching out to the community is an integral part of their mutual ministry. It is a part of their routine. Father Mike is a mature man with a fine sense of humor, a keen intellect, and a welcoming spirit. His wife, Nann, has a similar loving nature. They are fun people to be with, and they are not distant from the ordinary.

Shortly after he came to Holy Trinity, Father Mike undertook a unique personal civic mission to cultivate communication with ordinary folks. He made time in his busy schedule to commiserate with his fellow man, something he obviously deems important. Every week, he spends two hours on Friday morning at the local coffee shop simply to offer himself in conversation with his neighbors. Subjects for conversation are the choice of the visitor—or they can just play a game of Scrabble. This example of reaching out to the average person is a product of an environment set in real life. It is a stark contrast to the protected "by appointment only" routine of most Catholic settings. You can knock on Father Mike's door anytime, no appointment needed. If he's not there to help you, chances are Nan will. Our celibate Catholic clergy keep themselves tightly confined from the rest of us. Aristocracy does not pursue discourse with peasantry. The higher the rank, the greater the isolation and remoteness.

When was the last time anyone saw a Catholic bishop speaking with a common layperson? For me it has only happened with Bishop Thomas Gumbleton of Detroit. He is a person who has been able to resist the adulation and pomp of his rank. It is characteristic of him to maintain close contact with the lowly laity. Unfortunately, his resulting sense of reality, his pastoral persona, and the consequent impact on what he speaks has caused an obvious rejection of him by his Roman superiors. He does not toe the party line and is often persona non grata by the local bishop when invited to speak at some lay-sponsored event. He was punished by Rome following his testimony favoring an Ohio legislative effort to extend the statute of limitations for crimes of sexual abuse. The Curia accused him of violating the solidarity of *communio episcoporum*. Translation: "You're threatening the old boys' club." His punishment: Early retirement, removal as pastor of Saint Leo's, and he could no longer speak publicly without prior approval of the local bishop. Rome had spoken.

I would say that Bishop Gumbleton is one of those bright exceptions to what celibacy in the Catholic Church normally produces. There are other exceptions, of course, and they are not few, but it seems that somehow the Episcopal Church has managed to avoid the pitfall of celibate isolation. Also, they do not seem to have an Episcopal version of the old boys' club. Perhaps the inclusion of women has been helpful.

Were Episcopal leaders listening to the Holy Spirit? Were their Catholic counterparts listening? Once more, I sometimes think our Catholic leaders feel they don't *need* to listen. They seem to believe they virtually *are* the Holy Spirit. My Episcopal brethren obviously believe that the Holy Spirit speaks to us all, as opposed to the Roman concept of papal primacy. Pope John XXIII would probably have said that the Episcopalians have adeptly opened their windows to a refreshing breeze.

Not long after our move to Holy Trinity, and we founded the PFLAG Manistee group, Holy Trinity Church quickly offered its facility to hold our monthly meetings. It is something that would be unheard of in a Catholic Church. We are very happy with our experience in this small faith community. It is a very loving congregation. We also found some new and different things in the Episcopal environment. One was everyone wearing his or her own nametag on Sunday. It is a very helpful memory aid, particularly for us senior citizens, and facilitates a unique family atmosphere that would be difficult to match in our much larger Catholic gatherings. Our association with Holy Trinity and PFLAG has resulted in the beginning of work with other peace and justice groups in the area. It expanded our involvement in directions we had never planned.

This setting is one to which I think the Holy Spirit has led us. Holy Trinity's support of our PFLAG initiative is not a minor thing to us. Manistee is a small (population 6,500), blue-collar town, about 60 to 65 percent Catholic, and quite conservative; the opportunity for our PFLAG work is blatant and difficult. We have managed to draw a good portion of gay and lesbian kids to our group, but very few parents. The young people come because they are desperate for some form of support. The parents don't come because they are cowed by a faith and a culture that demonizes their gay children and preaches a homophobic rhetoric. Parents are terrified of being "outed." They are afraid to peek out of their closets; it is plain to see the fear, and the fear is a family affair. One young gay man telling his story at a recent PFLAG meeting related the struggle his parents had in accepting his announcement of his sexuality. He said, "My mom said to me, 'OK. So you're gay.

Well, fine, but how do you feel about the prospect of spending an eternity in hell?'" One can easily empathize with the angst of this parent and the pain inflicted on the child. It is a product of a faith built on fear, not love. It is a product of a celibate-led Church whose leaders have fallen into the proverbial "fortress mentality" and walled themselves off from reality. They are too often oblivious of the pain and hurt they inflict with their academic stance and righteous aloofness. They are incapable of understanding the effects of their dogmatic dictums and how far they've strayed from the love that Jesus proclaimed.

The loving gratitude shown toward Linda and me by PFLAG Manistee people has been overwhelming to us. We have managed to speak to some of the local public school teachers about school bullying, and have listened to the woes of some friends in nearby Ludington who are engaged in housing homeless kids. Some of these are young teenagers who have been rejected by their families and thrown out of their homes simply because they are gay. How can any legitimate Jesus-based faith justify such unloving actions?

We have been amazed at the number of other homeless people in such small communities. We had envisioned such problems as only a big city issue. Our learning and participation in community work is ongoing and intense. We have worked with several of the local Protestant communities who have warmly welcomed our endeavors. Indeed, the local Peace and Justice group gave us an award for our work in the community for LGBT people. It has inspired us with an increased enthusiasm for our commitment to not only the LGBT cause, but the broader community as well.

Throughout this experience, we were disappointed at the absence of the Catholic community from any participation in interfaith activities. Catholics are nowhere to be seen in efforts for charitable work in cooperation with other communities of faith. Whether justified or not, it projects an air of Catholic clannishness at best. While Protestant ministers get together for collective efforts on Manistee community needs, their Catholic counterparts reject or ignore invitations to participate. It is another manifestation of the Catholic practice to be exclusionary. It is a caste mentality—"us-against-them,"— and hardly a love-your-neighbor approach.

In defense the local Catholic priest, however, he is probably too overworked to join in. The local Catholic community has only one priest and one part-time assistant to handle the work of three parishes and the large Catholic population. This condition is a recent affliction due to the combination of the demise of three former pastors (old age) and the declining number of Catholic priests. It's definitely a harbinger of drastic changes to come.

Why are we suffering the debilitating loss from the priesthood? It is sad enough that celibacy promotes class distinctions and isolation of the clergy; but worse, fewer and fewer men are accepting the invitation to participate in the vaunted vocation of the priesthood. Some would argue that one major reason is quite simply the requirement for mandatory celibacy. Not surprisingly, our modern, more educated laity tends to reject the prospect of a life devoid of a loving relationship. Education is often a two-edged sword. It is easy to see from the large number of former priests, who are now married, that celibacy is a major concern for those considering the priesthood. It's definitely a contributing factor. Few would argue that aspect of celibacy.

"Marriage may often be a stormy lake, but celibacy is almost always a muddy horse pond"—Thomas Love Peacock, 1785–1866, English satirist and author

Celibacy has other negative impacts that are even more damaging. One may argue, and I would agree, that there are many clergy who successfully practice celibacy and live, in diverse ways, an outstanding and holy life. Indeed, I have known many such dedicated and wonderful clergy over the years who are obviously leading sensitive, compassionate, loving, and happy lives. Indeed, some of my best friends today exemplify celibacy at its best. Their lived examples of goodness in their ordained vocations would seem to defy any attempt at denigration of celibacy. Thomas Merton and Mother Theresa are celebrity examples of lives of celibate people who learned to love. Yet even they, despite their admitted perfection, did not experience intimate human love. Their alternative perfection is rare. There may be many such—many of whom I am unaware. My experience is limited.

Being celibate does not mean that no celibate person can ever learn to love or that celibacy per se is always a tragedy in process. I recognize that life is not that simple. I cannot know what the celibate who has achieved a modicum of perfection has experienced. I only know that person has missed intimate human love, whether it be a perfection to spiritual growth, or a detriment.

Yet, despite the reality of celibate success, it does not follow that celibate persons are unequivocally well equipped to minister as pastoral persons to the sea of Catholic laity. Nor does it follow that bishops and others of the hierarchy are better suited for their mission through the state of celibacy. The argument that the celibate state affords one an undistracted focus on the spiritual, is more than offset by the negative consequences of denying the clergy the reality of their sexuality and the experience of loving another human being. I stated earlier my belief that the core of celibacy's flaw is the denial of the experience of an intimate human relationship. Loving is so fundamental to the human condition that to deny it means for most, to inflict a stunting of the most basic of human learning. Loving is the essence of life.

I do not maintain that celibacy always denies a person the ability to know and comprehend love; it just makes it a great deal harder to learn, harder to achieve. For many it makes it impossible. It also separates the celibate into a class removed, and establishes the culture of clericalism, which has spawned so much evil. The subject of clericalism is beyond the scope of this book, but it is clear that celibacy promotes *isolation* and invents a fantasy world devoid of human reality. It is based on mostly academic theories and assumptions. It posits the stance that celibate clergy are fundamentally superior to the laity—separated from us ordinary folks, and they exist on a higher moral plane.

Celibacy, as an institutionally imposed affliction, is simply contrary to a Jesus-centered Christianity. It is reflective of a tribal mentality that divides the human family into separate and often opposing factions. It is essentially an anti-community concept that makes loving one another a remote possibility at best. If love is the core of Jesus' message, then not loving is antithetical to teaching love, a task that would seem primary to an ideal priesthood.

How can the loveless comprehend love? One would not expect to learn how to fly from a flight instructor who has not first flown thousands of hours himself. When I recall the ineffective attempt by a priest-counselor to help Trish and me during a critical time in our marriage, and my wife's negative reaction to his approach, I realize the difficult and often futile task for a celibate person to comprehend the issues in intimate relationships in any realistic way. The effectiveness of the institutional Church and its mission is diminished by mandatory celibacy, not enhanced by it. At the very least, it should be optional. As a serious distortion of the human condition, not a perfection of it, celibacy can be an obstacle to holiness and effective ministry to people in the real world. It is essentially a fantasy and it is the source of nearly all the other ills that have produced the sad state of the Roman Catholic Church today. It is the cornerstone of the "old boys' club," the hidden reality, the reality behind the rule.

The hierarchy would undoubtedly deny any association with celibacy and the sexual abuse scandal. Yet celibacy has been termed the greatest perversion of human sexuality, and the abuse scandal certainly reflects perversion. I'm not an expert on the subject, but it would seem likely that the celibate priesthood would tend to attract those who are sexually immature and it likely promotes an environment that enshrines such tendencies. Some psychologists state that sexual repression will often amplify one's sexual drive and result in distorted sexual obsessions. Rome's pathetic 2005 analysis that the cause of sexual abuse is gay priests ignores such probabilities and simply exposes the Vatican's ignorance. There are no studies to support their conclusion, and there is much evidence to refute it. In 2001, the American Psychological Association stated: "Despite a common myth, homosexual men are not more likely to sexually abuse children than heterosexual men are." [32]

Various pundits will argue otherwise, but they mostly have some antigay ax to grind. The APA would seem innocent of that flaw. My view is that the sexual abuse of minors is rooted in a severely stunted sexual psyche. In the Catholic priesthood, as dictated by

---

32 *Understanding Child Sexual Abuse: Education, Prevention, and Recovery*, APA 2001

Rome, the celibate environment attracts the sexually immature and nurtures immaturity in a make-believe world without sex. I'm inclined to agree that celibacy is a perversion, not an enhanced state of humanity. Celibacy realistically, is just one more obstacle to a vibrant priesthood for the Catholic Church.

I have some firsthand knowledge of the sexually immature cleric. Two of my daughters were molested when they were young girls by a Catholic priest who was a close friend of our family as we were all growing up. He was in many ways an effective priest and a good man, yet he was an abuser who eventually left the priesthood. I don't know the extent of his abuse—whether there were others beyond my girls who suffered his disturbing behavior. Fortunately, his unwanted sexual advances to my girls were firmly rejected by them and because of their own maturity, left no indelible scars—at least to my knowledge. It was not until years after the fact that the girls disclosed the abuse to me. When I questioned them about it, their comment was, "Dad, in some ways he's just an immature little boy."

My argument is not to equate celibacy with child sexual abuse, but rather to argue that celibacy is not a normal human state and most certainly not a superior one. On the contrary, it is an institutional affliction that is a distortion of reality. Rather than mandating celibacy, the Church should instead endeavor to establish a "normal" environment to attract normal people into the ordained ministry. Celibacy is not an advantage; it surely must be an attraction for those wishing to escape their sexuality and is, at best, a handicap to normalcy. The extent of the Church's adolescent sexual psyche among the clergy is dramatized by the broadness of the sexual abuse scandal. In a recent address, David Clohessy, founder of SNAP (Survivors Network of those Abused by Priests), stated unequivocally that the magnitude of abusers has been vastly underreported. His data project the number of abusers at 10 percent of the priesthood. This is far more than what our bishops admit.

Human sexuality in the magisterium's perspective is all premised on the dualistic conviction that the body and our human inclinations are evil. However, this is in contradiction to our belief in the Creator's observation, "and it is good." Male supremacy, misogyny, and celibacy concepts go hand-in-hand and have been haunting the Church for a long time. Historic backpedaling is not confined to such infamous errors as the Galileo affair. It has a significantly broader prevalence. Much has been written about the "Pastoral Rule" of Pope Gregory the Great in the sixth century, and whether or not he equated sexual pleasure within marriage with serious sin. Gregory's and the Church's defenders lament that we take things out of context to draw such conclusions. Yet, his words were plain: "The pleasure itself cannot be without sin." This commonly quoted phrase reflects a mindset of the time that seems ludicrous today. Despite legalistic contemporary arguments defending Pope Gregory, the traditional Catholic understanding of marriage is obviously distorted from reality by a celibate comprehension of it.

It should not be surprising that some men who are denied the most basic human relational experience will undoubtedly confront sexual distortions or maturity issues at some point. I am not an expert and I would not venture that I possess unique understanding. (I'm *ordinary*.) Despite this reality, I have formed some convictions about sex, a by-product of nearly sixty years of marital experience. I believe that, while sexual intercourse between loving spouses may be an ultimate expression of love, it is also an ultimate form of human communication allowing us to know the beloved. To love, one must first *know*. Knowing intimately is the honey in that flower we are attracted to by the sexual.

> *"Sex is communication, but only if what you want to communicate is unconditional acceptance."*[33]

The sexual drive under any circumstances is a very powerful human passion, which most folks struggle to control, even in legitimate circumstances. Certainly, the celibate state involves some

---

33 Bernard Apfelbaum, *Sexual Reality and How We Dismiss It*, presented as part of the panel, *What is Sex For?* Annual meeting, American Association of the Advancement of Science, San Francisco State University, November 1984, http://www.bapfelbaumphd.com/Sexual_Reality.html.

very difficult demands. The sexual repression involved confronts the individual with unique challenges that some do not handle well. The sexual abuse scandal reflects this reality, which Church leaders have yet to confront. The probability is that the abuse of minor children will continue. It is not a matter of <u>whether</u> our children are safe now (following Church pseudo-reform); it is more a question of, <u>how</u> safe our children are now?

Repression of the sexual drive and its effect on learning to love is not without consequences. Deny a person the experience of intimacy and human love for a lifetime and the resulting void will often as not produce sad distortions, not only in the persona, but also in the perception of reality. Those who are long celibate will tend to misunderstand the ancillary nature that sexual intercourse plays in intimate relationships. A limited academic perspective is the norm. If you haven't loved, chances are, you don't know love. If you haven't loved, the sexual aspect can seem very dominant. The more important characteristics of the unconditional giving of self and the overriding desire to serve the beloved have to be experienced to be understood. There is joy in loving, and it surpasses and is little related to sex. The celibate mindset certainly seems likely to contribute to the Roman obsession with genital-focused mores in human relations.

Human sexuality and relationships as understood and taught by the Church magisterium seem presumptuous at best and certainly don't correlate with my own experience of many years as a married person. At this point in my life, much of it strikes me as rather humorous. Labored arguments based on esoteric concepts of natural law are proclaimed as absolute truths. Often, natural law seems anything but natural. The definitions of these propositions are reserved as competent only to the magisterium. Not even theologians are deemed competent if they hint at any new understanding. Anyone who disagrees with the magisterium is simply said to be "not Catholic." End of conversation. Rome has spoken.

For me, Jesus Christ's law supersedes all other law, even Vatican law. It is the law of loving. I would also argue that it is a *natural* law for humans to love. For Church leaders to maintain that the natural law surrounding human sexuality is only understood by them is quite arrogant and absurd. Indeed, it seems that it is *least* understood by them. Lately, the Vatican has moved to the even more absurd position that certain issues may not even be discussed. I suspect that this precept is born out of fear—fear of reform, fear of the loss of control. It certainly reflects a denial of the possibility of any new knowledge—an absurd position. Interestingly, a married priesthood and women priests are two of those forbidden topics.

One could argue that Jesus was celibate and thus celibacy is the ultimate. Yet Jesus loved beyond any of us lesser souls. Admittedly, it is clearly evident that many celibate persons do in fact achieve a superior level of loving devoid of the sexual. Nevertheless, it is not a universal in the clerical world, nor does it seem to be the norm. It is also germane to note, that some biblical scholars describe their frustration over the limited knowledge we have concerning the historical Jesus. What really was Mary Magdalene's "special" relationship with Jesus? It's a moot point, perhaps, but there is no clear evidence that Jesus would prescribe celibacy for the priesthood today. Indeed, seven of the twelve apostles were married.

Celibacy, as a practical matter, in some ways is conducive to deceit. The sexual abuse scandal and attendant hierarchical cover-up is a classic example of such deceit, but it is also quite evident from a variety of studies [34] that celibacy defined as sexual abstinence is a facade for a large component of the clergy—estimated as high as fifty percent. Many who advertise as celibate are not. It is almost a joke. Sexual drive is a potent human appetite that entails considerable maturity to control. Failure to control it can breed multiple difficulties, which in turn, often leads to denial. Denial can lead to deceit. Once you lie, however, the sequence is bigger and bigger lies to conceal the initial falsehood. Soon deceit becomes so endemic that it is no longer recognized as deceit. The Roman Catholic Church is suffering from just such an affliction and is in dire need of a hearty dose of honesty. It will first require humility and reform.

Unfortunately, human sexuality is poorly understood at best and is not something readily attainable from any book. Sexuality

---

34 National Catholic Reporter, 4-28-2010, *Secret Sex in the Celibate System,* *Richard Sipe*

and human relationships are, for most of us, learned only from experience, and even then, the lessons are tenuous and obscure. Beyond that, few of us learn to truly love one another, even after a long lifetime. But if one is celibate, deprived of the experience of loving another human being, and burdened by the denial of one's own sexuality, the task seems virtually insurmountable.

Celibacy inherently promotes self-focus as one struggles to achieve an unnatural sexless existence, devoid of concern for a beloved. Because the human sexual drive is one of the most powerful passions and is difficult to control at best, Church efforts would be better directed toward efforts at improving our understanding of this proclivity and how to control it, rather than condemning nearly all aspects of a God-given nature.

Celibate males won't get this, but that does not negate what I am convinced is the reality: from celibacy, all other errors emanate. No meaningful reform is possible nor has ever been possible in the centuries of Church history without the experience of unconditional love for another human being. Love is the essence of the Jesus message and the chief characteristic that differentiates Him from the rest of us.

While I have known many celibate clergy in my lifetime, I have also known a few unmarried lay bachelors of many years. I have no way of knowing whether these men were sexually celibate just that they were celibate in the sense of not being married. They were clearly not in loving relationships. It has been my observation that these folks generally share a common trait unrelated to their non-clerical vocations, but more typical of their protracted single status. Their condition is similar to many of their celibate clerical counterparts. The common characteristic I have seen is a prominent self-focus of which they seem totally unaware. In colloquial terms it's called "the bachelor mentality." It took me a while to recognize the syndrome, and deduce the cause. To a man, it became obvious to me that what separated me from the long-term bachelor was the relationship that they did not have, but I did. It affected the very core of who they were.

One encounter I had as a younger man, impressed me greatly. I witnessed the case of a certain bachelor who finally married after many years of the single life. Before he married, he was generally recognized by his colleagues as something of a boor, an odd ball who just seemed detached from social reality and very self-focused. When he married, the subsequent transformation of his personality was rapid and startling. It was a dramatic change that astonished most of his friends and me. It took me years to understand what had happened to him. I ultimately realized that the impact of his new encounter with intimate human relationship was the cause of his amazing renaissance into a more loving, sensitive, and compassionate person. His new state enabled him to become a much more social person; a delightful person. I see a similar scenario displayed in our celibate priesthood, but devoid the positive outcome.

Yes, celibacy in the Catholic Church is proclaimed a sublime state. However, this self-ennobling perspective is one of the chief reasons that women are demeaned into second-class stature and celibate males preserve patriarchy as the cornerstone of the "old boys' club." It is critical to maintaining clericalism, the essence of the aristocracy. Gays are defined as disordered. Sexuality is reduced to an unfortunate fundamental of our nature, necessary for procreation, but mostly an affliction. Marriage is only for man and woman, entailing a sexual function needed for preservation of the human race—a necessary evil. In the hierarchy of values, what poses as a Church concern for love between spouses is offset by the conviction that marriage is definitely inferior to celibacy, and married people must follow the proscribed rules devised by the celibate on how to express one's sexuality.

The perspective that not loving is superior to loving goes a long way back and is part of a systemic distortion of human sexuality. From it flows the Church's misogyny. Any objective assessment of church history clearly reveals the lunacy of some of our Church's doctrinal proclamations. Women can't be ordained because they're the wrong sex. (Again, note Saint Thomas Aquinas, calling women "misbegotten males.") You have to have the right genitalia. Such a position will not be easily corrected. But make no mistake: this conviction about women still prevails, however subtle or denied.

Celibacy must cease before women will be ordained and misogyny ended. It is disingenuous to argue that the Church respects women as equals, or that Jesus' mother Mary is the proper role model. It is plainly obvious that women are not considered equal to men. The persistence of this historical position is manifested by the pope's recent declaration that we are forbidden even to discuss women's ordination. In the beginning of the twentieth century, when women's suffrage was being debated, it was opposed by many religious groups, but none more stridently than the Roman Catholic Church. It was plain to see that women's suffrage was seen as a threat. "Give them the vote, and the next thing they'll think they're equal to men" was the equivalent mantra. Celibacy and misogyny go hand in hand. Claims for a biblical basis are simply misleading mendacity.

There is less biblical support for the second-class categorization of women than there is for the support of slavery. Obfuscation and deceit disguised as God's will is still deceit. The misogynistic denigration of women fits right in with mandatory celibacy. The reality is that any relenting of this stance would risk destruction of the "old boys' club," and the hierarchy will not let that happen. Any discussion of the topic risks excommunication. So girls, put your hats back on, sit down, and be quiet. It's rather like asking a battered wife to tolerate an abusive spouse. (Marriage is for life.)

My own experience with married clergy and women priests is mostly with my Episcopal Church friends. It has been uniformly positive and has dramatically demonstrated the unique gifts women bring to the worship scene. If the magisterium were truly searching for truth, it would do well to consult its Episcopal brethren about the status of women.

Gays lesbians and other "sexually different" folks will also be denied the full love of Christ by the Church until it accepts the universality of the demand for loving relationships. The Church needs to understand that God created some people gay and that they too were created to love. Clearly, such loving is anathema according to Church doctrine. Here too, celibacy hinders understanding.

The celibate magisterium has even more difficulty handling sexual differences. The transgender don't exist; intersex is the source of special bafflement. The demand for the conformity to the Church-sponsored male-female heterosexual natural law concept defies the reality of the diversity in God's creation. God does not create uniformity, but seems to revel in diversity. Perhaps it's why we have so many different religions all addressing the same Almighty. On the other hand, celibacy explains the morph of the Catholic hierarchy into the aristocratic old boys' club, which focuses on the preservation of a patriarchal mindset and all the abuses that stem from it. If deceit is required to maintain it, then so be it.

All of which might lead the reader to ask, "If that's the way you feel, why don't you just leave the Catholic Church?" It's a question characteristic of the conservative elite. I have considered that question all the while I have also longed for and worked toward reform of the Church. To my conservative friends, I suggest they spend a little time studying Church history and try to exert some critical thinking in the process. I fail to see how an unbiased reading of Church history can support many of the outlandish Church claims as the sole possessor of infallible absolute truth.

No, I haven't left the Church. I've mostly stayed because of the gifted presence in my life of so many marvelous lay friends and exceptional clergy. I've stayed because I still find spiritual nourishment there. But more than that, I have lately come to realize that the reform I am praying for may already be happening. Nay, perhaps it *has* happened. I have been slow to recognize it. What I see that has happened is the impotent hierarchy has withdrawn, whimpering into their sheltered castles and pulled the drawbridge up behind them—firing off occasional defensive salvos of harsh condemning rhetoric. They have effectively cut themselves off from the rest of us and retreated into their little boys' club, enshrouded by a cloak of irrelevance while laypeople move on. They play their royal game of chess in their regal robes, sans any queen or princesses. They may get their media exposure, but most people in the pews are ignoring them[35]. I feel a sense of destiny to stay and work for reform in such an environment.

---

35   e.g. Estimates indicate 98% of Catholics reject Church teaching on contraception and nearly 70% approve of some form of same sex marriage. There are plenty of other areas where the laity reject the bishop's thinking.

A recent development among the laity, and the Church's reaction to it, illustrates the celibate bunker mentality. It is the formation of the ACC, the American Catholic Council.[36] ACC states on its website that:

American Catholic Council is a movement bringing together a network of individuals, organizations, and communities to consider the state and future of our Church. We believe our Church is at a turning point in its history. We recall the promise of the Second Vatican Council for a renaissance of the roles and responsibilities of all the Baptized through a radically inclusive and engaged relationship between the Church and the World. We respond to the Spirit of Vatican II by summoning the Baptized together to demonstrate our re-commitment. We seek personal conversion to renew our Church to conform to the authentic Gospel message, the teachings of our Church, and our lived context in the United States. Our reading of the "signs of the times," as we experience them in the U.S., our plan and our agenda are set out in our *Declaration.* We educate; we listen; we facilitate discussions and encounters; and, we build toward an American Catholic Council that will convene in Detroit over Pentecost weekend in June of 2011. At this Council we hope to proclaim our belief in the *Rights and Responsibilities* of U.S. Catholics.

The celibate hierarchy has no interest in what the laity thinks. It has already determined that ACC is not "Catholic." It hasn't come from Rome. Archbishop Vigneron quickly issued an edict "against participating in the American Catholic Council local listening sessions and national gathering."[37] The edict also included a proscription against any church in the archdiocese allowing ACC to use its facilities. It was followed by a directive to all clergy that any who might be entertaining the idea of attending the ACC conference would face potential dismissal if they did. The archbishop

---

36   The American Catholic Council: http://americancatholiccouncil.org/.

37   Jerry Filteau, *Detroit Archbishop Warns Clergy Not To Attend Catholic Gathering, National Catholic Reporter,* June 7, 2011, http://ncronline.org/news/faith-parish/detroit-archbishop-warns-clergy-not-attend-catholic-gathering.

obviously does not want any of us even talking about reform. The hierarchy simply doesn't need or want to listen to the laity. Of course, this contradicts Vatican II, but no problem. Vatican II is in the process of nullification. I suspect that the archbishop might have been under some degree of pressure and was not necessarily speaking from his heart. He too must conform. If it doesn't come from Rome, it isn't "Catholic."

I attended the June conference along with my wife and I observed hundreds of fellow Catholics, along with a few defiant lower level clergy, who obviously shared our discontent with our local Archbishop's view. His stance reflects a continuing attitude of confrontation rather than a sharing dialogue. He fails to accept that we are all sincere Catholics and instead opts to promote division amongst us. He clearly views it as a power struggle and an encroachment on his authority.

Papal stances too often seem to be a form of bullying that persecutes the pastoral, and rewards only blind loyalty. Consider that in mid-2011, Pope Benedict fired a very beloved bishop, William Morris of Australia, for the terrible offense of suggesting that the Church needs to consider *discussing* the possibility of married priests and women priests. His dilemma that precipitated this grievous sin: He has only sixteen priests to minister to 68,000 Catholics in his diocese. If my local archdiocese had the same number of priests per layperson as Bishop Morris's diocese has, my bishop would have to fire half of our existing priests. Now understand Bishop Morris's dilemma: He desperately needs more priests. He implores, "Let's talk about it!" But no, he's fired for the suggestion of exploring solutions. But turn the page back a couple of years: Benedict rescues the infamous Cardinal Law from persecution by U.S. civil authorities for being an accessory to the felony of child abuse through his cover-up, and then promotes him to a cushy job in Rome. Later, this supreme pontiff, successor to Saint Peter, reinstates the two bishops who his predecessor excommunicated for denying the Holocaust. (And they didn't have to recant.) This is blatant injustice. It is the earmark of a bully, not a pastor.

Few of us pay much attention to bleating bishops or popes anymore. They give the impression that they still think they are talking to uneducated children, and that the children are still listening. A mature, critically thinking adult laity does not seem to exist in their view. An example that comes to mind is the current introduction of the new missal in our archdiocese. Scheduled for the first Sunday in Advent, we laity are forced in the weeks leading up to it to practice like little children our new responses before each Mass. We are led to recite not once, but twice the "new" enlightenment. It is reminiscent of a first grade school scene. Apparently, the hierarchy does not understand that we have achieved literacy. The implication is embarrassing to any adult. I long for a place of worship where I am treated as an adult.

True, the bishops can still fire off their isolated cannons of excommunication and deprivations of the Eucharist, their occasional salvos of denunciations from their bully pulpits, and their control of Church property, but most of us ignore them and if necessary move on to some other Church venue not in control of the cardinal archbishops. The ACC met at Marygrove College for its 2011 Detroit-area listening session. Once again, the IHM nuns resisted. It was the women, the feminine, who were open to critical thinking. They were not intimidated. As the inbred incompetence of many of our bishops heralds the old order's demise, the priesthood dies. The institutional Church is collapsing, and the "old boys" seem to be blind to it. It is easy to see. The cancer of celibacy can be a fatal disease. Reform is possible but major surgery is needed. Mandatory celibacy is the first excision required.

Chapter 17

Change

"Nothing endures but change"
—HERACLITUS, 540–480 BC

Some folks never know when to hang it up. Others are prevented from retiring, either by financial circumstances or some other enforced lack of choice. Those who simply fail to recognize their age-inevitable obsolescence and have become more a hindrance to their chosen field than benefactor have truly rejected any acclaim for growing old gracefully. Society is constantly afflicted by such self-centered creatures. It is a common affliction to many of the famous who suffer from the effects of excessive adulation. When famous people retire and truly fade into anonymity, it is often an exception and a mark of real greatness. On the other hand, some of us refuse to relinquish our positions to those who are younger, thinking that somehow we are indispensable. It is often a product of pride or greed. This is probably one of the reasons why the pope has to die in office. It is axiomatic, I think, that change proceeds mostly from the young. New thinking is seldom born from old minds. Old age is a good reason to retire.

When the nonretirement phenomenon is inflicted by higher authority upon its aging subordinates through some false sense of institutional preservation, the consequences are even more repugnant. Growing old gracefully requires that the younger provide some facilitation for their elder's final task. The resistance to change in our Church has produced this sad and disgusting nonretirement syndrome more and more in recent years. It is one consequence of the priest shortage. It is a form of *elder abuse*, one more scandalous examples of nonfeasance of Church leadership.

We were on vacation in the southwestern United States. It was early spring and we had just come from a visit to the Grand Canyon. We had been joined by my daughter Tracey and her husband from San Diego and it was a delightful several days at nature's magnificent amphitheater. Now we had moved on to a small rural town in western Colorado to visit my fourth daughter, Nancy, and her young family. Linda and I had chosen to attend Sunday Mass at the nearby Catholic Church. It was the ten o'clock morning Mass, the only one scheduled for this small remote parish. We had arrived early and found ourselves being warmly greeted by a welcoming group of other early arrivals. We immediately felt comfortable and freely engaged in the community conversation. Inside, a small group was reciting the rosary prior to the start of Mass. Soon we were all seated in the main church awaiting the arrival of the celebrant. The congregation numbered perhaps little more than one hundred. The usual muffled whisperings of the congregants suddenly ceased, when finally, the celebrant appeared.

It was immediately shocking. A pitiful sight had emerged. An old, old, old man in priestly robes had appeared at the entrance of the main aisle. In a very slow procession down the aisle, he presented a scene that portrayed a desperate, painful, and agonizing struggle. It was obvious that he was barely managing the long, slow trip to the altar. I personally felt a wave of apprehension as I watched. He was a frail man who appeared to be a resident from some nearby nursing home. Looking to be well into his nineties, he shuffled very slowly, as if in pain, in an agonizing procession, bent over, trembling, and in a constant stoop; he supported himself by leaning heavily on a cane. Led by two lay cross and missal bearers, there were also two laypersons, one at each side, holding him by his arms to guard against any potential fall. It was a relief when he was finally seated in a chair behind the altar from where he sat to conduct the liturgy. The ensuing performance of the ritual was an obvious struggle—a halting performance as each segment of Mass seemed to present him with some new difficulty. His voice was barely audible, and his frailty was a continuing distraction. It was pathetic. This Mass was being celebrated by someone who seemed more victim than leader, someone who seemed in imminent threat of physical collapse. The congregation surely felt a mutual anxiety, as his every motion was fraught with the fear that this poor man might fall or worse. It was a nursing home scene, in every way distressing. His ensuing homily was clearly difficult for both him and his audience, as he read from a script at a barely audible level. I breathed a sigh of relief when it was all over and no tragedy had occurred.

This scenario is all too common in our Church today, a Church that fails every attempt at reform. I have seen celebrants at Sunday Mass who seem to have both feet in their final resting place, only waiting for the fat lady to sing. In one small rural parish, the pastor was wheeled in by wheelchair, from which he struggled through a brave imitation of clerical competence. His age-related physical disabilities and diminished oratory capability deprived him of any chance at dispensing a reasonable dose of spiritual sustenance to the congregation. The man passed on some months later. Is this a loving way of treating men who have given us a lifetime of service? Why would any sensible young person wish to dedicate themselves to such a potential for a demeaning end of life?

Such a scandalous phenomenon is a by-product of the hierarchy's refusal to introduce reform in the Church. The curse of a vanishing priesthood is a legacy of the vaunted Pope John Paul II and his predecessor, Paul VI. There is no hint that things will change soon. Church leadership remains entrenched in a fantasy—a medieval make-believe world. To address elder abuse, the papacy would do well to apply to itself and all clergy the very laws it lays on underlings who don't toe the party line: mandatory retirement at age seventy-five. Unfortunately, Rome has swallowed its own propaganda that the pope and his favored ones are beyond normal human nature. Church leaders have virtually declared themselves divine, and the rest of us suffer the hurtful consequences.

Elder abuse appears to be a little noted reality in today's Church, at least from my vantage point. The suffering victim priests seem sufficiently broad in numbers as to challenge the sexual abuse scandal totals. The aging clergy are obviously the primary victims, but the laity who suffer through a continuing deprivation of spiritual nourishment by more competent leadership are no less victims as well. The myopic refusal even to recognize this issue and the apparent sanctioning of such abuse would imply a deficient Church leadership at best. Any focus on priestly retirement issues and concern for elderly clergy seems nonexistent. In my own archdiocese, it is common knowledge that the retirement fund for elderly priests is essentially defunct due to the diversion of funds by an unaccountable cardinal. He has the funds to support anti–gay marriage initiatives and multimillion-dollar edifices to honor an aging pope, but cannot sustain retirement funding for his own priests.

Aging priests often face a bleak choice. The concept of priestly retirement is too often marked by a looming life of loneliness and semi poverty. The current alternative to "work till you drop" seems to be the common selection of many of our aging priests. It is not a very good way of showing our gratitude for a life devoted to service.

There are no guarantees when it comes to priestly retirement. Often outright abandonment is a real threat if one is seen to oppose the hierarchy in any active way. It seems a shameful and prevalent abuse that at the very least should engender some protest from the laity. We need to insist that an analysis is begun to ensure that retirement age priests are in fact appropriately tended to with loving gratitude. Nevertheless, such awareness and accountability are absent. It would require major change. The hierarchy is accountable to no one, and the laity seems entrenched in an historic passivity.

The paucity of newly ordained young clerics is behind the elder abuse. Younger men are not replacing older clerics because there are simply not enough new priests to go around. An added affront is the poor quality of many of those young persons who do make the choice for the priesthood. Seminaries today are mostly confined to the undeveloped world where education is a scarce commodity, but even in the developed world, they are producing a brand of unthinking automatons whose chief accomplishment seems to be doctrinal correctness. The preponderance, often display an adolescent maturity, and could be characterized as having a circus kewpie-doll intellect, whose string when pulled will produce the consistent response of the doctrinal party line and nothing more. There is little creative thought or sense of reality. Homilies are too often totally devoid of any hint of adulthood or critical thinking. The characteristic droning serves only to promote further lay boredom and escape. The younger generation is pushed further than ever from any committed engagement; their continuing exodus is only encouraged.

Some bishops have attempted to assuage this plight by importing priests from overseas where seminary production is prodigious. Too often, the result is a substitute who does not know the culture, has barely passable language skills, and usually displays deficient education manifested by adolescent-level homilies. It doesn't solve the problem, and only exacerbates the laity's frustrations. There must be exceptions to this sad state, but if there are, I have not witnessed any. I see mostly elderly priests who are too old and younger priests who are poorly equipped. Considering the state of the Church among the educated, the touted expansion in underdeveloped countries portends only a mass of poorly educated Catholics morphing the Church into a more cult-like entity. It's pathetic, and promises only further Church decline. The leadership of the Catholic Church is in ostrich mode. The Holy Spirit will have a tough time reaching such muffled ears.

Perhaps the Lord will find an alternative that embodies the laity as the solution. Indeed, why can't lay people celebrate the Eucharist? Do we really need the ordained? What will happen when there are drastically insufficient ordained? What if there were no ordained? What change would this precipitate? Will future change correct this void?

"A woman is mas occasionatus, a failed male…a female is deficient and unintentionally caused"
—Summa Theologica, 1, qu. 92, art 1, ad 1.

That official view of the feminine, as a doctrinal assessment, was articulated in the mid-thirteenth century by Saint Thomas Aquinas (my patron saint). The Church embraced this thinking at the time and, practically speaking, while well camouflaged, continues to proclaim a dogma of women's inferiority today. A patriarchal perspective by the Church, of course, is not an exclusively Catholic view. It is a stance secured in human history many a millennium before Saint Thomas, and is shared by many throughout the world today. Denigration of women is a common abuse. In some ways, then, the Church might be excused, since she merely reflects a longstanding culture, and other religions hold similar misogynistic views. Maybe so, but like it or not, times are changing.

Some four decades ago, my love affair with the water reached a pinnacle. Yielding to a lifelong obsession, my wife and I became power boaters and, having acquired a sizable cruiser, joined the Detroit Yacht Club and enlisted in the U.S. Power Squadrons. This latter activity became a dedicated form of public service for us, as we joined in the power squadron's focus on educating the public in safe boating. An interesting and unexpected consequence of this undertaking occurred, however. It marked a major step in my education on women, and in turn affected my faith journey. As the father of five daughters, I had already begun the reorientation of a perspective born from an all-male childhood. Despite my namesake's beliefs about the nature of women, I held a distinctly more moderate view, and I thought I was pretty progressive. My daughters managed to nurture not only this disposition, but they also tried to introduce a few new enlightenments as well. I certainly didn't expect though, that joining the U.S. Power Squadrons was going to be a new dawn for me in feminism. But it definitely was.

Joining the power squadron at the time required that each applicant first take a brief safe boating course followed by a written exam. It was designed to ensure that every member understood a modicum of safe boating principles. Trish and I both completed the same course and took the same final exam. As it turned out, she achieved a nearly perfect score, which was the highest mark in our class of some twenty-five students. While I also easily passed the exam, she managed to humiliate me by a good ten points. The result of this stellar performance was that I was invited to join the power squadron, and Trish was invited to join the lowly lady's auxiliary. This medicine did not go down well. Trish accepted her invitation to the lady's auxiliary with a smile that concealed an inner fuming. I could tell that this was not going to stand for long.

The U.S. Power Squadrons had long structured itself as an all-male organization not unlike our Catholic hierarchy. It was modeled after an historic but obsolete all-male U.S. Navy, and the boys were quite comfortable with this scenario. It wasn't long after Trish's initiation into the lady's auxiliary, however, that attitudes in the auxiliary began to change. Up to that point in time, only male members were allowed to teach public boating courses or serve on the executive boards as full-fledged officers in the squadron. The women were mostly relegated to the galley. There was no way I could mollify Trish's distaste for that medicine. While I'd occasionally noticed tendencies before, Trish's introduction to me of some undisguised feminism was a bit sudden and unmistakable. Soon my squadron male colleagues began commenting to me, something like, "Wow. That wife of yours is sure stirring the pot." I could only nod, or sometimes just shake my head. I knew when not to fight, and when to keep my mouth shut. Sometimes, silence definitely is golden. "These guys just don't get it yet," I thought.

Well, in less than two years, they were forced to get it. The U.S. Power Squadrons, after a prolonged and costly legal battle in the New York courts, succumbed to the feminine onslaught. Women were determined by the court to be equally as eligible for any of the benefits or offices in the U.S. Power Squadrons by reason of it being a public organization. It was henceforth no longer an all-male club. Now I'm not saying that it all happened because of Trish, but I think some of my buddies held some poorly concealed thoughts along those lines. Suffice it to say, the power squadron did very nicely with the women fully onboard. I hesitate to claim

that we were a much-improved organization, but our women definitely seemed more content. Before long, our squadron appointed
a woman to the rank of lieutenant commander and head of the
education committee. It became very smooth sailing. Change had
happened.

Yes, we call it feminism. It's a term that can still conjure a fury
of male anxiety among some. I'm sure it is seen as a creeping virus
among the hierarchy of my Church. Feminism is a term concocted
from a patriarchal perspective. Like Aquinas, we men tend to think
and act, shrouded in a cultural fog of very long standing. We just
don't see the forest. Nay, we don't even see the trees. Misogyny
is a prevalent and sometimes brutal fact that in some parts of the
world begins in the very young life of the victims. In Africa and the
Middle East, it is common practice to perform genital mutilation
on girls around the age of ten, ostensibly done to keep women
chaste. This barbarous torture is performed without anesthesia
and politely called "female circumcision." We men ought to be
ashamed of our male standards. Women are universally abused.
Patriarchy is sinful.

A characteristically male mantra is looking but not seeing. We
don't see all those single mothers out there raising children absent
their fathers. We don't see all those women performing with excellence on some job and then coming home to prepare supper for
the family while Dad watches the evening news or some sports program on TV. If she's lucky, he helps clean up the kitchen, but
chances are she puts the children to bed.

Then there's that thing we call "mother's love." No male can
compete with that. It's a unique virtue that is exclusively feminine.
It is normally always unconditional. It is never something you have
to look for or hope for. It doesn't hide. It seems unfathomable.
You can abuse it, refuse it, ignore it, or deny it, but you can always
retrieve it. It's always there. And you know it always exaggerates
your own goodness and virtues? A mother's love. What man can
match it? If God is love, then He must be a She.

There's also the love by a wife. It too will, most often, excel
beyond male performance. If I had to list all the loving things my
wife has gifted me with over these many years, I'd need another

lifetime to write it all down, then another to return them in kind. And every day brings new examples of it in my life. It's still happening. When Trish died and I later married my current spouse, Linda, I marveled at the amazing blessings that I once again enjoyed. My sister-in-law asked, "How did you get so damn lucky twice?" I couldn't answer that, but I think that most men, if they're paying attention and have any ounce of perception, would, with little pondering, admit that they too are *damn lucky*. Their wives probably do a better job of loving than they do.

When I think about women and the burdens we men often inflict on them, I often think of Mary, the mother of Jesus. Even He seems to have inflicted on His mother. The gospel stories of Jesus's mother experiencing first the loss in the temple, then the first miracle of the wedding feast are examples of more mundane inflictions, perhaps. Jesus replies to Mary's queries on those occasions sound rather curt as I hear them. Mary seems to shrug it off. But her greatest affliction must have been the torture and death of her son. I can't begin to imagine the pain that she endured as she witnessed the terrible beating and the crucifixion of her Son. When the Roman soldier asked Him to stretch out his hand, He complied without protest; the hammer came smashing down. He must have winced but apparently remained silent. What did that mother feel as she saw the blood gushing from her Son's battered body? What was she thinking? She must have been weeping, drenched in a grief so intense as to defy the imagination. It was a horror no parent should ever have to experience. Mary did, and she did it essentially alone, with no family to sustain her. No man, I suspect, can even imagine, because no man can love with a mother's love. It is women. Women.

Our modern culture tends to focus on the sexual aspect of women. We glorify the young bodies in so many ways. It is a marketing mantra. It's a relatively novel occurrence when we extol a woman's intellect. This is another unfortunate patriarchal proclivity of our society. I suspect if women rather than men dominated world leadership, we'd all be a lot better off. War would be a lot less palatable if the decision to send sons into battle were being made by feminine rather than macho minds. Yet, the sad reality is that many women who succeed in positions of leadership in today's world are often forced to emulate male role models in order to achieve their goals. Correcting our cultural bias still has a long way to go. Will change eventually come?

The Catholic Church's refusal even to consider the ordination of women reflects a cultural misogynistic bias more than any touting of some pathetic scriptural basis. It is the Church's great loss. My own experience hearing Protestant women ministers preaching confirms this. Somehow, women seem innately better at projecting and speaking to love, which is the essence of Christianity. The Catholic Church tends to have more of a fear focus, which is another reason why it doesn't want the women around. Hopefully, change is coming. Sooner or later, the Church will be dragged into a more intelligent reality. It's happened before, however grudgingly. It is clear that the Catholic Church today has no literal proclamation that "a woman is *mas occasionatus*," but its dogma on women is still very deficient and not much beyond that thirteenth-century stance. We have a long way to go.

Will the Church ever change her teaching on women? This question is one that I hear often from my women friends or family members. Often, too, I hear some of my more conservative Catholic friends say with a firm certitude: "The Church never has, and never will change her teaching on anything. The magisterium is guided by the Holy Spirit and cannot err, and thus cannot change her teaching on matters of faith and morals." Indeed, even my own archbishop once said to me, "Tom, if I could change Church teaching [on homosexuality] I'd do it in an instant!" I wish that on that occasion, I had replied, "Your Eminence, if it doesn't begin with people like you, where does it?"

The idea that the Church never changes her teachings is a common misconception, even among the hierarchy. But it is not supported by the historical facts. Actually, the Catholic Church has changed its teachings on matters of faith and morals many times over the centuries. The issues were pretty important, too. Change has come pitifully slow, but even a casual reading of history reveals many sad examples of serious errors by popes and bishops, Councils, and indeed, even some saints regarding official dogmas that are no longer held. Often those errors were generated in a culture of ignorance that affected the theological thinking of the time, but in light of today's understanding, clearly they were errors. They were errors that often inflicted great pain. Yet eventually, amazing changes quietly evolved. Claims to an immutable infallibility notwithstanding, the Church has changed its teachings in matters of faith and morals over time rather consistently. Most often, it reflected the expansion of human knowledge in general. To illustrate my point, let me mention just two notorious past teachings as typical examples of some major changes:

Slavery

The Church's long support for slavery can be traced from the earliest times through the modern era. The Holy Office issued this sad proclamation in 1866, *after* our own Civil War (during which Pius IX appeared to sympathize with the Confederacy):

> "Slavery itself...is not at all contrary to the natural and divine law...For the sort of ownership which a slave owner has over a slave is nothing other than the perpetual right of disposing of the work of a slave for one's own benefit."[38]

Earlier, in 1548, Pope Paul III proclaimed:

> We decree] that each and every person of either sex, whether Roman or non-Roman, whether secular or clerical, and no matter of what dignity, status, degree, order or condition they be, may freely and lawfully buy and sell publicly any slaves whatsoever of either sex, and make contracts about them as is accustomed to be done in other places, and publicly hold them as slaves and make use of their work, and compel them to do the work assigned to them. And with Apostolic authority, by the tenor of these present documents, we enact and decree *in perpetuity* that slaves who flee to the Capital and appeal for their liberty shall in no wise be freed from the bondage of their

---

38   Fiedler, Maureen, and Linda Rabben. *Rome Has Spoken*. New York: Crossroad, 1998, p84

servitude...but they shall be returned in slavery to their owners, and if it seems proper they shall be punished as runaways; and we very strictly forbid our beloved sons who for the time being are conservatori of the said city to presume by their authority to emancipate the aforesaid slaves—who flee as previously described and appeal for their liberty—from the bondage of their slavery, irrespective of whether they were made Christians after enslavement, or whether they were born in slavery even from Christian slave parents according to the provisions of common law. [39]

There are also incidents prior to the ones cited above that might support the claim that the Church opposed slavery. Yet these were more anecdotal than dogmatic. There has been an obvious historical inconsistency at best on slavery. A similar diversity of belief is typical of current teaching on homosexuality today. (Not all prelates agree with the Roman view). It is easy to recognize that today, the magisterium's understanding of slavery is unequivocal. It's evil. But at best, in prior centuries, there was much vacillating back and forth before the current position was achieved. It was an evolutionary process. It's salient to note, that even two years *after* the Civil War, in 1866, Pope Pius IX was still sympathetic to the Confederacy. This was the chap who first claimed infallibility, yet he was still clearly on the wrong side of the slavery fence. Change comes slowly.

Anti-Semitism

Then there was the problem of anti-Semitism. The history of anti-Semitism by the Catholic Church is sadly consistent over a very a long period of time. While a major embarrassment in today's perspective, it actually started in Saint Paul's time and continued through World War II. The Church, throughout its history, has viewed the Jewish people as "the Christ killers," despite the fact that

---

39   Motu Proprio, November 9, 1548. *Conffirmatio Statutorum populi Romani super restitutione servorum in Urbe. Statutorum Almae Urbis Romae*, Rome, 1567, VI, 19(B) from *"Slavery and the Catholic Church,"* John Francis Maxwell, p. 75, 1975, Barry Rose Publishers

it was Roman soldiers who actually did the deed. Discrimination against the Jewish people through official proclamations reflected this deep seated prejudice. It was pervasive and extreme enough to make plausible the roots of the Holocaust. There are in fact, several aspects of the Holocaust that had their birth in the Church's stance. The Star of David that the Nazis forced all Jews to wear had its origin established by the Council of Arles in 1234 [40] The Christ killer perspective was posited to all Jews for all time. It all started from distorted interpretations of Saint Paul's writing in I Thessalonians 2:15–16:

"Who killed both the Lord Jesus and the prophets, and harassed and drove us out, and continue to make themselves hateful and offensive to God and to show themselves foes of all men."

Yet this same great saint also wrote:

"There is no longer Jew or Greek, there is no longer slave or free, there is no longer male and female, for all of you are one in Christ Jesus" (Gal. 3:28).

The Jewish ghetto was invented by Pope Paul IV in 1555 [41] Sadly, there are many examples of the Church's anti-Semitism. Only the horrors of the Holocaust seemed finally to awaken the Catholic conscience. A couple of other examples:

Pope Gregory IX, 1239: "If what is said about the Jews…is true, no punishment would be sufficiently great or sufficiently worthy of their crime." [42]

Counsel of Basel, 1434: "Jews are to be forced under threat of heavy penalties to take on a form of dress by which they can be clearly distinguished from Christians. Moreover, in order to avoid excessive social intercourse, they must be made to dwell separate

40   Fiedler and Rabben, *Rome Has Spoken*. New York: Crossroad, 1998, p69
41   Ibid, p71
42   Ibid , p69

from Christians in their cities and towns, in places as far distant from the churches as possible. Nor may they on Sundays and other solemn feast days open their shops or work in public." [43]

One could argue that such edicts were effective models for the Nazi regime. It is reminiscent of Hitler's infamous Kristallnacht. No other world incident that I have experienced in my lifetime has left a greater impact on my mind than the Holocaust. I can still see the unbelievable evil so vividly displayed in the movie newsreels—the gaunt walking skeletons, the piles of naked dead bodies, the death camps—the utter incomprehensibility of it all. I was only sixteen years old when confronted with such repulsive horror. I could not understand at that time how such sickening atrocities could be inflicted upon one human being by another. I still can't. It defies rational thought. However slight its complicity in this horror, God have mercy on my Church.

The Church was very slow to change on this issue, and while there were some moderate, more kindly views over the centuries, they were rare and a very small minority. The Holocaust was the game changer. The Church's guilt of silence and reluctance to admit error is idiosyncratic. In recent times, we still witness pathetic attempts at whitewashing the Church's guilt. Many today would apply just such criticism to Pope John Paul II's recent *We Remember*. Thankfully, the current pope, Benedict XVI, is reported to finally proclaim in a forthcoming book that the Jewish people are not responsible for the murder of Christ, hopefully putting to rest a continuation of this source of anti-Semitism.

There were other changes. Catholic history is replete with many examples of terrible errors, crimes and injustices. Our dear Church has been guilty of genocide and persecution, ostensibly in the name of the faith. We tortured, burned at the stake, and employed war, most often in an ill-disguised goal of power and control. The Galileo affair is newly notable because it was our recent Pope John Paul II who finally apologized some 359 years later.

The bottom line is that infallibility, the party line of an unchanging, error-free Church, is a ludicrous myth, an absurd idea. Even

---

43   Ibid., p70

the papacy itself has been known to declare against the idea. Despite Saint Augustine's ancient dictum, "Rome has spoken; the issue is closed," unanimity in the matter is not in accord with history. Centuries later, Pope John XXII proclaimed in 1354 in papal bull "Quia Quorundam" that the concept of papal infallibility is a heresy. Much later, one of his successors, Pope Pius IX, evidently chose to ignore such contradictions. Attempts to ameliorate the infallibility concept by claiming it is only valid when the pope is speaking *ex cathedra* is simply obfuscation to cloak an irrational concept. It is easy to conclude from the manner of current pronouncements that the doctrine of infallibility is often poorly disguised as implicit in most anything the pope utters. The papal prohibition not even to discuss women's ordination comes to mind.

The Church has changed her teachings in the past many times, and is certain to do so again in the future. Clearly, the Holy Spirit is handicapped by having to work through human beings, with all our frailties and faults, but we are eventually led in the right direction as Christ promised. Change takes time—often lots of it—and prayer. The virtue of humility can speed things up, but often it is hard for us to follow where the Spirit leads. (Sometimes it seems especially hard for the hierarchy.) Again, the problem is being led where the Church does not want to go. The resistance to the Holy Spirit stems from the human element; people who are fallible all.

It is only fair to point out, however, that error is not an exclusively Catholic problem. It's endemic to us all. It's just that we Catholics are a big group with often embarrassing visibility. We tend to be a bit more vocal about our claims to unerring truth. It's a notorious reputation, and we seem to get more press because of it. Still, notoriety is better than obscurity, or as a wise sage once told me, "You don't get kicked in the rear unless you're out in front." In many ways, Catholicism is out in front. It's well to remember that Catholicism has an admirable record on social justice and other areas. It has spawned many renowned saints as well as many obscure persons who have led lives of heroic charity. It is an ongoing phenomenon.

Our constant prayer should be for the Holy Spirit to lead us—to enlighten our path and give us the courage to go where led. The Church has produced many wonderful people and has accomplished much good. We have received much from her. Yet, a mature faith comes not from a blind obedience to the magisterium, but a readiness to accept wherever the Spirit might lead. It can be difficult, often fraught with doubts and anguish. The path of a prayerful discernment of conscience and a willingness to go where we sometimes do not want to go, if not always easy, is always joyful.

Not knowing the mind of God, I personally try to follow the road signs I think I see—and be constantly aware. His greatest gift of course is Jesus, "the Way, the Truth and the Light." He has made many welcome impacts in my life. When I look back, I can see when He has carried me; I see all the many gifts I have received. I am certain that there are some I have missed and am unaware of. I realize, too, that one of the greatest of His gifts has been the blessing of a gay son, a son who has helped me greatly in my journey toward a mature faith, a son who has certainly helped me achieve a greater understanding of God's love. And, of course, just being who he is has also resulted in my realization that the Catholic Church's official teaching on homosexuality is wrong— wrong because it is opposed to love. I have too often witnessed how that teaching very effectively promotes hate, a condition that is the very antithesis of Christ's whole life of love. I conclude that Church leadership has lost its sense of humility and service. All this makes change difficult. However, change must happen. Change will happen in the Holy Spirit's good time. The retreat from the terrible errors of anti-Semitism and slavery foretell it.

Despite these bleak realities of the Church's shortcomings, the beauty of the people of God in the history of our Church is evident. It is also evident that the preponderance of wisdom throughout the centuries often emanated more from the laity, not those at the top. It has been an evolutionary process, however burdened by human failing. It continues to evolve. I am convinced that as members of that Body of Christ, we are more than ever obliged to persist as adult Christians, that we may at least contribute the wisdom of our experience. Our greatest failing would be to relax in the comfortable cave-like realm of passivity; an infantile faith;

a faith that entails only "pay, pray, and obey." We need whole congregations to rise up in simultaneous protest—a "Catholic Spring." It will require first and foremost, courage—a courage that follows His great commandment to love, even when it leads us in opposition to official Church teaching. It will require an activism. It is the way change happens. It may well produce another historic Reformation. Already there appears the seeds of a new Congregationalism forming among the laity along with some of the clergy. Change will happen. Our new age of information prepares us. The Spirit will prevail.

Chapter 18

Love

"God is love, and he who abides in love abides in God, and God abides in him"
—1 JOHN 4:16
"Whoever does not love does not know God"
—1 JOHN 4:8

As the aging process progresses, it inevitably stimulates greater and greater reflection. As this happens to me, I think a great deal about what I have learned. What is it that seems to rise above all the other lessons of life? What is most important? My answer comes easily. There is one lesson that stands out far more conspicuously than all else. It is love. The only absolute truth I recognize is the primacy of love. I have thought a lot about this. Every human condition that is lamentable can be resolved through love. All human aliments, injustices, poverty, and violence—all human evil would succumb to the antidote of love. I have experienced this amazing balm abundantly in my own life. It is marvelous to be the recipient of love, but it is even more joyful to love, to give of yourself. It perhaps took me too long to understand this, but I am grateful beyond description for the experience and the gift. I understand more every day the expression, "God is Love." Yet despite my experience, despite my convictions, I know that I have still much to accomplish in my ability to love. It seems to be a never-ending quest; my thirst for greater love is insatiable, even while my shortfall is persistent.

So, what is love? How do you define it? How do you describe love? I know that Saint Paul said it is the greatest of all virtues. He also was driven to describe it:

> Love is patient, love is kind and is not jealous; love does not brag and is not arrogant, does not act unbecomingly; it does not seek its own, is not provoked, does not take into account a wrong suffered, does not rejoice in unrighteousness, but rejoices with the truth; bears all things, believes all things, hopes all things, endures all things. Love never fails. (1 Cor. 13:4-8)

Along with Saint Paul, many poets and authors far more accomplished than I have described human love in the most eloquent words. Pope Benedict XVI in his encyclical *Deus Caritas Est* gives us an academic version. It says much to which I can relate. Yet, what can an ordinary man contribute? Can I add anything satisfying about love? Since it is the foremost lesson of my life, I have a need to express and pass on what I have learned about this treasured transcendent gift, despite my obvious limitations. Can I, from the perspective of an engineer—an ordinary man—that I make such an attempt?

What is it that have I learned of this great virtue? How would I describe it? I cannot. I do not possess the pen of a poet. It is impossible for me. I know only that as my life has progressed, I experience more and more the evidence for the primacy of this virtue. It far transcends all other human endeavors. It has become the focus of my faith and desires. I wish always to learn how to love more, for I have found life's greatest joy resides in loving.

None of us can love as unconditionally as God does. Some of us strive but mostly, we all fall short. Only Divine love achieves the pinnacle and beyond—beyond all understanding. But human love can mimic the divine. The central message of Jesus was love. More than anything else, to be a Christian means we must love. When one considers all the evils in our world today, and all our human failings, and then imagines how the virtue of love would affect this all, it is apparent that love is the solution to all human suffering. I know too that the most joyous and rewarding times in my own life have been the occasions when I have managed to love well.

Betty J. Eadie, in her book *Embraced by the Light*[44], recounting her near-death experience, forecasts that in the end, we will judge ourselves and our life. She predicts that "our biggest regret will be in recalling the times we could have loved, but didn't." Perhaps it could be added that our second biggest regret will be recalling those occasions when we could have loved *more*, but didn't.

I write this at a sad time in my country. Another shooting has taken place. This time the toll was six dead and nineteen wounded. The dead included a nine-year-old child, and the wounded included a U.S. Representative, who as of this writing, while recovering from her precarious clutch on life after being shot through the head will undoubtedly endure life-long disabilities. There is much commentary in the media about the roots of such evil. Political pundits have their position, one that seldom reflects self-examination. Others have attempted deeper understanding. While the shooter and his motive remain to be fully understood, whether emanating from a degree of insanity or a by-product of the continuing lack of civility in our political discourse, one thing is clear. It is definitely a continuation of a pattern that has existed in our country that goes far back in our history. Senseless killing in this nation occurs with relentless regularity. There is scarcely a period that one can point to and say, "That was a peaceful, loving time." Of course, our Civil War, with over six hundred thousand dead, is an exclamation mark in this terrible tale. It too began with political rhetoric not unlike today's.

Some argue that our gun laws, which allow such easy access to killing machines—devices whose sole design purpose is obviously to destroy human life in the most rapid and efficient manner possible—are the cause. My own take on all this seems different. I have not read or heard any authoritative source address what I

---

44   *Embraced by the Light*, Betty J. Eadie, Bantam Books, 1994

consider the fundamental issue. It is simply our national inability to love.

We have enshrined violence, the very antithesis of love, into our national culture. Violence has become so entrenched in our national being that it is no longer even recognized in some of its varied forms. It is everywhere one looks in our society. Our entertainment media is drowning in it. I watch in dismay at my grandchildren's obsession with violent video games in which the primary challenge of winning the game is to achieve the highest kill ratio. Technology has provided them with pocket versions of devices that can be carried everywhere and indulged in at the first hint of boredom. Family life has fallen victim to it in the form of divorce and spousal abuse. Violence in our sports is often the chief goal that everyone unwittingly accepts routinely as "part of the game." One can read the sports page any fall weekend and see that the best football heroes are often heralded for what is easily seen as their ability to be the most violent on the field of play. It is little different from the Roman killing spectacles of old. The acceptable mantra of violence has even invaded our churches. The abuse of children and ensuing cover-up, the castigation of gay people, the burning of the Koran are just a few of the current displays. (Actually, religion has one of the worst histories of violence.) The emotional defense of our right to bear arms is but one small shimmering ripple of the causative stone. The core problem is the rock of rejection we've dropped into the pool—the rejection of love.

We reserve the right to kill another to defend our freedom. Perhaps this is wrong. Nonviolence is more capable in achieving liberty and defending it. Gandhi tried to teach us that. Martin Luther King tried to teach us that. Has any war achieved what their nonviolent approach did? Even WWII was replete with excessive indulgence in pure killing violence—on both sides. While I'd admit to some fears of my own, relative to surrendering the right physically to defend my loved ones, I think it is long overdue to try a dose of loving too much. It's what I'd term the Christian option. It's never been tried in any national depth—anywhere. In America, it seems to be anathema. We have become a military-driven nation as our killing ability has become our primary financial investment and a powerful political element. We have essentially become reliant on our ability to be the world's most formidable killer to allay our national fears or protect our national interests. We think it protects us when, in reality, it probably does more to increase our vulnerability. I sometimes think that our overriding investment in our military will eventually be the cause of our national economic collapse. It seems plain to me that we really don't comprehend the essence of Jesus's message to "love one another," let alone practice it.

I must admit, however, that I too am a participant in that ideology of violence. My emotions rise in anger when I consider that terrible atrocity of 9/11. Are we to be denied the right to defend against those who are obsessed to destroy us? If we had turned the other cheek against Nazism, would we not all be in subjugation today? Is violence ever justified? I am reminded that Jesus used a whip on the temple moneychangers. Yet He also resisted organizing His followers to defend His own life, an action He could have easily accomplished. It is beyond my understanding. I place it on my overflowing shelf of life's insoluble mysteries.

It seems we all flounder in our understanding of God's love. Some religious denominations comprehend better than others do. Some seem to have no clue. The Westboro Baptist Church in Kansas, which preaches that "God hates fags," are at the extreme end of this deficiency. God hates? My entire life experience unequivocally tells me that God does not *hate*. I may not know or understand God, but I know what God is *not*. God does not hate.

This idea of loving and nonviolence has become a latter-day obsession of mine. I don't know where this focus has come from, except to admit that it is a gift of grace received along the way, and not through some latent superiority that has awakened in me. I also know that the experience of losing my beloved wife, Trish, was an experience in love. During her nine-month fatal illness as her caregiver, I had to do most everything for her, even some of the most personal things. I did what needed to be done with no thought of receiving anything in return, not even an expression of love from her. The doctor had cautioned me following her surgery that removing her tumor had necessitated injury to that part of her brain that controls emotions. He said to me, "Tom, you should understand that, because of the effects of the surgery on your wife's brain, she will probably not be capable of expressing her love for you. We have traumatized that area of her brain." Thus in the ensuing days as I gave every ounce of myself as lovingly as possible, I did it knowing I could expect nothing in return. It was a unique experience for me. Amazingly, I encountered an unlikely joy in it all. It was s grief-healing comfort that supported me for many months following her death, as I realized that for the first time in my life, I had given of myself fully, without expecting anything in return. I realized with a new clarity that the essence of loving is just such a mode: selfless giving. Unexpectedly, I had finally learned how truly to love. I had finally actually done it.

I have seen love and nonviolence in others: people who march in protest; the anti-war groups; the peace and justice folks. There are many, but too often, they comprise mostly an ignored minority. Gratefully, I see it in my own children. When I witness how uniquely loving all of my children are, I marvel and give thanks. Not too long ago, for no particular special occasion, my children spontaneously decided to get together—just the six of them—at a hotel in downtown Chicago. It was just for a weekend. Some of them had to fly from as far away as California and Colorado. The effort and expense, not insignificant, were secondary. They just longed to be together and enjoy each other's company, if only for a brief time. It was obvious that they *loved* one another. I see the same love today when we all gather at family reunions. There is a display of affection and harmony among them that has become a family earmark, one that seems too rare among other families. I am happy when I consider that Trish and I, if we're due any credit for this phenomenon, must have done a few things right.

When I meditate on the passion and death of Jesus, I am always struck by the meek and non-defensive manner in which He simply acquiesced to the centurion's nailing of His hands and feet. It was classic nonviolence; there was neither resistance nor struggle to escape the terrible torture. His whole ordeal is marked most by His silence and nonresistance. Even at the very end, He maintained this nonviolence, and culminated His death dirge with one final act of love: "Forgive them, Father; they know not what they do." However one describes it, this was Divine love. It was the supreme lesson in nonviolence. When I consider the theological view that Jesus died for our sins, it seems to me in some ways an irrational concept. How is the sin of Adam's disobedience expiated by our hideous murdering of God's only son? How can one sin then be excused by the commission of another, more terrible one? It seems an absurd idea that misses the central message of Jesus's passion. In a way, this concept enshrines violence that is the antithesis of love. Jesus's passion and death seems less atonement than a gift—a divine example of nonviolence and love. We have been given the capacity to try to do likewise. The essence of love is giving—unconditionally, without limit, even to the point of laying down one's life for the beloved. Being loved, however delightful, is not love. One can be a recipient of love, but to love is to give, and loving is the superior portion.

God's love for us is so difficult to comprehend. It is for me, I know. I have often meditated over one particular thought that has come to me in the past concerning this concept. It is one that helps me to comprehend a bit about God's love. Consider the following scenario: When I reflect on how deeply and unconditionally I love my children or my wife, I am impressed by the depth and intensity of that love. I know that my love for them knows no bounds. I love to the limit of my capacity to do so. Yet, when I imagine standing before my Maker at the moment of my final judgment, I know that I will be unable to say, "I loved more than You."

When I survey the nighttime sky, think of the incomprehensible immensity of the universe, and then wonder at the awesome string theory of the nano-cosmos—when I realize how much science has discovered, yet how little we still know—I am struck by the awful power and the infinite essence of the incomprehensible Creator. I realize the arrogance of thinking one might know the mind of God or, for that matter, the ultimate truth. I am also struck by the utter insignificance of my own existence. I am less than a grain of sand on the ocean beach. Yet somehow, we seem to matter. We matter because God loves. That is surely the greatest incomprehensible—God's love. It's there; I know it. I sense it.

My life's experience has displayed it so vividly before me. It over-whelms. It dispels my fears. It is more important than all other creation. It is an attraction so powerful that few can resist. Is this presumption? I don't think so.

Then, of course, I do fear God. Who could not? His infinite jus-tice, His omnipotence, one would have to be a fool not to fear the Almighty. Yet His love wipes away fear. I am left with calm and a confidence that He will never abandon me. Jesus said, "Fear not." The psalmist says, "Though I walk through the valley of death, I will not fear." This for me then is the ultimate gift of the Creator— God's love. I may stumble through this life and be guilty of many failings, but I know God loves me still, and I am safe.

Truly, to consider that God loves us to an extent we cannot comprehend is the greatest of comforts and an irresistible invi-tation to reciprocate. We have only to accept and engage in the learning process. This belief of mine, in the absolute primacy of love, is the most profound discovery of my life. It is the single most important legacy I wish to leave my family: Love is not about the *me*; love is about the *you*.

"With love comes understanding and together they are they answer to everything"—Gandhi

Chapter 19

Bullied

"But he that shall scandalize one of these little ones...it were better for him that a millstone should be hanged about his neck, and that he should be drowned in the depth of the sea"
—MATTHEW 18:6

It was late Friday afternoon, and it was already getting dark outside. A light snow was falling and Janet was worried. A while ago, she had arrived home from her position as a nurse in the triage unit at the local hospital. Her husband, Matthew, the pastor at the nearby Baptist church, was upstairs in the library preparing his sermon for the weekend. However, their son, Derek, was not home from school yet. She was worried because he was nearly two hours overdue and it was unlike him to be late. She knew not to disturb Matt when he was working on his sermon, but maybe this was different. Maybe she should talk to Matt. It was getting to the point she couldn't wait any longer. Before she could decide, the front doorbell rang. When she opened the door, she saw a frightening scene. Directly in the doorway stood a tall police officer, his dark uniform and bright silver badge clearly announcing bad news. "Mrs. Duncan?" the officer asked. "Is your husband home?" "Yes," she replied, "he's upstairs." "I think you'd better get him," the officer said.

Janet, sensing urgency, called out to her husband: "Matthew! Please come; come quickly." In a moment, Matt was at Janet's side, frowning at the sight of the police officer. "What is it?" Matt asked. "What's wrong?" "It's your son, Reverend. I think you both better come with me."

"Oh my god!" Janet gasped, and immediately the tears started rushing out. "What is it? What's wrong? Is he all right?"

The drive to the hospital was a benumbing blur as the patrol car raced, siren blaring, the short distance to the local hospital where Jan worked. They arrived with a screeching halt and saw an EMS vehicle parked at the emergency entrance, its flashing red lights announcing a tragedy. Another police car stood by, its flashing lights adding to the drama. As the police officer helped Matt and Janet out of the car, the school principal, Mr. Paulson, was there and immediately began repeating: "Oh Mrs. Duncan, Reverend, I'm so sorry, I'm so sorry, Derek has, has…terrible, terrible…oh!" At that moment, the EMS unit lifted out a Stokes stretcher from the rear of the EMS vehicle. The stretcher carried a small body bag. Janet glanced at it, shrieked out a scream, and fell into Matt's arms. Their nightmare had begun and would not end with the coming dawn.

Derek was sixteen years old. He was a slight, soft-spoken young boy, small in stature for his age, just barely five feet tall and weighed ninety-two pounds. Both Matt and Janet would proudly inform you that he was a very bright boy who nearly always excelled at virtually anything he did. They would also tell you how gentle and sensitive he was—quiet, a delight to his parents in every way. In recent months, however, Jan and Matt had noticed a change in Derek's demeanor. He seemed withdrawn and complained frequently of not feeling well. After school, he would often go directly to his room, close the door, and not be seen until called to dinner. They began to wonder if he was depressed. They had taken him to the doctor, but no ailment was found. They tried to get him to talk about it, but Derek wasn't talking.

What Matt and Jan didn't know was that Derek's small stature and quiet demeanor had proven to be the source of much trouble for him in recent months. It had really all started in late middle school. Derek had become a target for some school bullies. They had interpreted Derek's slightly effeminate persona as homosexual and quickly labeled him the class queer. The derisive "faggot" and similar slurs soon escalated into shoving, punching, and tripping. Mom and Dad were mostly unaware. Earlier, they had gone to school authorities more than once when Jon had come home obviously the victim of some physical altercation. Yet mostly, bolstered by school authorities who attempted to allay their fears and assured them that it all was not a really serious problem, they shrugged it off as an inability to prevent boys from being boys. Once, the principal had told them that, "Your son is perceived as gay. There's not much we can do about that. Our hands are tied." That hadn't set well with Mathew, as the suggestion that his son might be gay held special affront for the reverend. He knew that Derek had been raised in a thoroughly Christian environment. That Derek might be gay was insult on top of injury. They said nothing to Jon about their encounter with the principal. It was just not something they wanted to confront. Besides, there was no way Derek could be gay. He was a good kid who had been instilled with the best Christian values. In desperation, at one point, while not having consulted a professional counselor, Jan and Matt on their own, had talked about moving Derek to a private school, but found that the only one in the vicinity catered mostly to children with special needs. They had concluded that might be an even worse environment.

Derek's life had become unbearable for him. He was living a life of constant fear, an incessant dread and a feeling of terrible loneliness. He really had no friends, but he knew he could do something to end the misery. There was a way. Finally, on a day when two boys had spit on him, kicked him several times, and told him he didn't deserve to live, he decided to act. Following his last class that Friday, he had gone back to his homeroom at school after everyone had left. Then he sat down and wrote a note to his mom and dad and left it on his teacher's desk. The note read:

Dear Mom and Dad,

I'm very sorry. I just can't stand my life anymore. I have to do this. There is no other way but to end it. There's no hope, I just want out of this. I hate my life and who I am. I know the misery will never end. I am an abomination to everyone, even you, if you really knew me. Please don't worry and just try to forgive me. I love you both always.

Derek.

Derek then took a small length of rope, on one end of which he had fashioned a very efficient noose, with a simple knot at the other end; he had used a chair to place the knotted end over the top of the classroom door, closed the door firmly to contain the knot, placed the noose around his neck, and kicked the chair from under him. The task was well accomplished; the deed could not be undone. The school maintenance worker found him some time later, as he made his closing rounds before leaving. Mr. Paulson was just about to leave when the grisly discovery was made.

The unending nightmare that followed for Jan and Matt is an all too common scene in America. Their misery, which will take many years to ease, is a small part of an ongoing tragedy that seems to evoke little national concern. The bullying stories continue almost daily.

Recently Fox News reported:

Teen Boy Commits Suicide in Greensburg, Indiana after School Bullying (2010):

Billy Lucas, 15, hung himself in the family's barn in Greensburg, Indiana Thursday, Sept. 2, according to the local Fox News station. Apparently, students at Greensburg High School bullied him for being gay, though he had not come out. Billy's mother found her son. "People would call him 'fag' and stuff like that, just make fun of him because he's different basically," student Dillen Swango told Fox News. "They said stuff like 'you're like a piece of crap' and 'you don't deserve to live.' Different things like that. Talked about how he was gay or whatever."

The Center for Disease Control (CDC) has reported: "In 2004, suicide was the third leading cause of death among youths and young adults aged 10–24 years in the United States, accounting for 4,599 deaths. [45]"

While it might matter little to the parents whether their child was gay or straight when confronting the reality of their child's suicide, it is important to know that if your child is homosexual, he is three to four times more at risk for suicide than his heterosexual counterparts, according to the CDC.

The stories of children who end their lives are always heart wrenching, but all the more so when the cause is bullying. The reason for this is that bullying-related suicide most often implies inattention or poor communication on the part of parents, and malfeasance or misfeasance on the part of school officials or teachers. Adults have failed in their responsibilities. Often it is a reflection of a cavalier attitude about the school bullying issue in general. No sense of urgency is seen. The attitude that "boys will be boys" is often heard. This and similar dismissive comments are classic examples of shirking the most serious of adult duties. It is often an abuse of one's position.

The New York Times, reporting on the suicide of a fifteen-year-old Phoebe Prince, of Springfield, Massachusetts, noted that the district attorney claimed: "The investigation revealed relentless activities directed toward Phoebe to make it impossible for her to stay at school," Ms. Scheibel said. "The conduct of those charged, far exceeded the limits of normal teenage relationship-related quarrels. It was particularly alarming," the district attorney said, "that some teachers, administrators and other staff members at the school were aware of the harassment but did not stop it. The actions or inactions of some adults at the school were troublesome," Ms. Scheibel said, "but did not violate any laws." [46]

No, they "didn't violate any laws," but that's little comfort to Phoebe's parents. I have personally witnessed just such excuses

---

45   CDC, National Center for Health Statistics; 2007
46   New York Times, March 30, 2010, p14

for complacency, most often in the legislators of my own state of Michigan. When Linda and I lobbied our state legislators for the passage of an antibullying bill, and were able to convince one lone Republican legislator to support our cause, his Senate counterpart was in a more dismissive mood. He said simply, "I'm not going to support a bill that puts more responsibility on school administrators." He wasn't interested in solving the bullying problem. Teen suicide was not a concern for him. In reality, the Republican Party in my state has consistently pandered to a group of people who demand that sexual orientation be excluded from any anti-bullying edict. Their opposition seems to be a religious issue promoted by a few fanatics.

In addition to the politicization of school bullying, a new threat has developed. In addition to the historic verbal and physical modes, we now have cyber bullying. It portends perhaps an even greater threat. Ivan Herring wrote in Heritage Newspapers:

One of the most basic instincts in the animal kingdom is the desire of a parent to protect one's offspring. How often have you heard someone say, "She's like a momma bear protecting her cubs"?

A problem is that we, as modern humans, don't always know when our children are in danger. In this information age of instant gratification and the world at your fingertips, we are often not aware of our children's plight, and when we do suspect something, they usually don't want to openly discuss it with us.

...We tend to ignore that these electronic marvels have made our children equally accessible to those who seek to do them physical or emotional harm, or take advantage of them financially. No matter how hard we try to be a good parent, the evening news still seems filled with stories of violence, drugs and sex facilitated by the perpetrator using the new electronic media, especially mobile phone texting.

...Today the average teenager in possession of a mobile phone sends and receives more than 3,300 text messages per month, according to the Nielsen Co. (Heritage Newspapers, Opinion, February 26, 2011)

Herring goes on to describe software that will ostensibly protect electronic media from such threats. The application is currently available through www.amberwatchsafetext.com. [47]

Another broad approach to reduce bullying, cyber or not, and the consequent destruction of young lives, would be for our country to turn from homophobia and fully embrace inclusivity. More realistically, local school boards need to establish some firm anti-bullying policies so that teachers have some supportive guidelines. If nothing else, it is logical self-interest. School districts would be warding off the possibility of punitive civil actions that often follow bullying tragedies.

Waiting for legislative action can prove costly. The sexual orientation component of bullying has become so politicized that statewide policies are consistently blocked. Our politicians are immobilized as misguided religious fanatics threaten them with retribution if their false agenda isn't precisely adhered to. More than that, we need to shed our xenophobia, and reject violence and our complacency toward it. It would involve loving one another, a seldom-practiced, true-Christian value.

Sadly, The Roman Catholic Church is largely complicit in the phenomenon of bullying. In some ways it is guilty of encouraging violence against LGBT young people. It does this through the demeaning dogma of *disordered* and *intrinsically evil* while ignoring any effective policy of promoting its own doctrine of the dignity of all people. It is a hypocrisy steeped in ignorance.

---

47   Sentry Parental Control Software is available at http://www.amberwatch-safetext.com./.

Chapter 20

A Different Path

*"Inspired by Your unconditional love for all of us, we believe
our families are Fortunate Families, because all our children are
created in Your image"*
—FORTUNATE FAMILIES PRAYER.

W ho understands or can predict the serendipitous ways of
the Holy Spirit? Events in one's life have of way of inter-
connecting that we never anticipate. Nor do we often even
recognize the interconnections until they are long past. In the
summer of 2000, Trish and I traveled to Notre Dame, where I was
scheduled to give a talk to a weekend alumni gathering. My talk
was essentially a retelling of my experience of discovering that I
had a gay son, the ensuing angst and recovery, both spiritually and
emotionally, and how it had impacted my life. It was well attended
and received. The large lecture hall was nearly full and I spoke
with a passion, born of a deep conviction that people needed to
hear about the bad things that were happening to some of our
children. I recall one attendee speaking to me afterward. He was a
psychiatrist who apparently felt deeply sympathetic for what I was

saying, and urged me to continue my efforts. It was encouraging feedback.

I had been invited to speak at Notre Dame not just because I was an alumnus, but also because sometime earlier, Trish and I had met a couple from South Bend, Indiana, at a national PFLAG convention, Hank and Nancy Mascotte. Hank was also a Notre Dame alumnus and when we had met at the convention, I related my story to him. He suggested at the time that I should tell it at a Notre Dame alumni gathering the following summer. He said he would try to arrange it. But this meeting had more than one serendipitous effect.

The following fall, Trish and I attended the annual Call To Action weekend conference in Milwaukee. Call To Action is a group of like-minded progressive Catholics from across the country who work persistently for Church reform. During that conference in 2000, in the course of socializing with Hank and Nancy, who were also attendees, they introduced us to Casey and Mary Ellen Lopata, a couple from Rochester, New York who were long-time activists for the LGBT community. We all got to know each other at that conference, particularly in the spirited conversation over dinner on Saturday night. Little did I realize at the time how dramatically Casey and Mary Ellen would affect me in the future. They would go on to later demonstrate how much just one couple's efforts can impact a world that sometimes seems so deficient in compassion for the oppressed. Their activism would come to provide Linda and me with invaluable resources in our own actions to support the LGBT community. It was the Catholic focus that really got our attention.

Casey and Mary Ellen had founded a group called Fortunate Families in 2004. It is a Catholic-oriented ministry comprised of a small number of lay people organized as a board of directors, and supported by a group of more than 140 "Listening Parents" that is now international in scope. It accomplishes a ministry to Catholic families with LGBT children that is unique in the Church. Rather than focus on doctrine, their goal is to provide their fellow Catholics with a compassionate and pastoral support found nowhere else in the Church quite so effectively. Fortunate

Families has a website, [48]that is a treasure trove for those seeking information and support during what is often a critical time in the life of their families. While one can find authentic Church teachings at this site, the emphasis is on the positive aspects of the Catholic perspective. The mission statement displayed at their website says in part:

> ...We promote and facilitate personal, meaningful, and respectful conversation, especially within our parishes and with our pastors and bishops. We stress the significance of our personal stories as a source of grace within our families and as a witness for justice in our civic and faith communities...

Recently, one of their board members, Deb Word, wrote a letter to a Minnesota archbishop. It was in response to a recent incident in the Twin Cities. The local archbishop, John Nienstedt, previously from Detroit, had issued a very antigay edict opposing gay marriage, and espousing a state constitutional amendment to achieve such an end. He spent thousands of dollars sending 440,000 DVDs promoting his conviction to the people in his diocese. When that edict met considerable pushback from his flock, he then further affronted hurt parents of gay children by denying the Eucharist to those wearing rainbow ribbon pins at Mass the next Sunday. His action drew national attention and reaction. Deb was moved to write:

> Dear Bishop,
> I house discarded LGBT youth; eight so far this year. I have bandaged a child who has been beaten. I have prayed over the nearly lifeless body of a child who attempted suicide. I house, feed, counsel and love these children. I speak at vigils, write letters to fundamentalists, and remind clergy not to tell these children that they are hell bound because of their orientation. You might call me a gay activist. I am, and I would ask you to join me. Do you have a homeless shelter that will reach out to LGBT youth in your diocese? Nondiscrimination clauses in schools and hiring?

---

48   Fortunate Families website: http//www.fortunatfamilies.org

Oh and…I wear a rainbow pin every day because… I believe that the rainbow is a symbol of a promise from God. I believe we are all His children, and have an inheritance in that promise. I believe that wearing it reminds those who would deny my child a place at His table that they don't own the guest list. I believe that wearing it gives hope to a gay youngster that there are adults who can love him. I believe that wearing it gives parents an open door to talk to me about their gay children; and that leads to affirmed and healthy children. I believe that it starts the conversation with those who are ignorant of the struggles of gay folk.

So, if you see me in your communion line with a rainbow cross, or pin, or peace sign, I would hope you realize that wearing the pin is my way of reaching out to the marginalized, and reminding them that they are welcome, loved.

When I serve as extraordinary minister of the Eucharist, I wear it to remind me not to judge anyone who comes forward, but instead to share with them the table of the Lord.

We are all God's children, He loves us all.

As events transpired, Linda and I, just a short time we after we were married volunteered to be listed on the Listening Parent network. Before long, we were contacted by a young, visiting Asian student living and attending school locally, who was desperate to become a Catholic. He came from a Buddhist background and happened to be transgender, a condition the Church effectively fails even to recognize. Why this young person with such an unlikely background wanted to become a Catholic rather mystified us, but he needed someone to help him in his quest—someone who would understand his sexuality and guide him in his journey of faith. It seemed providential that he had come to us, and we were delighted to help. Linda and I eventually became his godparents for his subsequent baptism at Easter. It was an amazingly rewarding experience for the two of us. We've had other contacts through the network, which have given us similar joy.

In the fall of 2010, Fortunate Families held a national conference for Listening Parents titled "Joining Hands, Reaching Out."

Many of our Listening Parents traveled long distances to attend. It was a fruitful gathering, which produced much inspiration for our work. One mother from a small town in northern Michigan attended the conference. Her name was Mary. She was another example of the Holy Spirit at work in us, and I want to tell you about her. Mary had recently attended a meeting of PFLAG Manistee, the group that Linda and I had started and currently head. She subsequently became a member, and like many of us, she has a gay son whom she deeply loves. She wanted to become an advocate for him and others like him in the GLBT community, and at one of the PFLAG meetings, she heard about Joining Hands, Reaching Out, the Fortunate Families gathering that Linda and I were planning on attending. She decided to attend the conference as well and to find out how she could help spread the word for support of her gay son. Mary is a Hispanic woman, and mother of three children. She has lived a relatively quiet life in her small town and has recently been studying and working hard to achieve her high school diploma. Her love for her son was primary and unconditional, but she had certainly not been an activist in LGBT issues. That was about to change.

After her experience at Joining Hands, Reaching Out, Mary was transformed. She was suddenly energized into an activism that released a pent-up desire for justice—a justice for her son that had always been latent in her heart. In a recent conversation with Mary, she spoke about her life after the conference and we were amazed. It seems she learned the value of telling her story and she has been doing that very thing ever since, in an unremitting fashion. In recent weeks, she has met many times with the pastor of her local Catholic parish. At those meetings, she has told the pastor about her son and how he has been alienated from the Church even though her son continues to work in a very Catholic manner for those less fortunate in his Chicago community. She told him how angry she was to learn how her Church sends negative messages about gay and lesbian people.

At the Joining Hands conference, Mary was appalled to learn that the Knights of Columbus had been misusing funds contributed for the care of the needy, by instead supporting the United

States Conference of Catholic Bishops' anti–marriage equality campaign. The Knights have contributed millions of dollars to restrict the freedom to marry in state-based political battles ranging from Maine to California.

Mary was particularly incensed because she had recently become aware of a local agency in her hometown that offered shelter and support to homeless youth. Many of these homeless kids were gay and lesbian children whose families had refused to accept them. Mary realized that the agency could have used that money to support these kids, so she went back to her pastor and told him, "The Knights ought to be ashamed of themselves for contributing to political campaigns which deny marriage rights to gay and lesbian people when there are gay kids running around in the woods without food or shelter because they can't go home."

Her complaint did not fall on deaf ears. Because of Mary's persistence, her pastor informed the local Knights of Columbus about the gay and lesbian homeless kids and the Knights responded by providing some twenty warm jackets for them. Mary has become a force to be reckoned with. Sometimes the ordinary laity can make a difference.

In addition to her advocacy with her pastor, Mary intends to volunteer her home as a safe place for LGBT kids as soon as she finishes requirements for her high school diploma. Mary's new mission to tell her story and to work for justice for LGBT people is a direct result of two lay people, who years before undertook a most unlikely task. Casey and Mary Ellen Lapota are traveling a path which the Roman Catholic Church leadership has wandered from. It is the path of love.

That pastor in the small Northern Michigan town of Ludington exemplified a compassionate and loving response that I would term truly Christian. He was on a different path. There are many other clergy like him, but very few at the hierarchical level. Linda and I encounter many white-collared Samaritans. One of the most generous is ones is Fr. Gerry Bechard of St. Simon and Jude Church in Westland Michigan. On every occasion, when we need a place to meet or a pastor to console and support an LGBT person in need, he has been there to give of himself. His parishioners uniformly reflect his mission of love and compassion. He is truly a one of Jesus' professionals, upon whom Jesus must be smiling.

In contrast to this scenario, consider an experience I encountered in the spring of 2005.

I had been writing Cardinal Adam Maida, Archbishop of Detroit, as part of an extended exchange between us beginning in the fall of 2004, on the issue of homosexuality and the Church's insensitive position. (I touched on this correspondence in Chapter 15.) During our exchange, the Cardinal had referred me to the local chapter of Courage. He said in part:

> ...there is outreach for persons who are homosexual and wish to be Catholic through a group called *Courage*; for family members there is a related group called *Encourage*.

The Cardinal had recommended that I have my son contact the pastor of St. Joan of Arc Church in St. Clair Shores, Michigan, one Father Michael Bugarin, the chaplain of Courage for the Detroit area. Ironically, shortly after the Cardinal's recommendation, an article appeared in the *Detroit Free Press*, relating the story of an encounter by Father Bugarin with two lesbian women who were attempting to register as parishioners of St. Joan of Arc. Surreptitiously, I was drawn to this article by the reporter himself, who had somehow gotten my name and called me, in order to get my reaction to the incident as the father of a gay son After reading the article, I was greatly disturbed. It cast the Church in a very negative light, and portrayed Fr. Bugarin as completely insensitive to the spiritual welfare of the two women, and totally lacking in empathy. It was distinctly at odds with the Cardinal's past assurances of the clergy's sensitivity, and his recommendation that Fr. Bugarin was very pastoral toward gay persons. My natural and immediate reaction was skepticism. I was sure it must be a distorted account.. I did provide my comments, but vowed to personally contact the two women to hear their story first hand. The result was a letter written to me by the two young women. It said in part:

...."Cheryl and I went to Saint Joan of Arc Parish in St. Clair Shores to register as new members. When we entered the office I introduced myself as Mary Horon and this is my wife Cheryl Mathers, the lady obviously knew we were a gay couple from the very beginning. We were asked to complete the membership and that was all we needed to do; we were parishioners and our envelopes would be mailed shortly. Because we have been happily married, since December of 2000 by a Vermont Civil Union, we strongly felt that it was appropriate for us to complete the membership card as "any" married couple would do. Cheryl and I crossed out the "husband " title and replaced it with "wife"; we hyphenated our last names and answered all of the questions asked of us. The lady took our card and asked who Mary was, because I was the one who was raised as a Catholic, baptized, and confirmed as a Catholic, and have attended Catholic schools since second grade. Cheryl was interested in becoming a Catholic and the lady said she would mail that information along with our envelopes.

After two weeks we had not received our envelopes and I made a call to the church to inquire about this. The lady put me on hold for over ten minutes and came back to say she would call back. Another two days went by and no envelopes or return call were received from the church. I called again, then put on hold, and then was asked to speak to Father Michael Bugarin but he happened to be in a meeting. I called back another two times but was not able to speak with him at those times. Finally Father Mike called back "because he was asked to call Mary". I introduced myself and he said "Oh yes, you're the gay lady", I corrected him by saying " actually we are a gay couple and we would like to become parishioners of Saint Joan of Arc church" and we haven't received our envelopes as of yet. Father Mike replied by saying "No, I cannot allow that, this is a family oriented church." I said no problem we are family. Father Mike paused for a second and said, "I cannot have gay people here, you obviously won't hide it and God knows you're a sinner." I explained to Father that my marriage is sacred and that God loves all of us, and we should not judge one another but love one another. Father then said , "I'm sorry, you are not welcome here", I asked what are you saying Father Mike?" He stated: "You are not to come in my church!" My reply was: "The sign you have in front of the church doors that says "all are welcome" is a lie!" Father continued to speak of sin and repeated that he did not want us there. I then realized I was dealing with a homophobic man and said " Mike, I forgive you, and may God forgive you for what you are saying". He then began to speak of church law about homosexuals and that his robe protects him, I then said: " When you die you will not be able to hide behind your robe." He was silent, and then I said God bless you and Good bye."

After reading this and the balance of the letter, I concluded that the Free Press article seemed mild and low key by comparison. It left me very troubled and more convinced than ever, that the Holy Spirit is thwarted by a dogma driven Church. The naivety and presumptuousness of Mary and Cheryl notwithstanding, I continue to hope for a more loving response than this incident portrays. In today's conservative environment, I am not hopeful.

I never contacted Fr. Bugarin for his version of events, as every encounter I have had with *Courage/Encourage* people, either before or since, has been a sour one that reinforces the righteous, doctrinaire, and pharisaical mindset exemplified by Father Bugarin above. It is interesting to note that he is now *Monsignor* Bugarin. It seems that only acerbic traditionalists are promoted in today's Church—It pays the ambitious to tout the party line.

These negative tales I've related are not strident exceptions. Indeed, it seems I weekly hear or read of similar stories of abuse by the clergy beyond the infamy of the child sexual abuse scandal. The recent denial by a Colorado pastor of the entry of a child into the local parochial school because the parents were lesbian, is matched by an incident just last week. As the *Huffington Post* reported it:

A Maryland-based priest is garnering heat in the blogo-sphere today after allegedly denying communion to a lesbian parishioner attending her mother's funeral ...Father Marcel Guarnizo of Gaithersburg's Saint John Neumann Catholic Church reportedly covered the bowl containing the Eucharist as the woman, who is identified only as Barbara, approached him. "I cannot give you communion because you live with a woman and that is a sin according to the Church," he is quoted as saying. To add insult to injury, Fr. Guarnizo left the altar when she delivered her eulogy to her mother. When the funeral was finished he informed the funeral director that he could not go to the gravesite to deliver the final blessing "because he was sick."

Sick he certainly is. Is "brood of Vipers" far off the mark?

Chapter 21

The End Game's Rearview Mirror

"For I am convinced that neither death nor life, neither angels nor demons, neither the present nor the future, nor any powers, neither height nor depth, nor anything else in all creation, will be able .to separate us from the love of God that is in Christ Jesus our Lord"
—ROMANS 8:38–39

I consider it realistic, not maudlin, to recognize my onrushing mortality. It's clear that my twilight is here. "The shadows are lengthening for me." [49] I look at the calendar and the number of days or years I might have left, and I know that it is so. At eighty-two, the conclusion has to be that my time is short. I feel good physically and seem to have good health, but that's a minor assurance, for clearly, this body is getting old. The end game is upon me. The numbers don't lie.

So what's it like to know that death is probably near? Does it make any difference? Does it affect the way one feels, thinks, or acts? Maybe because my health seems so good, it's not an answer

---

49   Taken from General Douglas MacArthur's farewell address to Congress, circa 1951.

that I can accurately assess. But since I do feel that my journey is near the exit gate, I ask myself the questions: Are you ready? Have you done what needs to be done? Should you change anything? It's not too late yet—maybe. What message do I want to leave with my loved ones? There are many questions for which there may be no confident answers, but it makes sense to take stock—to make any last minute preparations or changes if I think it necessary or prudent. I've just recently taken to visiting my lawyer to update my trust and last will and testament, but that's just the material issues with which my chil.dren will be saddled. I want to make it as easy for them as possible. The larger issue is, what's beyond for me? What prudent preparations are needed? Is there anything I need to do that hasn't been done? Is there something I need to say? Last confessions are for the last moment, and I'm not at that point yet, even though that too may be imminent. Actually, I'm not sure I'll even want that. It may not even be a possibility. I don't know that yet. But I do see the numbers. Mortality is an ever-approaching reality that seems quite near. So take stock I must.

The thought that seems uppermost to me is, What have I learned? Have I lived what I have learned? Has my faith, as I have lived it, truly reflected an honest pursuit of a conscience driven conviction? Have I achieved adulthood? Have I really gone where the Spirit has tried to lead me? I would reply to these queries with a prayer of hope, hope that I have not been presumptuous, and hope that I have listened, hope that I got it right. I conclude that once again, certitude is not an option.

Most of life is spent looking toward the future. There may be times when we turn to the rearview mirror, reexamining our regrets or enjoying those momentary delights of some past accomplishment. But forward is our most frequent focus. These end years seem different, however. The rearview mirror engrosses my attention, demanding constant concentration.

Despite the caution to "live the present moment," my mind seems persistently to follow its own

agenda. At eighty-two, I experience much of this rearview-mirror syndrome. Some might call it nostalgia, and while nostalgia implies a longing for things past, my end game brings me little longing. The reflection I dwell on is my trail of faith and where it has led me. It is a mental video that does include some recollection of past pleasantries and fond memories—the marvelous nuns who taught me as a child, the ongoing *celibate* saints who live their moments in dedicated service to us ordinary folks—there is definitely a delight in this indulgence. I have encountered so many wonderful people in my journey. These images cannot escape my view, but this is the limit of my nostalgia.

There is another, more mesmerizing mandate. It is the obsession to synopsize the meaning of it all and to reach some measure of conclusion. The questions keep repeating: What have I learned on this journey? Does it matter? Is there value in it? If so, so what? There is that old demanding dictum: Knowledge gained needs be knowledge shared. I seem haunted by some nagging notion to react to what I see in my mirror. It is the reason for writing this memoir. It is an unremitting challenge—a video game that I have yet to master (a skill that has always eluded me), but play I must. So I look into the mirror, and this is what I see:

I have always liked history. I recall that when I studied Church history I did not like too many of the things I read. I saw too much abuse of power, too much pharisaical hypocrisy and downright evil. It has forced me to recognize that the institution, rather than being infallible, is sometimes constituted by bad individuals not immune to human frailties. It is a history that evokes more shame and less admiration than when I started. Eventually I found it impossible blindly to accept the Church's vaunted claim of absolute, infallible truth. I learned that an early pope, John XXII, in his bull "Quia Quorundam" of 1324, essentially declared that the concept of papal infallibility was a heresy, but this teaching changed over the centuries. Today, the trend of creeping infallibility is a poisonous fruit of those seeds planted so long ago. It is a dogma clearly refuted by the many historical errors that unmistakably highlighted the Church's past fallibility. It seems that this pitiful papal presumption has been most often consigned to imperious men. We ordinary folks suffer the scars, and it's an ongoing affliction.

History records many mistakes and terrible sins. The abuse of the gospel and the mendacity of past and current Church leadership were often appalling. Yes, I saw failings; most were typical human failings, common to us all. Yet I also saw many great and wonderful people in the Church's past and in the present. I have read of sinners but also of saints. I decided that most of us have chosen to focus on the saints and ignore the failings. This is probably good, and largely, I have followed that path. I feel that to be nonjudgmental requires me to forgive and try to focus on the good. "Who is without sin?"

Yet I also am driven not to be part of any cover-up. When I "looked at the data," and saw how too many of our Church leaders succumbed to the fog of adulation that afflicts those in positions of power, I recognized that this is an ancient malady very much alive and pervasive throughout our culture today, and not just in my Church. I realize that all of the issues I relate involve their culpability, not mine. Who am I to judge? Would I have done better had I walked in their shoes? More importantly, what have *I* done? Where have *I* gone wrong? What would history say about people like me, ordinary Catholic that I am? What should I do before the end to rectify any of my own errors?

I conclude that at the very least, there is one major remaining task: Avoid the error of silence. I must speak out always and everywhere on the issues of today and work with all my energy for reform—to make my Church more Christ-like. I am driven to cry out, to make my views heard.

Looking in that mirror, one thing is clearly visible: I have enjoyed uncommon blessings throughout my life. I may be ordinary, but I think many of my blessings have been extraordinary. In addition, those extraordinary spiritual incidents, while few in number, have left indelible impressions that have profoundly affected my faith in ways that are hard for me to articulate. They've made me puzzle over why I was given such unique graces.

I acknowledge, that I haven't always been the "good boy" that I might have started out to be, and that my "lead me into temptation" prayer was definitely answered in the affirmative— and not always to my eventual acclaim. God, the Holy Spirit, and Jesus—*They* have always been there for me, sometimes in spectacular fashion. God's love has been unmistakable. It has not been invisible to me. Divine grace seems to have been an amazing gift to me continuously. Regrettably, my response to grace has sometimes been one of some presumption, maybe to a fault. I'm certain, too, that there were times when I wasn't listening, when my response to grace was zero. Often my response to it was not always adequate or enthusiastic. Too often it was tentative. I recognize that the greatest wrong or failure of my life was excessive self-focus. There were too many times I could have loved more—my greatest regret. I was too eager and obsessed with being loved. I failed to comprehend the adage, "You want to be loved? Be loving."

Of course, my personal failures have been painfully plentiful, but I lack the humility to list them all. So, as I don't intend to apply for sainthood, I simply claim the privileged golden rule of silence in these areas, while maintaining that my greatest failing is also the most common among us all: I could have loved more.

Perusing my mirror further: As one might expect, a recurring scene is the diorama of colorfully clothed ecclesiastical figures clouded by my dark and depressing cynicism, and I wonder: Is this some kind of resurgence of self-idolatry I feel? Is it some misguided prophet paradigm I am afflicted with? Cynicism it surely is, as it has immersed me in a sea of scorn for much of the Church leadership from whom I've sought spiritual refuge over a lifetime. They have largely failed me. They have left me to discover my loving Master on my own. When seeking the way, they have too often shown me distorted precepts that led me down a wrong path, away from His love. Their arrogant self-interest very nearly deprived me of one of God's greatest gifts to me—my son. Am I now to be silent about this?

No! How many are even at this moment being misled? Am I to be silent over this veiled holocaust, this persistent atrocity that defends a cult of condemnation—a militant attempt to exclude so many of the Creator's souls? No! I cannot be silent. I cry out against those Roman chiefs who proclaim my son is "disordered." No! They themselves are the disordered ones. They are virtual henotheists—ones who believe in God but subtly profess other deities to which they have appointed themselves, the supplementary deities. It is an arrogant posture.

It is a damning view I see. Yes, perhaps I exaggerate, but it is my view from the pew. I have seen too much violent injustice stemming undeniably from my Church leaders. They who are supposed to be all-inclusive suffer a cult of exclusivity. They are supposed to be loving and pastoral, yet they abuse children, denigrate the sexually different, openly shut out sinners and defraud those whom they should be assisting; they secure for themselves the highest places in the community. I reject them. I reject their self-idolatry. I stand apart from some of the Church's most basic doctrines. I make no excuses for it; their fundamental aristocratic tenants, I openly reject; I herein declare, my denial of:

- Infallibility—an absurd ruse; infallibility belongs only to the Divine.
- Celibacy—the root of the curse of clericalism from which all other ills flow.
- No women priests—blatant misogyny, as if worship is somehow dependent on genitalia.
- Homosexuality as an objective disorder—a pathetic misunderstanding of human sexuality born of ignorance.
- Contraception—a product of a deficient celibate mindset, which is sex obsessed.

There are other areas where I see through a different lens. The institutional Church structure and governance reflects a dictatorship that denies any voice of the Holy Spirit channeled through the laity and a doctrinal theme that seems focused only on the negative, not on the primary virtue of love.

Yet in the same breath I also openly declare my belief and commitment to my Catholic faith. I do hold to the truths expressed in *The Apostle's Creed*. I do believe in God, the Father Almighty, Creator of heaven and earth, and in Jesus Christ, His only Son...I believe in the Holy Spirit...in life everlasting...and most importantly I believe in God's unconditional love for us all

Many of my fellow pew dwellers hold similar views. They, like me, essentially ignore the prattling bishops and simply try to find spiritual nourishment and live their lives according to their graces received and similarly sans any input from the magisterial aristocracy. I know many of them. They get no press but they don't care.

My mirror definitely displays a transformation. It is a transformation that injects me with an unlikely enthusiasm in my end game. Regardless of the source or cause, the lens through which I now see the world reveals so much injustice, violence, and lack of love that I am compelled to cry out in protest to the limit of my small voice and aging energy. I have a new awareness. I am no longer the quiet Catholic I once was. I've gone from cave dweller to town crier. I admit to the folly of crying out possibly the wrong thing at times. I also admit that I can be rightly accused of excessive stridency in my rhetoric. I know that those who criticize are subject to critique. But "by their fruits you will know them." At this stage of my life, the one thing I want to avoid is silence. I have witnessed too often the tragic consequences of the silence of good people. That's one fault I'm not going to indulge, despite the associated risks. I am determined to let the "data" be my script.

My perception of the Church is harsh, perhaps, but when I consider the terrible violence throughout the world today, I most often see the opposition to it comes from the feminine among us, not the Church, which seems only timid in opposing this evil. It sees evil where there is no evil and seems blind to its own internal evil. The Church's reality is a persistent pattern of self-interest—of protecting the hierarchy at the expense of the victims.

Even worse in my judgment, is its tragedy of silence. When the focal point of the Boston sex abuse scandal, Cardinal Law, was moved to Rome with a virtual promotion in order to escape possible civil prosecution in the United States, the ensuing outcry seemed muffled and sparse—much too silent. Even general society seems to bow before the myth of an infallible, flawless pope. The observer who chooses silence when witnessing such corruption can be justifiably classified as an accessory to deceit. We all have an obligation to cry out. I have witnessed in my own lifetime unspeakable crimes stemming from the silence of good people. Silence is the greatest failure of the ordinary man. Unfortunately, the consent of silence remains an ongoing failure.

Martin Luther in the fifteenth century was an example of a good Catholic who refused to be silent. Today's Martin Luthers are being ignored by Church leadership, just as he was. The reforms of Vatican II are slowly being erased by a hierarchy that struggles to return to medieval castles and unchallenged control. As with Martin Luther, reform is once again rejected.

Yet change is coming. As I witness the dying priesthood in developed countries and the broad decline of in the presence of pastoral hierarchy, I realize that the evidence for change is plain to see. What this portends is difficult to predict. I know that a new structure will arise, hopefully one that is transparent, honest, holy, and focused on loving as Christ loved—focused on the gospel. I have begun to understand how my Church is not unlike myself. She too is comprised of mostly ordinary people, clergy and lay alike. I am no better than the Church, and the Church is no better than I am. I reckon that most members of the hierarchy may be trying to do their best by the light that they are given to see, and the understanding they have been given to comprehend. One major advantage that I have, however, is that I do not have to suffer their burden of adulation. On the whole, I am not optimistic that a good outcome will prevail anytime soon.

These conclusions and observations have propelled me to an activism that some may say is anti-Catholic at best. Yet it is my Catholic upbringing that has made me who I am. Despite the negative realities, I remain Catholic. I will die Catholic. I still go to Mass every Sunday. I go not only because it's the boat they sent me in; not only because the destination shore is now in sight; but more than that, I go because I still need spiritual sustenance on a regular basis. I *want* to worship every Sunday. I go because it is where my spiritual home is. I go not out of fear, but out of love for the God who has given me such abundant grace over so many years. I go because the Spirit leads me there. Yes, sometimes I go to my Episcopal Church up north, but that's an irrelevant difference. The Spirit has led me there as well. The Spirit may yet lead me into different church environment. If so, I will go.

I look away from my mirror and conclude from what I have seen that my journey to a self-reliant faith has been scary at times, but no longer. The risk of placing everything in God's hands has been a challenge to any sense of courage I might claim. It may have been easier when I let the Church do my thinking and set the rules—when I was a silent cave dweller. It certainly was not as satisfying or as joyful. Taking the reins to set my own direction has required more faith and more thinking by far than just following the leader, as I did when I was a child. While it has been frightening at times, the joy I am experiencing in these end times exceeds anything I could have wished for or anticipated. The "second half" of life that Richard Rohr so eloquently describes in his book *Falling Upward: A Spirituality for the Two Halves of Life* is definitely the better half. I feel a great sense of calm and satisfaction at this point. I expect death to be a happy experience. I am confident that I have sincerely tried to do my best despite my failures. I feel satisfied that I have made a small contribution toward the evolution of love—at least to those around me. I have tried to follow where the Spirit leads, and lately I am doing even better at that.

I will persist. I wish to always respond to God's every grace to the limit of the capability I have been given. Pursuit of the love of Jesus is a call to a joyful journey I cannot resist. Those who would claim they have a better path revealed only to them are no longer my navigators. I have a new compass. I pray for the continued vitality to follow it. I pray also for continued time to do God's work as the Spirit reveals it to me. The future, whether long or short, will be a continuation of what I have been doing.

For the end that's coming, I fear not. Fear is not a factor because the God who has blessed me so for a lifetime, the God who has so dramatically revealed Divine love to me, will not abandon me at this end-time of my life. On the contrary, the uncommon vitality I have been given in old age and the grace to become an activist reinforces my convictions. Despite my ranting against the institutional Church, and the terrible failures I witness in her, I rejoice in my activism and stubbornly insist that I am still Catholic. I revel in the prospect that I will remain Catholic—but perhaps just an ordinary Catholic.

I recognize that my journey has been unique to me. It's easy to observe that everyone's journey is unique, and clearly, mine is not necessarily better or worse than anyone else's. I know that others may well have had experiences that would lead them to far different conclusions than my own. My conclusions and understanding are limited by the constraints of my experience and knowledge, and those constraints are just one reason why my beliefs are not absolute. It is a limitation that is universal to the human condition. It is quite startling to me to witness how my siblings' lives have differed so much from mine. We came from identical backgrounds but our lives and conclusions are so amazingly different. In many areas, we have reached distinctly opposing views. It is the reason why we try to avoid talking politics or religion at family gatherings. I see similar uniqueness in the lives of my own offspring. The challenge to each of us is to be aware that our understanding is different from everyone else. I believe that rather than just rant our personal views, we should also attempt to expand the depth of our understanding. We must listen—to each other. It is the basis of civil discourse and that is important.

As the distant shore approaches, and I reflect on my evolving faith, my many contrary convictions, and disputes, I try to view it all with a sense of humor and not to take them or myself too seriously. We only know according to the light we are given, and are all guilty of our follies and failures. Like Saint Augustine, I know I cannot understand many things. When I compare myself to others, I conclude that I have been dealt mostly aces and many graces, but I am guilty of ignorant follies and many failures—perhaps just an ordinary Catholic. Yet that's OK. We are a ubiquitous lot.

I smile at the idea that any of us can know the mind of God in this life. Saint Augustine got it right when he said, "God is not what you imagine or what you think you understand. If you understand you have failed." And I realize how this voyage has transformed my faith in unimagined and profound ways—how far different I am from when I started out, how for some reason, God seems to have showered me with uncommon good fortune. I realize that the older I get, the more questions I have—questions for which the answers become fewer and fewer. I realize that life is unpredictable, and in many ways not fair. Yes, every journey is different and an amazing maze of twist and turns. I know that while mine, too, has wandered, it has been a journey of joy, a faith of love, a journey of an ordinary Catholic.

It is most certainly the path that the Spirit has led me on—different from yours perhaps, and maybe a destiny decreed by God's love. It is a faith I hold most dearly in my heart and soul, with unwavering confidence in the surety of the outcome. It is a faith that I confidently expect will see me safely through my end game. It is a story of so many blessings received, so much love showered upon me over a lifetime. I have seen the amazing love from the all-loving God who loves us all beyond anything we can imagine. My destiny I embrace with confidence—with an unremitting joy and an eternal gratitude. No other conclusion can I make than says the ancient hymn:

"No fears can shake my inmost calm...How can I keep from singing?"

* * *

Bibliography

Berry, Jason. *Render Unto Rome*. New York: Crown Publishing, 2011.

Bokencotter, Thomas. *A Concise History of the Catholic Church*. New York: Doubleday, 1990.

Campbell, Antony F. *God First Loved Us: The Challenge of Accepting Unconditional Love*. Mahwah: Paulist Press, 2000.

Carroll, James. *Practicing Catholic*. New York: First Mariner Books, 2009.

———. *Constantine's Sword*. New York: First Mariner, 2001

Carroll, James. *Toward a New Catholic Church*. New York: Houghton Mifflin Company, 2002.

Couzzens, Donald. *Sacred Silence, Denial and Crisis in the Church*. Collegeville: Liturgical Press, 2004.

Crosby, Michael H. *The Dysfunctional Church: Addiction and Codependency in the Family of Catholicism*. Notre Dame, IN: Ave Maria Press, 1991.

Fairchild, Betty, and Nancy Hayward. *Now that You Know*. Orlando, FL: Harvest Books, 1998.

Fiedler, Maureen, and Linda Rabben. *Rome Has Spoken*. New York: Crossroad, 1998.

Johnson, Elizabeth A. *Quest for the Living God*. New York: Continuum International, 2007.

Kung, Hans. *The Catholic Church, A Short History*. New York: Random House, 2003.

Lopata, Mary Ellen. *Fortunate Families*. Victoria: Trafford Publishing, 2003.

McNaught, Brian. *On Being Gay: Thoughts on Family, Faith, and Love*. New York: St. Martin's Press, 1988.

Morris, Charles L. *American Catholic: The Saints and Sinners Who Built America's Most Powerful Church*. New York: First Vintage, 1997.

Nelson, James B. *Embodiment: An Approach to Sexuality and Christian Theology*. Minneapolis: Augsburg Publishing, 1978.

Nelson, Thomas A. "God Gave Me a Gay Son." In *The Best Catholic Writing 2005*, edited by Brian Doyle, 67–80. Chicago: Loyola Press, 2005.

Nugent, Robert, and Jeannine Gramick. *Building Bridges.* Mystic: Third Publications, 1997.

O'Murchu, Diarmuid. *Adult Faith.* Maryknoll, NY: Orbis Books, 2011.

Rohr, Richard. *Things Hidden.* Cincinnati, OH: St Anthony Messenger Press, 2007.

Salzman, Todd A. and Michael G. Lawler. *The Sexual Person.* Washington, DC: Georgetown University Press, 2008.

Spong, John Shelby. *Here I Stand.* Morristown, NJ: Harper One, 1999.

Sipe, A.W. Richard. *Celibacy in Crisis! A Secret World Revisited.* New York: Taylor-Routledge, 2003.

Spong, John Shelby. *The Sins of the Scriptures.* New York: Harper Collins, 2005.

Sullivan, Andrew. *Virtually Normal.* New York: Vintage Books, 1995.

White, Mel. *Stranger at the Gate.* New York: Plume, 1994.

Wills, Gary. *St. Augustine.* New York: Penguin Putnam, 1999.

———. *Papal Sin.* New York: Doubleday, 2000.

———. *Why I Am a Catholic.* New York: Houghton Mifflin Company, 2002.

Wilson, S.J, George B. *Clericalism.* Collegeville, MN: Liturgical Press, 1992.

Made in the USA
San Bernardino, CA
13 December 2013